ADJUSTMENT AND EQUITY IN DEVELOPING COUNTRIES

GENERAL EDITOR
Christian Morrisson

ADJUSTMENT AND EQUITY IN CÔTE D'IVOIRE

By
Hartmut Schneider

in collaboration with

Winifred Weekes-Vagliani, Paolo Groppo
Sylvie Lambert, Akiko Suwa, Nghia Nguyen Tinh

DEVELOPMENT CENTRE
OF THE ORGANISATION FOR ECONOMIC CO-OPERATION AND DEVELOPMENT

ORGANISATION FOR ECONOMIC CO-OPERATION AND DEVELOPMENT

Pursuant to Article 1 of the Convention signed in Paris on 14th December 1960, and which came into force on 30th September 1961, the Organisation for Economic Co-operation and Development (OECD) shall promote policies designed:

— to achieve the highest sustainable economic growth and employment and a rising standard of living in Member countries, while maintaining financial stability, and thus to contribute to the development of the world economy;

— to contribute to sound economic expansion in Member as well as non-member countries in the process of economic development; and

— to contribute to the expansion of world trade on a multilateral, non-discriminatory basis in accordance with international obligations.

The original Member countries of the OECD are Austria, Belgium, Canada, Denmark, France, Germany, Greece, Iceland, Ireland, Italy, Luxembourg, the Netherlands, Norway, Portugal, Spain, Sweden, Switzerland, Turkey, the United Kingdom and the United States. The following countries became Members subsequently through accession at the dates indicated hereafter: Japan (28th April 1964), Finland (28th January 1969), Australia (7th June 1971) and New Zealand (29th May 1973). The Commission of the European Communities takes part in the work of the OECD (Article 13 of the OECD Convention). Yugoslavia has a special status at OECD (agreement of 28th October 1961).

The Development Centre of the Organisation for Economic Co-operation and Development was established by decision of the OECD Council on 23rd October 1962.

The purpose of the Centre is to bring together the knowledge and experience available in Member countries of both economic development and the formulation and execution of general economic policies; to adapt such knowledge and experience to the actual needs of countries or regions in the process of development and to put the results at the disposal of the countries by appropriate means.

The Centre has a special and autonomous position within the OECD which enables it to enjoy scientific independence in the execution of its task. Nevertheless, the Centre can draw upon the experience and knowledge available in the OECD in the development field.

Publié en français sous le titre :

AJUSTEMENT ET ÉQUITÉ
EN CÔTE D'IVOIRE

*
* *

Foreword

This work is one of a series produced under the Development Centre's programme on "Structural Adjustment and Equitable Growth". Following approval by the Centre's Advisory Board, a macro-micro model was developed and refined. This was published as a Development Centre Technical Paper (No. 1) in 1989. The model was then modified and applied to a number of developing countries and the results are being collected in this series. When completed by the end of 1991, the series will include a number of individual country studies and an overall synthesis volume.

SPECIAL OFFER

For the purchase of eight books to be published in the ''Adjustment and Equity in Developing Countries'' Series (Ecuador, Chile, Ivory Coast, Ghana, Indonesia, Malaysia, Marocco. {Synthesis}):
(41 91 00 1)   FF835   £110.00   US$198.00   DM320

ALSO AVAILABLE

Adjustment and Equity in Chile   *by Patricio Meller* (1992)
(41 91 16 2) ISBN 92-64-23619-3   FF130   £17.00   US$31.00   DM50

Adjustment and Equity in Ecuador   *by Alain de Janvry, Elisabeth Sadoulet, André Fargeix* (1991)
(41 91 15 1) ISBN 92-64-13539-1   FF130   £17.00   US$31.00   DM50

Adjustment and Equity in Malaysia   *by David Demery, Lionel Demery* (1992)
(41 91 20 1) ISBN 92-64-13601-0   FF130   £17.00   US$31.00   DM50

Adjustment and Equity in Morocco   *by Christian Morrisson* (1991)
(41 91 21 1) ISBN 92-64-13589-8   FF130   £17.00   US$31.00   DM50

Development Centre Studies

External Trade and Income Distribution   *by François Bourguignon, Christian Morrisson* (1989)
(41 89 03 1) ISBN 92-64-13250-3   FF190   £23.00   US$40.00   DM78

Table of Contents

List of Tables

7

List of Figures

Acknowledgements

This study was made possible by assistance from the Swedish International Development Authority and we are grateful for this support.

We benefited from the help of a great many people in the preparation of this study, and we should like to thank them here. First of all, we thank Côte d'Ivoire authorities for having made the results of the 1985 Household Survey available to us. In Bertin Gbayoro they gave us a very knowledgeable discussion partner for our preliminary analyses.

We would particularly like to thank Christian Morrisson for his frequent advice, and François Bourguignon and Jean-Claude Berthélemy whose knowledge of Côte d'Ivoire statistics was very useful to us. Michèle Fleury-Brousse and Armelle Le Clec'h gave us very valuable help with computing and statistics. We also thank Odile Vincent for her analysis of family structures. Concerning Chapter VI, we thank Catherine Beaumont for her comments and Jeanne Picquart for her help in preparing this chapter. Finally, we thank the Centre National de la Recherche Scientifique of France for permitting Nghia Nguyen Tinh to work with the Development Centre

Preface

This study is part of the Development Centre's project on "Adjustment Programmes and Growth with Equity". It is of special interest for several reasons: Côte d'Ivoire was long considered a brilliant model of development based on agriculture, but in fact it seems to have entered an impasse from which it will be difficult to emerge. A particular effort has been made in this study to analyse employment, the agrarian system and family structures in some depth.

This work is thus the fruit of a multidisciplinary effort to which an agricultural engineer and a sociologist have contributed in addition to the economists. It has also benefited from the co-operation of the Côte d'Ivoire government, which in particular authorised the analysis of the 1985 Household survey.

The history of adjustment in Côte d'Ivoire is a long one, for it dates back to difficulties that appeared in the late 1970s. It shows that these are not simply a deviation from normal, as might be thought for certain other countries, but are part of a more complex and far-reaching process, to which both internal and external factors are contributing. This character of the problem has not always been recognised, and some commentators have spoken of an end to the crisis in the mid 1980s. We now know that this was unfortunately only a temporary improvement and the factors causing imbalances in this economy and in the markets for its principal export products have since gained the upper hand again.

While the Côte d'Ivoire government has sometimes acted rapidly and vigorously, it is clear that the measures and their implementation have not always gone far enough. But it must also be recognised, as shown by the street demonstrations on the one hand and the authors' analysis on the other, that the State has often had little room for manoeuvre. The use of a computer simulation model has clearly brought out a number of dilemmas. For example, among the austerity measures, it is the reduction of public service wages that seems preferable to all the other possibilities examined. But we know the resistance the government recently encountered when it announced drastic measures along these lines. Another dilemma appears in the following terms: according to the model, a devaluation would have positive economic and social effects (income distribution and poverty), but could be envisaged only if Côte d'Ivoire withdrew from the CFA Franc Zone. However, such a move would threaten to reduce seriously the confidence of the investors the country so desperately needs.

In view of the importance of the stakes and the difficulty of the task, the authors have resisted the temptation to propose simple solutions, but present arguments likely to be of use for determining measures which, in the longer term, offer the hope of overcoming this crisis that has lasted far too long.

Louis Emmerij
President of the OECD Development Centre
December 1991

Executive Summary

The structural characteristics of the Ivorian economy and the functioning of its public finance system have created a "disequilibrating dependence" in this economy. This is a twofold dependence: first, exports are very heavily concentrated on two agricultural products, coffee and cocoa; second, tax revenue also depends to a large extent on these same two products. This is not an ineluctable dependence stemming entirely from Côte d'Ivoire's natural resource endowment, but rather a dependence reinforced by the development strategy pursued for many years.

It is true that this strategy brought a certain prosperity to Côte d'Ivoire as long as world market conditions for coffee and cocoa were favourable. Nonetheless, we find that this economic prosperity was not accompanied by social development (educational attainment and health) comparable with that of other countries at the same economic level.

The prosperity caused a certain euphoria and development policy ambitions that can be judged with hindsight as exaggerated. This state of mind led to other disequilibria which took the following forms: public over-investment, too much state involvement in the enterprise sector, lack of strict management of public finances in general.

When world market conditions for the export crops deteriorated, the government acted rapidly to reduce certain expenditures, notably investment. However, its ability to act effectively was limited, on the one hand by the lack of instruments for tight management, and on the other by the sheer weight of its many commitments. The situation was then further aggravated by two factors outside government control: the interest rate increase on the international financial markets (increasing debt servicing costs) and the drought of 1983.

This résumé of the structure of the economic and social disequilibria is the background for our analysis of the impact of the crisis and the adjustment on employment and wages, and more generally, on the population's standard of living.

Employment and wages

The adjustment programmes acted in "classical" fashion by reducing public expenditure and domestic demand. Furthermore, they included specific labour market measures. These programmes acted on both the modern sector and the traditional sector, though in a more indirect fashion as regards the latter.

Civil service employment continued to increase during the adjustment period (at an annual average rate of 3.5 per cent between 1981 and 1987), while it fell by over a third in the enterprise sector. The adjustment therefore did not affect the overall level of civil service employees, but it did substantially reduce their real wages (down 20 per cent over the period). By contrast, the level of real average wages was maintained in the enterprise sector.

While there is thus a sharp contrast between the civil service and the enterprise sectors, there are also considerable variations within the latter.

While employment fell in all branches of activity over the period 1980-85, the fall was less in manufacturing industry than in the "formal non-tradeable" sector and in primary product exports. The "construction" branch lost as much as 85 per cent of its jobs, mainly because of the reduction in public investment. There was thus a significant change in the sectoral breakdown of employment.

The adjustment measures, notably the disindexation of wages and liberalisation of employment, did not lead to more intensive use of labour in enterprises or even to its stabilisation. At most, they made it possible to reduce enterprise losses and budget deficits. This effort to re-establish equilibrium, while necessary, did not take place in a sufficiently dynamic economic context for it to trigger renewed growth in improved structures.

Standard of Living

Overall, the rural population was rather better placed than the urban population with respect to the adjustment measures. Among these measures, the most restrictive such as the reduction of public investment and the freeze on civil service wages concerned above all the urban population, while farmers benefited from several increases in the prices of coffee, cocoa and cotton as from 1983. Even though the increases in the nominal producer prices were not sufficient to prevent a fall in real prices due to inflation, the producers of cash crops, as a group, nevertheless saw their real incomes increase over the period 1980-86, thanks to an increase in production of over 33 per cent.

In urban areas, the standard of living of people in the informal sector is more difficult to assess than those in the formal sector. While for the latter the impact of the adjustment measures was relatively direct through employment and wages, this impact was largely indirect for those working in the informal sector. It made itself felt partly through a fall in demand for the goods and services supplied by the informal sector to households and enterprises. The poor are over-represented in this sector: while 50 per cent of all the households in Abidjan belong to the informal sector, the proportion rises to 75 per cent in the case of the poor in this town.

In the urban areas the adjustment not only affected the standard of living of the relatively well-off persons in the formal sector, but also that of persons on average poorer and even more numerous, working in the informal sector. The majority of the workers in this sector are women.

The impact of adjustment on the standard of living of different population groups was also analysed through the structure of their expenditure. This varies between town and country on the one hand and between rich and poor households on the other. The increases in the controlled consumer prices for rice and bread, which formed part of the adjustment measures, are the most striking examples of differences in impact very much to the disadvantage of the poorest groups. Thus the price of rice was increased much more than that of bread (34 per cent as against 7 per cent), while poor urban households spend a greater share of their income on rice than on bread.

The analysis of school enrolments over the period 1975-87 throws a more general light on the social effects of the crisis and adjustment. The fact is that the number of children at school, after a large increase during the 1970s, increased at a rate lower than that of population growth after 1982.

Simulations of policy alternatives

A numerical model, at the same time both macro- and microeconomic, was applied to the case of Côte d'Ivoire between 1980 and 1986. This made it possible to study, within a coherent framework, the effects of different possible adjustment measures on the principal aggregates and on income distribution. The simulations concerned the two major problems in Côte d'Ivoire during the 1980s: reduction of the budget deficit and the question of the exchange rate necessary to balance the current account.

Five different measures to reduce the budget deficit by the same amount were compared: reduction of public investment, reduction of current government expenditure, and reduction of civil service wages on the one hand, and increased taxes on production and primary exports on the other. All these simulations have recessive effects at first, but show good results for the target parameters of the adjustment policies: budget deficit, current account deficit, balance of trade. From the poverty standpoint, expenditure reduction policies are less painful than tax increase policies. It should be noted, however, that there are some limits to the comparability of these simulations. Thus a variation in the level of public expenditure has a direct effect through demand, while a change in the tax rate causes induced effects through its impact on the tax base itself. Furthermore, part of the operating expenditure in fact has long-term effects that make it a sort of investment in human capital. In the simulation model, however, these expenditures are seen as having an effect only during a given period.

Among the expenditure reduction simulations, it is the reduction in civil service wages that seems preferable to all the others, though it should be noted that poverty increases with respect to the reference level, while inequality is diminished.

The second set of simulations was aimed at reducing the external debt by depreciating the exchange rate, either by devaluing once and for all, or through letting the exchange rate float. In both cases there is a strong revival of the economy accompanied by a reduction in inequality and in poverty. But inequality gets worse as from 1984 in the case of a floating exchange rate. While the first of these simulations seems very favourable, it should be noted that both make the assumption of firms being able to borrow abroad, which is not very likely in practice. If this assumption is abandoned, the results become much less favourable.

At the end of this simulation exercise, we noted three points: the instability of the Côte d'Ivoire economy, which means that no one measure can durably improve the situation in all respects; the question of the credibility of the economic authorities and the sensitivity of the results to assumptions made about access to new foreign loans; and the Côte d'Ivoire authorities' lack of room for manoeuvre in the short term.

Towards a durable adjustment

The most general conclusion of our analysis is that adjustment is a complex process, with multiple endogenous and exogenous factors that combine and sometimes reinforce one another. We can therefore not expect simple and rapid solutions. Rather, adjustment should be seen as a lengthy process consisting of redefining and implementing a development strategy having many components. Furthermore, this task is not simply technical, but highly political. The government does not control all the action variables and thus has to find ways to incite economic agents to change their behaviour in the desired direction; it also has to be able to anticipate any resistance likely to arise.

It must be admitted that in Côte d'Ivoire a good many basically correct measures were decided upon, but they were not all applied, and some were implemented too late and incompletely to produce the desired results. In addition, there are certain structural characteristics that have not been modified and which, as a result, have preserved or made worse certain existing imbalances.

In the first place, the structural vulnerability of Côte d'Ivoire must be stressed. As we have shown, the heavy concentration of exports on very few primary products remained virtually unchanged during the 1980-87 period. The diversification of exports, which was envisaged by the development programmes, for the most part still remains a dead letter. This is a matter of identifying viable and practicable alternatives. Creating or reinforcing the structures that could promote this diversification is thus one of the measures that needs to be implemented. Here it is necessary to ensure that the existing price structure, insofar as it is controlled by the government, does not prevent such an adjustment.

Another field where vulnerability must be reduced and some sort of equilibrium re-established is that of food crops. The Côte d'Ivoire authorities recognised this necessity as early as the beginning of the 1980s (food plan) but did not act with sufficient resolve to achieve the desired result. This is certainly a long and complicated task that involves changes in the traditional agrarian system, but it is well worth embarking upon energetically. In this way it would be possible not only to re-establish the balance of production, but also achieve an improvement in the situation of socially disadvantaged groups in both rural areas and near urban areas. Once again this type of adjustment requires attention to the existing level of prices, partly determined by the exchange rate system and by international competition that is sometimes unfair. If a devaluation cannot be carried out under the present monetary regime, perhaps well-targeted protection through import taxes should be considered. In this way, it would be possible at the same time to mobilise certain resources to promote productivity in the food crop sector. In addition, if favourable general conditions could be created in this sector, it would probably constitute an example of adjustment based largely on the mobilisation of local resources.

The fiscal system which is largely based on export taxes is another domain requiring measures to reduce vulnerability. This system has transmitted fluctuations of the main export markets to the public budget, which has need of greater stability. Furthermore, through the receipts of the *Caisse de Stabilisation et de Soutien des Prix et des Productions Agricoles* (CSSPPA), this system has even removed certain tax revenue from any tight management control. Through seeking a more stable tax base and more complete control over revenues and their utilisation, it would be possible to reduce this type of vulnerability which is at the same time a source of inefficiency.

The large fall in public and private investment is a worrying feature of adjustment, as it has been in Côte d'Ivoire. Comparing adjustment in the CFA zone countries with other sub-Saharan countries, Devarajan *et al.* (1990) have explained this phenomenon as follows: the impossibility of a nominal devaluation for the member countries of this zone has practically obliged them to adjust more by reducing expenditures than by the reallocating resources that would result from the relative price changes following a devaluation. Adjustment by reducing investment has serious consequences for the future and cannot go on indefinitely. Even if it is assumed that some of the scrapped investment projects were not economically viable, others will be sadly missed from the stock of real capital on which future growth depends.

Once again, therefore, the question arises as to whether a monetary regime that does not allow nominal devaluation should be retained. This is a very controversial question and the answer must, of course, also take account of the stabilising effects of and the confidence inspired by this regime. If the regime is retained, it will be necessary to seek other methods of stimulating a reallocation of the factors of production to make it possible to re-establish the desired balances. Taxes that increase import prices together with export subsidies could possibly play this role. While such measures can change prices in the desired direction, it must nevertheless be stressed that private investment will not react unless the whole set of measures is considered credible and there is a general climate favourable to investment. Investors must be persuaded that they will not run too high a risk if they invest.

Any measure leading to increased efficiency of production of goods and services is likely to facilitate, directly or indirectly, adjustment in its different forms. For example, enterprises that produce at a lower cost become more competitive on the international market and/or make it possible to reduce the price of intermediate goods on the domestic market. Administrations that can provide the same service at lower cost help to reduce the budget deficit and the burden that the state imposes on taxpayers, and hence enterprises, and the outcome is as in the previous example. Thus there must be a continued search for greater efficiency in all fields, already begun in different forms in Côte d'Ivoire. However, this effort, and hence the resulting adjustment, cannot be durable if it does not take account of the consequences for certain persons or social categories in the short term, and for the future of the society as a whole.

While the austerity imposed in Côte d'Ivoire facilitated the restoration of certain balances, it is not necessarily synonymous with increased efficiency and the future has been compromised in various ways. In order for the adjustment to be equitable and durable, it is necessary to propose measures that can, for example, offer employment to those who have lost their jobs, and ensure a certain minimum of education and health care for those who might be deprived of these benefits. These measures can cushion the negative impact of adjustment at the individual level and spread the cost more evenly over the society. This is also a field where external aid can be useful (like in the PAMSCAD programme in Ghana) to provide support until the adjustment starts to bear fruit and the country is able to meet the cost of such redistribution operations on its own.

Chapter I

Structure of the Economy and Incomes

A. Introduction

In 1980, Côte d'Ivoire was leading the sub-Saharan African countries with a per capita GDP of $1 150 and in the middle of the lower middle-income countries (classification in the World Bank, World Development Report, 1982, excluding Gabon). This situation was the result of strong GDP growth since independence (1960) on the order of 7.2 per cent a year. This period was also charactcriscd by considerable openness to foreign capital and foreign workers (both African and non-African), concentration on agriculture for export and substantial State involvement in the economic sector.

In 1987, Côte d'Ivoire was still among the lower middle-income countries but on a lower ranking, with a per capita GDP of US$740. Among the sub-Saharan African countries it had been overtaken by Botswana, Cameroon and the People's Republic of the Congo. These figures, even though far from the whole picture, do illustrate in dramatic fashion the changes that had taken place in the economy as a result of external and internal factors. In this report we shall try to clarify as far as possible their respective roles and the evolution of the situation of different population groups. The final question we shall consider is to what extent alternative policies could have made the necessary adjustments at lower economic and social costs.

In this chapter we describe the main features of the Côte d'Ivoire economy at the beginning of the 1980s. This forms the background for an analysis (in Chapter II) which adopts a more historical approach and attempts to explain the appearance of the macroeconomic imbalances. The stabilisation and structural adjustment measures adopted to counter these imbalances are the subject of Chapter III. On the basis of that we can make a more detailed analysis of the effects of adjustment policies and the economic and social situation in the subsequent chapters, using on the one hand a macro-micro model to simulate alternative policies and on the other the findings of various surveys and in particular the 1985 Household Survey.

When considering economic measures and in the analysis, a distinction is generally made between stabilisation and structural adjustment, the term stabilisation being used for measures aimed at demand (and acting mainly in the short term), and the term structural adjustment for those aimed at supply and often requiring more time for their implementation. In practice these terms partly overlap. In order to simplify the presentation, in what follows we shall use the term adjustment for the whole range of measures, except where we wish to stress the specific nature of one measure or another.

B. Structure and growth of production and foreign trade

Agriculture occupies a very important place in the Côte d'Ivoire economy, much more important than in the average middle-income country, whether African or not (see Table I-1). While there is a long-term trend for the agricultural share of GDP to fall (from 47 per cent in 1965 to 36 per cent in 1987), the 1980s seem to have interrupted this fall. Similarly, the fall in the service sector share between 1980 and 1987 runs counter to the trend generally seen in the development process. Côte d'Ivoire is also atypical among the middle-income countries in its openness to foreign trade, as shown by export and import shares much higher than the average for these countries.

GDP growth slowed considerably at the beginning of the 1980s, reaching an annual average of only 2.2 per cent. This is very much lower than the rate of population increase, 4.2 per cent. In industry there was even an absolute fall in production, accompanied by an even greater fall in employment (see Table I-2).

The great weight of the public sector in the Côte d'Ivoire economy can be clearly seen in different ways, even though it is difficult to make comparisons on the international level. Together, the State and the public enterprises account for over 59 per cent of total investment, but less than 6 per cent of employment and 17.5 per cent of GDP.

In **agriculture**, Côte d'Ivoire has been marked by the agricultural export model adopted during the French colonial period and continued after independence. The traditional export crops are coffee and cocoa, forest crops, and since independence, also cotton, cultivated in the savanna, and other export crops promoted in the forest zone and the coastal regions (rubber, oil palm, pineapple, etc.). The effect of this policy is that exports are heavily concentrated on primary products. They accounted for 86 per cent of total exports in 1987 (as compared with 93 per cent in 1965), while for the average lower middle-income country these figures are 27 per cent and 59 per cent respectively, excluding fuels, minerals and metals (see World Bank, World Development Report, 1989).

However, among these primary products, the roles of coffee and cocoa were reversed between 1965 and 1986. Coffee's share of exports fell from 38 per cent in 1965 to 20 per cent in 1986, while cocoa's share increased from 17 per cent to 39 per cent (including processed products and intermediates goods). Building timber also fell from 27 per cent to 7 per cent (see Berthélemy and Bourguignon, p. 373).

Côte d'Ivoire's agriculture at the beginning of the 1980s was also characterised by a relative stagnation in yields, notably for the main export crops. In the case of coffee, there was even a fall due to a lower compensation for a working day than for cocoa (see also Chapter V). In this situation, the state's dependence on the revenue procured by export crops through the Caisse de Stabilisation et de Soutien des Prix et des Productions Agricoles (CSSPPA) is doubly worrying for the producers. They face domestic fiscal burdens and international market forces which the CSSPPA cannot cushion indefinitely, as was seen in 1989.

Coffee and cocoa prices are controlled by the CSSPPA in the following way: the CSSPPA fixes a producer price at which dealers and exporters purchase the product. The CSSPPA also announces an authorised export price, and keeps the difference between these two prices less a gross margin allowed to intermediaries.

The ratio between the price paid to the producers of coffee and cocoa on the one hand and the cif price received for exports on the other has tended to deteriorate, averaging 0.36 for coffee and 0.48 for cocoa for the period 1983-85 as against 0.47 and 0.52 respectively for 1971-73. Thus the CSSPPA's receipts were positive between 1970 and 1986 and in good years (rise of the world market price) amounted to over 30 and even as much as 44 per cent (1977) of total government revenue (see Table I-3).

The CSSPPA receipts were used to finance a great variety of agricultural and non-agricultural investments (see *la Côte d'Ivoire en chiffres*, 1986-87) and were therefore not available to compensate for the very sharp drop in world prices after 1986.

Although food crops (cereals, cassava, yam, plantain) occupy an important place in the primary sector (about 50 per cent of the value added of agriculture, forestry and fisheries), domestic production is increasingly unable to meet the food needs of the population. Food imports therefore increased in relation to total imports during the 1970s and 1980s from about 7 to 8 per cent to 15 to 20 per cent (see *la Côte d'Ivoire en chiffres*, 1980-1981 and 1986-1987).

The state is virtually omnipresent in **industry** through para-statal and mixed enterprises. It holds a majority share in important industries like oil and gas extraction, sugar, oil, tobacco and rubber processing, and also transport. Of the total number of enterprises registered by the *Centrale des Bilans* (using the standard accounting plan) Ivorian public capital amounts to 69 per cent, Ivorian private capital 9 per cent and foreign capital 22 per cent (1983 figures, see Brochet and Pierre, p. 84).

Table I-4 shows the continuing preponderance of the agro-alimentary industries, though their relative share has fallen below the 33 per cent recorded in 1981. Longart (1989) identifies the structural problems of Côte d'Ivoire industries at the beginning of the 1980s under four heading:

1. Reduced competitiveness of enterprises due to inflation and a complex system of quantitative restrictions on imports to protect the import substitution enterprises;

2. Discrimination within the industrial incentive system in favour of sales on domestic and regional markets;

3. Low level of integration of the industrial fabric because the incentive system did not encourage either relations between sectors or the densification of production processes;

4. Inadequate promotion of local industry due to institutional weaknesses.

The quantitative restrictions on industrial sector imports were extended during the 1970s. Thus the number of industrial products subject to import authorisation rose from 86 in 1973 to 426 in 1982, representing about 38 per cent of total imports. In practice, the effects of the quotas varied considerably from one branch to another, for example, from very restrictive in textiles to virtually no effect in industries where the quota was fixed at a level higher than import requirements.

Another characteristic of the industrial sector is its heavy concentration. In most branches, between one and three firms alone account for over 50 per cent of the value added. Domestic competition is therefore limited, and both tariff and non-tariff barriers provided protection from international competition.

Despite these obstacles, imports in the foreign trade of Côte d'Ivoire (see Table 8.5) are dominated by manufactured products. A large proportion, notably machinery and transport equipment, have no domestic competitors. Another point to note is the increasing proportion of food products in total imports. Rice imports make it possible to keep the consumer prices at a relatively low level. Until 1979, these imports accounted for 40 per cent of consumption but this had risen to approximately 80 per cent by 1983.

In exports, the preponderance of primary products remains impressive (86 per cent in 1987). The increased weight of the two main products, coffee and cocoa, together making up 59.5 per cent of the total in 1987 as against 51.2 per cent in 1980, gives grounds for concern in view of the mediocre outlook for the international markets for these products. These figures include processed products and intermediates goods, whose share increased from 5.5 to 8.3 per cent between 1980 and 1987. The diversification of exports, which has been one of the objectives since before 1980, is not yet reflected in the statistics, because the 8.5 per cent fall in building timber was entirely compensated by the increase in cocoa intotal exports. The share of other primary products, processed or otherwise, has thus remained steady at about 20 per cent. This stagnation in global and relative terms obscures opposing trends in different products, both in volume and value terms. Thus between 1980 and 1985, the export volume of latex increased by 82 per cent while that of canned fruits fell by 61 per cent. In value terms, latex exports increased by almost 120 per cent, while those of canned fruits fell by almost 10 per cent and total exports doubled. Canned fish increased more moderately with a 50 per cent rise in value which was, however, below the average (see BCEAO, Statistiques économiques et monétaires, nos. 350 and 354, 1986).

Looking at foreign trade as a whole (Table I-6), it can be seen straight away that there was a surplus throughout the period 1975-85 in the balance of trade, but that the current account balance was continually negative. This is a reflection of Côte d'Ivoire's dependence on foreign labour and capital. Annual transfers for these two factors alone have exceeded FCFA 200 billion since 1979 and amounted to more than FCFA 400 billion in 1985 (rising from 10 to 13 per cent of GDP). The other item weighing on the current account concerns transactions in "non-factor" services (transport, insurance, etc.) which also exceeded FCFA 200 billion a year between 1980 and 1983. While it is clear the fall in the terms of trade as from 1977 (see Table I-6) was an important factor in the deterioration of the foreign trade situation, it also made itself felt in sequences of events (reduced export income leading to increased indebtedness and debt servicing) associated with the overall economic policy, which it is premature to discuss in this introductory Chapter.

C. Public finances and monetary regime

Côte d'Ivoire has a complex system of public finance. It has three main budgets and a certain number of "decentralised" budgets:

1. *Le Budget General de fonctionnement* (BGF), which covers current expenditure;

2. *Le Budget Special d'Investissement et d'Equipement* (BSIE), which covers government investment expenditure but also contributes to the investments of public enterprises;

3. *La Caisse Autonome d'Amortissement* (CAA) which manages the internal and external public debt.

The allocation of taxes to these budgets as well as the "decentralised" budgets is fixed by law. The main factor for flexibility in this system, which could otherwise appear rigid, is the *Caisse de Stabilisation et de Soutien des Prix et des Productions Agricoles* (CSSPPA), whose importance for public finance and the situation of export crop producers has already been stressed (see Table I-3). CSSPPA surpluses may be freely allocated to different budgets and even to non-budget purposes. This flexibility makes it difficult to interpret statistics based on the formal budgets because of the sometimes very large CSSPPA surplus.

The taxes collected amount to about 20 per cent of GDP (see Table I-7), the most important one being that on imports (representing 38 per cent of total taxes in 1981). This is one of the taxes on international trade which together bring in about 50 per cent of the tax take. The export tax mainly concerns three products (coffee, cocoa and building timber). Non-traditional exports are virtually exempt. Among the other taxes which should be mentioned are a payroll tax paid by non-agricultural enterprises at the rate of 12.5 per cent on the wages of Ivorians and other Africans and 20 per cent on those of non-African expatriates. In addition, non-agricultural workers pay a tax on their wages (about 2.5 per cent) levied before income tax, the average effective rate of which is on the order of 4 per cent.

Public enterprises contribute very little in the way of surpluses (and more often deficits) to the tax revenue. The figures in Table I-7 in fact overestimate this contribution because they do not take account of the direct subsidies paid to these enterprises and included in current expenditure.

The relative share of total current expenditure showed a certain tendency to rise after 1980. This trend is partly explained by the maintenance of current activities while real GDP fell after 1981. But within this category there were both increases and declines. The item that increased the most was interest payments, which reflects at the same time the increase in the debt and the rise in interest rates (this is discussed in more detail below).

Unlike current expenditure, the investment expenditure share fell regularly after 1978, corresponding to a reduction in its two components, government investment and public enterprise investment. However, it is not easy to trace the evolution of these investments because those included in the BSIE do not cover all public investment. Until 1985, public enterprises could in fact obtain financing outside what was provided for in the programme law for investment. This decentralisation of financing decisions contributed to the uncontrolled growth of the Côte d'Ivoire debt.

While the outstanding debt and new loans were already considerable before 1980 (amounting to as much as 60 per cent of GDP), they subsequently increased even further, reaching a maximum of 100 per cent of GDP in 1983, with a debt service representing 43 per cent of exports. The weight of this burden gave rise to a rescheduling in 1984, which cut the cost of debt servicing by half (see Table I-8).

Côte d'Ivoire's financial and economic situation is also conditioned by its membership in the l'Union Monétaire Ouest-Africaine (UMOA) whose currency, the FCFA, is tied to the French franc by an exchange rate fixed at 50:1 and managed by *la Banque Centrale des Etats de l'Afrique de l'Ouest* (BCEAO).

Under an agreement signed between France and UMOA Member states in 1973, France guarantees unlimited convertibility between the two currencies, through an "operations account" that the BCEAO maintains with the French Treasury. In return, the governments are subject to strict limits on their borrowings from the Banque Centrale. The BCEAO has several instruments for controlling the quantity and conditions of credit in Member countries: (1) maintenance of minimum reserves, limits on advances to governments, refinancing ceilings, standards for the evolution of ordinary credits; (2) sectoral credit policies, prior authorisation for credit granted by the banks and (3) interest rate policy, fixing identical rates for all Member countries. Normally banks and financial institutions do not have the right to have a debit balance on their accounts with the BCEAO. The credits granted to the government by the Banque Centrale are deducted from the general refinancing ceiling to arrive at a ceiling open to banks and financial institutions. The BCEAO has created an inter-bank money market which accepts surplus deposits from banks and subsequently lends them to other banks within the UMOA. Côte d'Ivoire banks have been the biggest net borrowers on this market.

An important principle of the UMOA is the free circulation of capital within it and with France. However, transfers are subject to a tax of 0.25 per cent. Capital flows to or from places outside the franc zone are in principle subject to the agreement of the BCEAO and the Côte d'Ivoire government, but in practice there are few restrictions.

D. Product and factor markets

Looking at the overall situation on the principal product and factor markets in Côte d'Ivoire, we find marked state presence and intervention in certain fields and great openness to the exterior and lack of intervention in others.

Thus in the export crop sector, the state intervenes to fix the producer prices for coffee, cocoa, cotton (and partly for rubber) but leaves the collection and marketing of these products in the hands of authorised traders. In forestry (where the capital is 80 per cent foreign) the state simply issues operating licenses.

In the case of food products, where the output is consumed by the producers or traded on local markets the state only intervenes to fix the price of rice on both the level of production and that of consumption. However, there is a free market that is bigger than the official market. Rice sold to consumers on this latter market (imported rice) is considered by consumers to be inferior and this is reflected in a price differential between the two markets.

The market for industrial products is characterised by production oriented more towards the domestic market than to exports and by effective protection that increased during the 1970s. The state intervenes in the functioning of this market in many ways, for example, by investing in enterprises, providing incentives and through fiscal measures.

The labour market (discussed in more detail in Chapter IV) is characterised by a dualism between the traditional sector and the modern sector. In this latter there is considerable rigidity due to the existence of minimum wages for all categories of employees, limitations on dismissals, and the existence of social welfare and employment taxes.

Lastly, we have seen that the financial market is very open thanks to the UMOA system. The mobility of financial capital in this system is further facilitated by the presence of subsidiaries of French commercial banks. However, the policy of keeping interest rates low has perhaps encouraged flight of capital and discouraged mobilisation of local savings. At the same time, since the long-term financial market is fairly narrow, the general openness of the system enabled foreign loans to be contracted in virtually uncontrolled fashion before the introduction of the adjustment measures.

E. Employment, incomes and poverty

The difficulties of defining and applying with any precision the concepts of "labour force" and "participation rates" in a country like Côte d'Ivoire are well known. They are essentially due to the absence of complete statistics, the existence of a large subsistence sector in rural areas, and the importance of the informal sector in urban areas.

We shall therefore use orders of magnitude and major trends that broadly converge even though there are divergences in details between the different sources. A first observation concerns the high proportion of people employed in the primary sector (59 per cent in 1985), which is higher than the rural population for the same year (52.7 per cent, see Tables I-9 and I-10). There are thus agricultural and forestry activities that occupy part of the population defined as urban, something which is in fact confirmed by analysis of the household surveys.

A second peculiarity is the large proportion on non-Ivorians in the total population (over 25 per cent and rising), which results in substantial transfers in the form of migrant remittances. The great majority of the non-Ivorian population is made up of immigrants from neighbouring countries who have unskilled jobs in rural and urban areas. Thus they provide about 60 per cent of the forestry workers and over 80 per cent of the agricultural workers in the modern enterprises in these sectors. Nevertheless, on the whole the non-Ivorians tend to be more urban than rural and together with the internal migrants they contribute to the growing urbanisation. The population of Abidjan is thus increasing at an annual average rate of 10 per cent.

The influx of migrants also explains why the increase in the active population was substantially higher than the increase in the total population (5.6 per cent as against 4.2 per cent over the period 1980-85).

As regards the sectoral breakdown of the active population, we have already noted (Table I-2) a decline in the modern sector. This decrease is both absolute and relative, while in the primary sector an absolute increase of about 100 000 persons employed has not prevented a fall in the relative share of this sector due to the very considerable increase in the numbers working in the informal sector.

The differences between the two minimum wages, SMIG and SMAG (for the non-agricultural and agricultural sectors respectively) and the wages effectively paid by enterprises in the modern sector (see Table I-11) give some indication of the inequalities in incomes in the different milieux. But as there can be multiple sources of income, and notably income in kind in rural areas, the inequalities in total income are probably not so great as the inequalities in wages. Nevertheless it is clear that on average agricultural workers (except in the modern food producing sector) are the most disadvantaged and civil servants the most advantaged. It should be noted, however, that the self-employed in the informal sector are not covered by these data.

For Ivorians and other Africans the inequalities in incomes also correspond to a difference in educational level: the higher the educational attainment, the greater the remuneration (see Table I-12). However, the same educational level does not guarantee equality of incomes between groups. Thus non-Africans are highly privileged by remuneration that is much higher than those of others. However, while the inequality factor (defined as the ratio between pay at the same educational level) is on the order of 6 for the lowest levels (though there are very few non-Africans at this level), it falls as educational attainment increases and is 1.7 for those with higher education. These 1979 figures indicate the advantages of progressing in the educational system, but they do not take account of the unemployment among those with diplomas that appeared during the 1980s.

The inequalities can also be demonstrated in a different way, through comparing the percentage of total income for households in different strata of the population (see World Bank, *World Development Report*, 1989). The distribution for 1985-86 is as follows:

Poorest	2nd Quintile	3rd Quintile	4th Quintile	5th Quintile
2.4 %	6.2%	10.9%	19.1%	61.4%

The ratio between the poorest quintile and the richest is about 1:26. Comparing these data with those for other developing countries (see also J. Lecaillon *et al.* for earlier years) it can be seen that income distribution in Côte d'Ivoire is relatively unequal.

Measuring inequality using the Gini coefficient put Côte d'Ivoire at an average level in 1959 with a Gini of 0.46, while the data for the 1970s gave a Gini of between 0.52 and 0.54, thus indicating increasing inequality at a relatively high rate during the 1960s and 1970s. On the basis of 1985 data, an income Gini of 0.49 can be obtained (by dividing the Gini coefficient of expenditure calculated by Glewwe by 0.88), thus suggesting a reversal of the earlier trend.

Glewwe (1987) analyses inequality in Côte d'Ivoire on the basis of the (adjusted) per capita expenditure provided by the 1985 Household Survey, using different measures. They all show that inequality is greatest in Abidjan and least in the Western Forest, which is a region of recent colonisation. Taking Côte d'Ivoire as a whole, however, inequality is greater than within any of its regions, which implies very great inequality between regions. This contributes roughly 10 times more to total inequality than that between ethnic groups or between nationals of different African countries. Even more important than regional inequality, is the inequality between educational levels, which according to this same analysis accounts for between 27 and 37 per cent of total inequality.

The 1985 Household Survey data were used extensively by the World Bank to analyse poverty by population deciles, notably with a 10 per cent and 30 per cent poverty line (cf. Glewwe, Kanbur, etc.). Glewwe found the following distribution for average per capita expenditure (FCFA):

	Poorest decile	Deciles (1-3)	Total population
Expenditure on food	32 200	47 100	105 500
Total expenditure	45 000	70 000	216 500

We add our own analysis based on these data in Chapter V. In the absence of any other comprehensive analyses of poverty at the beginning of the 1980s, we can nevertheless use certain welfare indicators to define Côte d'Ivoire's position (see Table I-13).

On the whole, the health and education indicators show Côte d'Ivoire as being rather below the average for middle-income countries. Nevertheless, even during the crisis years the majority of these social indicators improved. The daily calorie intake per inhabitant constitutes the exception, for it fell between 1980 and 1986. This trend reflects the considerable population increase and the growing difficulty in meeting food requirements either through domestic production or through imports.

Note

1.   Section based largely on Berthélemy and Bourguignon, 1989.

Chapter II

Origins of the Macroeconomic Imbalances

A. Introduction

The origins of the macroeconomic imbalances are to be found on the one hand in the structural vulnerability of the Ivorian economy that we briefly described in Chapter I, and on the other in exogenous and endogenous factors effecting the functioning of this economy. While these different origins can be distinguished from an analytical standpoint, they are in reality closely enmeshed and their disequilibrating effects can successively reinforce one another.

Thus the heavy structural dependence on coffee and cocoa exports of Côte d'Ivoire's economy was reinforced during the 1970s, with increases in the sown area of 100 per cent for cocoa and 40 per cent for coffee between 1970 and 1980. The increased dependence on these crops was stimulated by favourable world and domestic prices which allowed the government to obtain tax and other fiscal revenue from these crops while paying the producers sufficiently high prices to encourage them to increase production. The functioning and the importance of the CSSPPA (briefly explained in Chapter I) caused the government to maintain and even strengthen a production and export structure that threatened to disrupt the entire economy if there should be a long-lasting decline in the market.

Among the endogenous factors there is a system of tax and other fiscal revenues highly dependent on export crops. Conversely, the world market can be seen as an exogenous factor, whose price and demand fluctuations have a direct and strong influence on the volume of fiscal revenues and, more indirectly, on producer incomes. In addition, as a factor further aggravating the structural disequilibrium, there is a certain rigidity associated with perennial crops. It is difficult to envisage the premature uprooting of coffee and cocoa plants except in situations of dire distress. A less radical reaction by producers that can increase flexibility in the short term in response to a fall in profitability of these crops is to reduce the amount of effort put into maintaining the plantations and harvesting the crop.

An increase in public expenditure, notably in investments, during boom periods is another link in the chain of "disequilibrating dependence" that can be identified in Côte d'Ivoire. These expenditures generally involve recurrent costs which become a heavier burden when the financial situation deteriorates and the costs of several years of investment are accumulated. In addition, there is a certain inertia in the planning and implementation of investment projects, which prevents rapid adjustment of expenditure to income, except by abandoning current projects, which often means the complete loss of any expenditure already made.

B. External shocks

Côte d'Ivoire suffered a first shock as a result of the oil price increases of 1973/74 which were passed on to the import prices and caused a deterioration in the terms of trade. However, this first shock was more than compensated for in 1977 when the terms of trade improved by 73 per cent as compared with 1975. Table II-1 shows the evolution of the three main export products. The price increases were higher for coffee than for cocoa. The increases were temporary, however, with a fall in the terms of trade for total exports as early as 1978. The effect of the fall in export prices was subsequently aggravated by the price increases of imports caused by the second oil shock of 1979. The impact of the shock on the world coffee and cocoa markets was felt all the more strongly in Côte d'Ivoire because these products weigh very heavily in the exports (see Table I-5). Furthermore, the simultaneous (in 1978) fall in the terms of trade and in coffee production reinforced the negative impact. It should be noted that the producers were protected from this reversal of the world market after 1977/78 because the nominal prices they received remained stable or increased (for real price trends see Chapter V-2).

Another external factor that acted less suddenly but contributed significantly to the deterioration of the situation was the increase in interest rates for the external debt, which rose from about 8 per cent in 1976 to 12 per cent in 1980.

C. Internal disequilibrium factors

The main internal factor behind the crisis was the extremely rapid increase in public investment (see Table II-2). In real terms, public investment increased by 250 per cent between 1975 and 1980. It rose from 15 per cent of GDP in 1975 to 21 per cent in 1978 and was still 14 per cent in 1980 (see Table I-7). Total public investment increased from 22 to 24 per cent of the GDP between 1975 and 1980, with a peak of almost 30 per cent in 1978. In the years 1977-78, public investment was over 70 per cent of total investment.

As the investment boom coincided with the coffee and cocoa boom, it might be thought that the latter was responsible for the former. In reality this is true only to a limited extent, because substantial investments had been decided upon as early as the preparation of the 1976-80 Plan, which had been encouraged by the CSSPPA surplus of 1974. Investment expenditure in 1977-80 nevertheless exceeded the Plan figures, this under the influence of a certain euphoria because the improvement in the terms of trade was interpreted as a durable phenomenon rather than being temporary.

Table II-3 shows the differences between the 1976-80 Plan figures and the actual figures, in the field of investment among others. It can be seen that the planned figures for investment and financing were exceeded only in the public sector, while the private sector remained very much below the forecasts. It is partly because of the hesitancy of the private sector that the public sector accounted for such a large share, of the external debt too. The fact is that the income from the coffee and cocoa boom was not sufficient to finance the expansion, but it was not until after 1979 (when the CSSPPA receipts had substantially fallen) that foreign loans reached a maximum, covering over 90 per cent of public investment (see Table II-2). Thus for two or three years the coffee and cocoa boom had made it difficult to perceive the imbalances that had been looming for quite some time.

Besides the increase in the volume of public investments, it is also necessary to consider the quality of the investment projects. In fact it turns out that investment projects, often on a very large scale, like SODESUCRE in the sugar sector, were not always profitable. What is more, the emphasis placed on the development of the North and of infrastructure could hold out the promise of benefits only in the longer term.

In agriculture, 37 per cent of the public investment was used for developing sugar crops (without counting the processing plants). This was a very large project which took a long time to implement. The capital-output ratio alone, 5.8 (on the basis of the planned 1985 production), bears witness to this.

The main infrastructure investments construction of two hydro-electric stations, roads and the development of the telecommunications network. When work started, a dynamic response from the private sector was counted on, but this never materialised. At national level, the dominance of big investment projects and the inadequate response of the productive sector resulted in a marginal capital-output ratio of 4.1 during the period 1976-80, as against 2.9 in 1965-70 and 3.4 in 1970-75.

The preponderance of big projects with long lead times can clearly be seen in Table II-4, as can the cost overruns. These overruns reflect the lack of control over public expenditure, due to the functioning of the CSSPPA (see Chapter I above) and to spending by public agencies and enterprises decided on a decentralised basis even where it involved foreign loans.

A second factor of internal disequilibrium (after the excessive public investment) was the fall in private savings during the 1970s from 11 per cent of GDP on average during the first half to 5 per cent during the second half of the decade (see Table II-5). This fall was not foreseen in the Plan and is to be explained by several factors :

a) increasing remittances by foreign workers;

b) a relative increase in food prices of about 50 per cent between 1976 and 1980, reflecting a growing imbalance between the agricultural sector and the rest of the economy, this increase influencing not only the capacity to save of households, but also that of enterprises, because wages were indexed on food prices;

c) an increase in the interest rates for loans contracted abroad by enterprises, which reduced the profits available for savings.

A corollary of the fall in private savings was accelerated private consumption. This grew at 9.2 per cent a year between 1975 and 1980, as against 6.4 per cent for the economy as a whole.

The demand created by investment and consumption naturally affected imports, which increased at an annual average rate of 13.2 per cent during the period, while total exports increased at a rate of only 4.6 per cent. The food products share of imports doubled between 1975 and 1979, to reach 18 per cent. The government responded to the increased competition from imports by quantitative restrictions in the form of quotas and prior authorisation requirements in the industrial sector.

As regards the financial consequences of the imbalances that appeared in the second half of the 1970s, we have already mentioned the indebtedness that helped to aggravate the current account deficit. In 1979, part of the deficit was financed through foreign loans by the Ivorian commercial banks. Finally in 1980, when this deficit reached 18 per cent of GDP, the foreign assets in the Banque Centrale were exhausted and the operating account with the French treasury was in deficit for the first time since independence. Thus the growing imbalances had led Côte d'Ivoire into a financial impasse.

Another financial consequence of the imbalances was the acceleration of inflation, which reached an average annual rate of about 16 per cent between 1974 and 1980 as against 5.7 per cent during the preceding ten years. However, part of this inflation was due to foreign trade: price increases in the industrialised countries, and hence in imports, and price boom for the main exports. Nevertheless, inflation in Côte d'Ivoire exceeded the import price rises and the effective real exchange rate (import price/Ivorian GDP deflator) fell as a result by about 4 per cent a year between 1974 and 1979. There was thus a loss of purchasing power for non-indexed wage earners and a loss of international competitiveness because of relatively high inflation.

Monetary policy was on the whole fairly lax and did not really try to damp down this inflationary pressure. Access to external credit for investors, the commercial banks and the government was easy and contributed to the external indebtedness, while interest rates were fixed at a fairly low level by the Banque Centrale, causing capital to seek better yields elsewhere. The first big loan (FCFA 30 billion) by the banking sector to the government was in 1979. The (gross) government debt with the Banque Centrale reached FCFA 78 billion in 1980.

In conclusion, we can trace the origins of the crisis and its evolution to a series of imbalances, whose effects were cumulative and sometimes reinforced one another. Thus the structural disequilibrium of an economy and a fiscal system depending very heavily on coffee and cocoa was aggravated during a period when the world market was favourable. The euphoria caused by the external boom stimulated existing investment ambitions. These two phenomena would probably by themselves have been enough to push up inflation and hence reduce the competitiveness of exports and create a pressure in favour of imports, in short external disequilibrium.

This external disequilibrium, whose origins in part were domestic, was further reinforced by external factors (lower cocoa and coffee prices and higher interest rates) as well as domestic factors (lack of strict budgetary management, low efficiency of public investment, and a lax monetary policy that was also inappropriate in the field of interest rates). In the process, the budget imbalance caused by the domestic investment boom contributed to external disequilibrium because of the growing indebtedness necessary to cover the deficits.

Chapter III

The 1981-86 Adjustment Policy and its Main Economic Consequences

A. Introduction

Côte d'Ivoire's adjustment policy involves a fairly long and complex process which began shortly after the coffee and cocoa boom in 1977-78 and has been going on ever since. It is not simply a reaction to the shocks and imbalances of the 1970s; its implementation has been accompanied by climatic shocks and by the sudden changes in the world market during the 1980s (see the Chronology annexed to this chapter). It has consisted of a series of programmes aimed at restoring financial and economic health, at both macroeconomic and sectoral level. While austerity has been the key word (and the response to the excessive and sometimes poorly chosen expenditures of the past), efforts have also been made to improve the efficiency of both public and private management. Austerity concerns the management of investment and credit as well as the multitude of inefficient public enterprises, some of which have been closed down or privatised. For the private sector, the main objectives have been to increase competitiveness and productivity. Social objectives, notably for equity and poverty, are virtually absent from these programmes. At best, account is implicitly taken of them through assuming a "trickle down", i.e. the idea that in the final analysis everyone will benefit from a revival of growth resulting from a reduction of imbalances.

B. Principal objectives

Confronted with a financial crisis due to the fall in world coffee and cocoa prices in 1978, the Ivorian authorities reacted rapidly by adopting an initial one-year action programme that started in April 1978. It included the cancelling or postponement of certain investment projects and increasing taxes. This first set of measures was extended in the orientations of the economic and financial programme for 1981-83, which was the major component of the adjustment policy. It formed part of the agreement with the IMF and was also the basis (in its macroeconomic aspects) for the agreement with the World Bank on the first structural adjustment loan (PAS I).

The general objectives of the programme were:

— progressive reduction of the public finance deficit to 6.2 per cent of GDP in 1983 (as against 11.4 per cent in 1981);

— progressive reduction of the external current account deficit to 8.4 per cent of GDP (as against 16.7 per cent in 1981);

— progressive stabilisation of external debt servicing at about one quarter the value of the exports of goods and services.

a) Macroeconomic measures

A set of budgetary and monetary measures with the accent on reducing absorption was followed by measures concerned with foreign trade. These latter consisted in modification of the trade regime aimed at improving international competitiveness and reducing certain rents due to protection. These measures, in combination with the sectoral measures, were intended to permit a certain reallocation of resources towards sectors producing tradeable goods, even if this reallocation does not explicitly appear among the objectives.

Budgetary measures

In addition to reductions in expenditure, notably investment, and increases in revenues through an additional fiscal effort, there were institutional reforms. These were necessary to implement the austerity policy, which implied greater control over public expenditure and greater budgetary discipline.

Two major new tools were therefore created:

1. A consolidated public sector account, covering all public finance (Treasury, *Caisse Autonome d'Amortissement*, CSSPPA, funds for specifically earmarked revenues, social security, public establishments and a representative sample of public enterprises).

2. A *Comité de Coordination Financière et de Controle des Investissements*, which draws up and updates a monthly summary of the consolidated accounts of the State, the monetary situation, external assets and the public debt servicing schedule. This Committee also sets conditions for new public investment projects and draws up every month a systematic inventory of public sector arrears. Thus any slippage through falling into arrears can be identified and eliminated.

Greater control of public expenditure also means tighter programming and control of public investment, here using a triennial complete list that includes both public and parastatal projects. The control procedures are intended to give preference to economic investments and pay closer attention to recurring costs.

The reduction of expenditures was mainly to the detriment of investment expenditure. This was reduced from FCFA 415 billion in 1978 to 174 billion in 1985. This reduction is even more impressive when compared with total expenditures (see Table I-7) because nominal current expenditures doubled over the same period. The increase was due in the first place to increased interest payments (up from FCFA 36 to 295 billion) and wages. Despite the wage freeze, this item of expenditure still increased by about 10 per cent between 1982 and 1985. Several other measures concerning both expenditure and revenues were implemented (see the Chronology annexed to this Chapter) and made it possible to reduce the overall deficit of public sector consolidated operations from 11.4 per cent of GDP in 1981 to 7.8 per cent in 1983 and 5.8 per cent in 1984. The reduction of the deficit thus occurred more slowly than initially planned in the objectives.

Monetary policy

Monetary policy was aimed at limiting inflation and indirectly the balance of payments deficit, by means of a credit ceiling. A particular sub-ceiling was fixed for the public sector in order to maintain a sufficient volume of credit for the private sector. The Banque Centrale pursued an interest rate policy aimed at making domestic financial investments competitive in order to prevent the flight of capital, which is very mobile within the franc zone. In line with this aim, the tax on bank interest (tax on services) was reduced in three stages from 25 per cent to 10 per cent.

b) Sectoral measures

Among the objectives of these measures a distinction can be made between those concerned more specifically with public enterprises and those concerned with all sectors. For the former, it was a matter of rationalising relations between the state and its enterprises and eliminating their shortcomings as regards costs and profitability. Management studies of 15 of these enterprises led to restructuring plans for ten of them between 1982 and 1984. As a result, the consolidated operating surplus of the public enterprise sector more than tripled between 1982 and 1985 (from FCFA 13 to 42 billion). This process of improving the management of public enterprises continued after 1985 and reduced the volume of transfers from the treasury to these enterprises.

Industry

A certain number of measures were taken to encourage exports (subsidy of 20 per cent of value added) and to unify and generally reduce the levels of import protection. These measures were intended to make the industrial sector more dynamic and competitive (see the Chronology annexed to this chapter).

These measures were introduced as from 1984. While they did perhaps help the revival of the industrial sector as from 1985 (industrial production had fallen by 7.5 per cent a year between 1980 and 1984), they had at best only limited success. Even the export subsidy seemed to suffer from a lack of credibility that it would be maintained, so entrepreneurs hesitated to make the investment necessary to benefit from the export possibilities.

On the institutional level (*Ministère de l'Industrie* and *Centre d'Assistance et de Promotion de l'Entreprise Nationale*) the planned strengthening did not materialise. The reforms also encountered opposition from industrialists who had previously enjoyed a high level of protection. What is more, the appreciation of the FCFA against the dollar, while potential competitors like Ghana and Nigeria were devaluing their currencies as part of their adjustment processes, led to the reintroduction of quotas and reference prices for imports in 1988.

Agriculture

According to the policy declarations, this was the priority sector, but, as indicated by the Chronology annexed to this chapter, the measures mainly concerned export crops and rice, which benefited from incentives.

As regards the public enterprises in the agricultural sector, the reorganisation of SODESUCRE seems to have been successful, as this company now manages to cover its operating expenses, though this is on the basis of domestic sales prices well above the world price. It also seems that considerable progress was made with regard to the functioning of the companies that organise the producers and this also benefits food crops.

However, little was really achieved in the research programme and its links with agricultural advisory services, or the medium- and long-term strategies for which studies had been planned. This is all the more worrying since the agricultural sector greatly suffers from imbalances linked to the heavy concentration on coffee and cocoa and to the virtual stagnation of the food sector. The evolution of the agricultural system and the situation of producers during the adjustment period are analysed in greater detail in Chapter V.

Housing

In this field, the policy of the 1970s was to build dwellings and have them managed by public and semi-public enterprises. These dwellings were designed to satisfy the needs of the medium and high income groups and benefited from subsidies that were a considerable burden on the state budget.

To eliminate this source of deficits, the government greatly reduced the subsidies to housing for civil servants and gradually sold off the dwellings and closed down or reorganised the enterprises active in this field. The *Direction du Contrôle des Grands Travaux* (DCGTX) was given the job of running a new system of housing construction that gave pride of place to private promoters and the mobilisation of savings for access to ownership through commercial banks.

Energy

In the context of the third structural adjustment loan, a certain number of measures were envisaged to make this sector more efficient. This involved improving co-ordination within the sector and between the several ministries concerned, pricing, and investment programming.

Oil production failed to live up to the hopes placed in it, reaching its peak in 1983. However, the *Société Ivoirienne de Raffinage* (SIR), a mixed economy entity, was successful, for it is no longer a burden on the Treasury and has even succeeded in reducing the ex-refinery price to consumers from about 200 per cent of the equivalent price for imports (excluding taxes) to about 135 per cent.

Studies were undertaken in several areas, but without leading to the solution of some persistent problems. Thus *Energie Electrique de la Côte d'Ivoire* (EECI), which is a heavy burden on the state, has not been restructured and continues to suffer from among other things, considerable arrears in payment by administrations, municipalities and public enterprises.

C. Economic consequences

Although the application of certain measures decided as early as 1981 met with resistance and took several years to become effective (for example the alignment of wages in public enterprises) Côte d'Ivoire did on the whole adhere strictly to the austerity measures. The reduction of public demand brought a reduction in real terms in private consumption, private investment and hence also imports as from 1981.

As regards real GDP, there was stagnation in 1980/81 and a subsequent fall until 1985 (see Tables III-1 and III-2). With an annual average population increase of about 4 per cent and an annual fall in real GDP of 4 per cent between 1981 and 1984, per capita GDP must therefore have fallen steadily over three years at the rate of about 8 per cent a year.

Taking the period 1980-87, it can be seen that industry was the sector hit the hardest, for its annual rate of growth was negative (-2.4 per cent) over the whole period (see Table I-1), while in agriculture and the service sector, the growth rates were halved (as compared with 1965-80) but remained positive. Within the industrial sector, mining and textiles continued to grow, but then went into decline after 1983 and 1985 respectively (see Table I-4). The sector that was hit hardest and fastest was construction and public works, where value added fell by 74 per cent in real terms between 1979 and 1984.

In addition to the substantial depressive effect resulting from the cut in public expenditure, industrial enterprises suffered financially from the accumulation of arrears by the government. These "forced loans" to the government (whose ability to borrow from the banking system was limited to 20 per cent of the preceding year's tax take) reached a (cumulative) level of 10 per cent of GDP by the end of 1983.

There were four main reasons for this practice of paying greatly in arrears, and these same reasons explain why at first (1981-83), the public sector deficit persisted despite the reduced expenditure. The coffee and cocoa markets remained unfavourable, seriously limiting CSSPPA receipts (see Table I-3). The burden of external debt servicing became heavier, reaching 43 per cent of exports in 1982. Under the influence of the depression, tax revenue fell as a percentage of GDP (from 22.3 per cent in 1981 to 18.4 per cent in 1984) despite the increases in certain tax rates. Finally, the additional income that was supposed to be generated by oil production as from 1982 never materialised.

These same reasons prevented any substantial improvement in the current account balance before 1984 (see Table I-6). It is important to remember that most of the factors working against an immediate and significant reduction in the budget deficit and balance of payments deficit following the reduction in public expenditures were exogenous and thus quite independent of the policy pursued by the government. It was only after an improvement in the terms of trade in 1984 (aided by debt rescheduling and more favourable weather conditions) that an impressive reduction in these two deficits was achieved. Thus the consolidated public sector deficit fell to 2.8 per cent of GDP in 1985, and the current balance nearly reached equilibrium in the same year (according to Bougerol it was even in surplus as early as 1984).

However, the existing austerity policies were augmented in 1984/85 by additional austerity measures which included further reductions in spending for hiring new civil service personnel and on student grants in higher and secondary education. New civil service recruitment was cut by a reduction of about 30 per cent (from 4 132 to 2 782) in admissions to schools providing training for the public sector. Furthermore, the number of student grants was reduced by 50 per cent for higher education (from about 3 800 to 1 900) and by 30 per cent for secondary education (from 58 000 to 41 000). These latter measures indicate that young people denied access to relatively privileged jobs and to secondary and higher education had to bear part of the burden of adjustment.

The reduction of employment in the modern enterprise sector from 243 000 to 165 000 between 1979 and 1984 makes it possible to identify another substantial group of people who were directly affected (see also Chapter IV).

On the whole, it was the urban population who seem to have been more affected than the rural population by cuts in incomes. Thus it is estimated that during the period 1978-85, the urban population lost 45 per cent of their per capita income in real terms and the rural population, 27 per cent (from an initial level which was very much higher in the towns of course; see also Chapter V).

To conclude this analysis of the adjustment process, a number of observations can be made. To begin with, the validity of the multiple restructuring measures cannot be called into question in general terms, but it is clear that the adjustments did not take place as rapidly as hoped. Moreover, it was exogenous factors that finally determined the timing and way in which certain balances were restored. This draws attention to a very worrying third point, i.e. the fragility and vulnerability of the Ivorian economy. Despite considerable progress in many areas, notably as regards public enterprises, an adjustment of the basic structure of this economy still remains to be accomplished in order to reduce this vulnerability and create a more favourable and durable foundation for economic growth.

Chronology of the Major Events and Measures 1977-87

1977/78 Boom in world coffee and cocoa prices.

1978/79 Initial austerity measures in the form of cancellation or postponement of investment projects.

Fiscal measures: increased taxes (VAT, taxes on services, tobacco and fuels).

1979 Second oil shock.

1980 International Coffee Agreement introduces export quotas.

1981 Adoption of an austerity operating budget (preceding the stabilisation and adjustment programmes under the aegis of the IMF and the World Bank in the same year) with a limitation on the increase in expenditures to 5 per cent in current francs and the following specific measures:

— Petrol tax increase of 10 per cent;

— Increases in tariffs and prices:

a) electricity: +7.5 per cent;

b) railways: +9 per cent for passengers, +11 per cent for freight;

c) water: +8.3 per cent and +5.3 per cent in two stages;

d) transport: SOTRA +25 per cent; AIR IVOIRE +15 per cent;

e) rice: consumer price +10 per cent;
    producer price for paddy -20 per cent.

— Measures affecting wages: alignment of public entity wages on public service wages, which are frozen.

1981 Record harvest, with 7.5 per cent growth in the primary sector.

1981 Agreements with the IMF (January) on a 1981-83 stabilisation programme under the Enlarged Financing Facility (EFF) for 485 million SDRs and with the World Bank (December) on a structural adjustment loan (PAS I, of US$150 million).

At the level of **macroeconomic management**, these two agreements (to be followed by several confirmation agreements in 1984-88 and PAS II and PAS III in 1983 and 1986 respectively) overlap one another and are aimed at:

— tightening budgetary discipline and consolidating public finances, among other things by setting up a committee for financial co-ordination and investment control;

— limiting external borrowings;

— limiting domestic credit, including for the public sector.

As regards public enterprises and sectoral policies, several measures were envisaged in PAS I and partly extended in PAS II and PAS III. We summarise here those that were actually implemented:

— **Public enterprise management**: Closing down 16 public enterprises (between 1978 and 1982), control of local and foreign loans, management audits, preparation of rehabilitation plans, (undertaking) reorganisation, increased tariffs, financial restructuring of the three main public enterprises in the agricultural sector (including the settlement of arrears).

— **Agricultural policy:** encouragement of the production of export crops and rice through increasing producer prices (between 1981 and 1984) for coffee and cocoa (+33 per cent), cotton (+43 per cent, but at the same time, abolishing subsidies on fertilisers used in cotton growing), oil palm by small growers (+35 per cent) and paddy rice (+33 per cent, accompanied by an increase of 23 per cent in the consumer price). The price for small producers of rubber is oriented towards the world market. Privatisation of the public sector activities in rice processing and marketing.

1982	Increase of 10 per cent in the minimum wages of the private and semi-public sector; freezing of the base ceiling for the calculation of social insurance taxes.
1983	Severe drought.
1984	Maintaining or extending external debt with the Clubs of Paris and London.
1984/85	Confirmation and extension of **austerity measures:**

— Limitation of operating expenditure to 1 per cent above the 1983 level in current francs;

— Reduction of public investment expenditures in real terms for the fourth consecutive year;

— Reduction of civil service recruitment based on reducing admissions to vocational schools preparing for it from 4 132 to 2 782);

— Reduction of the number of grants available for higher education by 50 per cent (from about 3 800 to 1 900) and for secondary education by 30 per cent (from 58 000 to 41 000);

— Continuation of the freeze on civil service remuneration for the third consecutive year;

— Reduction of the subsidies for civil servant housing and sale of public sector housing to individuals.

Commercial and industrial policy

— Promulgation of a revised investment code (1984);

— Raising of the reference values serving as a basis for the export duties on coffee and cocoa;

— Increased import duties and specific tax on fuels;

— First phase of the customs duty reform, reducing effective protection to about 40 per cent on products representing over 80 per cent of the industrial value added;

— Adoption of a system of export subsidies based on value added (not brought into force until 1987) and replacement of quantitative restrictions on imports by a temporary increase in import duties;

— Increase of 25 per cent in the cost of electricity, public transport in Abidjan and water;

— Increase in the prices of bread (+7 per cent) and petrol (+8 per cent).

1986

— Record cocoa harvest, increasing receipts from cocoa exports by 25 per cent.

— Multi-year rescheduling of the commercial debt (MYRA).

1987

— Collapse of world coffee prices, causing a fall of 40 per cent in receipts from coffee exports;

— Stopping of interest payments to creditors of the Paris Club and London Club.

— Increase in import duties, due to the financial crisis, increasing the level of effective protection to 52 per cent.

Chapter IV

Employment in a Period of Adjustment[1]

A. Introduction

The austerity policies pursued by the Côte d'Ivoire government since 1981 form part of the economic treatment of the crisis. On one hand, the contraction of domestic demand and the attempt to achieve greater efficiency by eliminating unnecessary jobs, among other things, certainly had negative effects on employment and wages, while on the other hand liberalisation of the functioning of the labour market was suposed to work in favour of labour, very abundant in Côte d'Ivoire. These two effects do not necessarily cancel one another out in a given period and two series of vital questions need to be asked:

— What jobs were eliminated and created by sector and by skill level in the short and medium term? What was the trend in wages for the different categories?

— In the medium term, what economic structure needs to be established so that in the future there will be an improvement in the labour market and in equity for the different occupational categories?

The replies to the first questions require an analysis of the general characteristics of the labour market and its situation before the adjustment and of the specific measures affecting labour. Then there has to be a quantitative study of the different effects on employment, skill levels and remuneration. While the answer to the second question has to take the historical analysis undertaken in this chapter into account, it is given only in terms of the simulations made using a general equilibrium model where the main relationships, both macroeconomic and microeconomic, can be taken into account (see Chapter VI).

In this Chapter, analysis centres on the modern sector because of the statistical opaqueness of the traditional sector and much more complete data are available for the modern sector.

The introductory section describes the labour market before the adjustment; the second describes the adjustment measures concerning labour; the third presents a chronological analysis of the main effects of the adjustment on employment and skill levels and the fourth section studies the trends in wages and the labour-intensity of production.

B. The labour market before adjustment

Before the application of the adjustment measures the labour market was characterised by a great heterogeneity and a twofold pressure on the labour supply.

1. Wage disparities and segmentation of the market

As in the majority of developing countries, an economic dualism is reflected in the labour market. The modern sector is made up of the public sector, enterprises and services to households, while the traditional sector is divided into informal urban and rural components. After a brief look at the functioning of the labour market, we shall analyse internal migration and immigration and then the segmentation of the labour market in the enterprise sub-sector.

a) General functioning of the sectors within the dualistic framework

Within the traditional sector, the informal urban and rural components have in common free competition of the economic agents while functioning on a family basis or with very few employees. Negotiation between employer and employee takes no account of the legal minimum wages: the guaranteed minimum interprofessional wage (SMIG) in the towns and the minimum agricultural wage (SMAG) in rural areas.

In the towns the informal activities are made up of industrial subcontracting, traditional crafts and retail trade. In subcontracting payment is by piece work based on requirements and is accompanied by vocational training and possibly the loan of machinery and/or the supply of raw materials. The craftsman may exercise his activity on a subcontracting basis, but generally supplies goods or services directly to consumers. Although classified in the traditional sector, his activity may be based on the recovery of industrial by-products or the wastes of modern consumption. The small trader, and in particular the itinerant vendor, generally pays a lump sum tax either to occupy a place in the market or in the form of a license. There are also urban agricultural activities due to the broad definition of "town".

While the urban informal sector activities are often carried out by self-employed workers there are also a good many wage earners in the sector (family labour or other) and apprentices. Because these activities are not officially registered and because they may be carried out in fixed premises, in itinerant fashion, or at home, it is not possible to give any figures for the different types of employment. What is more, the phenomenon of multiple activities makes it impossible to have any precise statistics (see Oudin 1986).

In rural areas, a distinction can be made between family labour in the agricultural sector and agricultural wage earners. These latter may be employed by the month or by the day. The SMAG (guaranteed minimum agricultural wage, see Table V-3) varies according to the crop and appears to be little respected. While wages may be higher than the SMAG during periods of serious labour shortage, there are traditional practices which limit wages of workers who want to settle in a village, whether they be internal migrants or immigrants. These practices consist of promising a plot of land after a certain period of work remunerated at a relatively low wage. However, a growing scarcity of land imposes increasingly long waiting periods which are unacceptable unless the wages are raised. Thus this system is tending to give way to regular wage labour.

In rural as well as urban areas, the members of a single household and sometimes even a single person may work in both the modern sector and the traditional sector. We shall analyse the rural and the informal urban sectors in more detail in Chapter V.

The other component of the dual economy is the modern sector. All employment in this sector must be reported to the Ministry of Labour by the employer. This procedure implies respect for labour legislation, mainly consisting of legal minimum wages according to occupational category, compulsory taxes and various regulations. Employment in domestic services is distinguished by advantages in kind provided by the employer household, but conversely by greater dependence on the part of the employee. The civil service is characterised by job security, wage rigidity and a lack of information on recruitment for job-seekers. Regardless of the ministry, all posts are defined in uniform fashion according to the professional category, grade, level and family situation. This system takes no account of specific and complementary skills or qualifications but only of the main diploma. Promotion is generally by competitive examination.

The production sector is made up of the private sub sector and by the mixed or parastatal sub sector. Employment conditions are governed by labour law and collective agreements. A very detailed nomenclature is used to fix a nominal minimum wage according to occupational category. This wage is indexed on inflation at the discretion of the government. The Labour Office, one of whose functions is to make the market transparent, lacks the resources to fulfil its responsibilities and does not get enough co-operation from employers and those seeking work.

In addition to the dualism of the modern and traditional sectors, there is the contrast between the savanna zone of the North and the forest zones of the South. An additional element is introduced by the concentration of modern activities in the Abidjan region.

b) Regional disparities and Ivorian prosperity

The two migratory movements, from the bush to the town for the Ivorians and the immigration of Africans from neighbouring countries, can be explained by regional disparities and Ivorian prosperity.

There are both push and pull factors behind the rural exodus. Although they are relatively minor, rural push factors do exist in Côte d'Ivoire. Regional disparities in the availability of health care and services together with the lack of cheap transport induce young people to leave rural areas. In addition, according to Mr. Bala Keita, the Ivorian Minister of Education, "Ivorian schools teach people to hate agriculture".

. At the same time, towns and especially Abidjan have the attractions of high wages and of concentration of modern jobs. In 1980, the rural SMAG was only about one-fourth of the SMIG applicable to urban jobs (see Table V-3).

The urban pull is accentuated by the virtually total concentration of modern sector jobs in the towns. In 1979, over three-fourths (78.2 per cent) of the formal sector jobs were in the Abidjan *département*[2]. Before the recession, these jobs had an annual rate of increase (4.5 per cent) higher than those of the informal and traditional agricultural sectors (3.7 per cent)[3].

Immigration from neighbouring African countries results from factors: ethnic and demographic on one hand and economic and political on the other. On the ethnic level, the fact that the Ivorian mosaic straddles boundaries facilitates integration of immigrants, especially after a long period of shared life under colonial administration and the building of the Abidjan/Ouagadougou railroad. Demographically, the low population density in Côte d'Ivoire (32 inhabitants per square kilometre) is a another factor attracting and maintaining the flow of immigrants.

The fact that internal migration and immigration both involve mainly young men results in an above average male-female ratio in the towns and a fairly favourable dependency ratio in the country as a whole. This latter ratio expresses as a percentage the number of people outside working age (under 15 and over 65) with respect to the number of people of working age. This is less than 100 per cent and represents a fairly low demographic burden (the average for Africa is 190 per cent). On the economic level, the dual migratory movements have made agricultural production fairly competitive as a result of the low rural wages. Immigrants send some of their income to their country of origin. The second major consequence of these migratory movements is the growth of the informal sector.

All in all, there are three contradictions associated with the labour market. The first stems from the need to increase the remuneration for rural work and the consequent risk of inflation which would reduce international competitiveness. The second contradiction lies in the difficulty of reconciling the requirements of labour law and the development of the urban informal sector. The third is the conflict between dedication to regional economic integration and the Ivorian threshold of tolerance towards immigrants, this being likely to be lowered by the crisis and unemployment.

c) Fragmentation and Ivorianisation

Both the civil service and firms make extensive use of expatriate staff, whose high qualifications and spirit of enterprise helped to make the Cote d'Ivoire a flourishing showcase of Europe in West Africa. The other side of the coin is a fragmentation of the labour market. The fact is that the wage differentials between Africans, Ivorian or others, on the one hand and non-Africans, European, Lebanese and Syrian on the other, are so great that increasing the Ivorian share of employment appeared perfectly in line with the way things should develop: the Ivorians like the great majority of peoples emerging from colonisation aspired to economic independence, represented by holding the capital of enterprises and their key posts. In particular, the active Ivorian population, and above all young people emerging from schools and universities, exercise a considerable pressure on the labour market, reflecting their legitimate desire for occupational attainment. However, Ivorian prosperity was based on economic liberalism towards foreign capital and human resources.

At a given educational level non-Africans have a remuneration 70 to 600 per cent higher than Africans. The gap is greatest at the lowest educational levels, and paradoxically reaches a factor of 10 between these two communities in the "not stated" educational category. There are several possible explanations, but false declarations and refusals to respond appear to be the main reasons for the apparently enormous differences. In any event, the wage gap at the lowest level of education is of little significance in view of the small number of non-Africans at this level. The lack of equivalence in diplomas and professional know-how justify the more reasonable wage differentials found at the higher education level (see Table I-12).

This division in favour of non-Africans in the enterprise sector makes it is clear that the very high level of Ivorian ownership of capital has not been matched on the employment side. In fact, the Ivorian share of capital largely became a majority share within a five-year period, rising from 40 per cent in 1975 to 62 per cent in 1980. During this same period, the proportion of Ivorians in the total enterprise sector labour force increased only slightly, from 58 per cent in 1975 to 64 per cent in 1980 (see Table IV-2). However, according to a 1979 survey[4] the non-African labour force increased between 1974 and 1979 (from 9 476 to 9 805 people). Thus it was not a case of "Ivorianisation" of jobs, but the creation of additional jobs for Ivorians. A more detailed analysis reveals that the low level of Ivorianisation of employment appears to stem from three causes. First, while the control of capital is shared between the Ivorians and the non-Africans, jobs are occupied by Ivorians, non-Africans and other Africans. Even if the expatriates had all handed over their jobs to Ivorians the proportion of the latter would still only have been 63 per cent in 1975 and 68 per cent in 1980. Second, the legal protection of workers prevents an expatriate with a labour contract of indefinite duration from being replaced by an Ivorian without good reason. Lastly, although there are many unsatisfied job demands by qualified Ivorians, a certain category of supervisory posts cannot be filled by anyone without adequate experience. The managers of enterprises also hold manufacturing secrets and have personal standing vis-à-vis foreign suppliers and clients.

More detailed data show that the proportion of Ivorians in management and supervisory jobs has increased more rapidly as we move down the professional hierarchy: senior managers, middle managers and supervisors. If we examine the trends in the non-African labour force and non-Ivorian capital, we see that there has been a gradual disengagement of non-Africans at all levels, more or less in parallel with that of capital (see Table IV-1). It is also possible that the relatively slow pace of Ivorianisation of management posts is partly due to the desire for on-the-job training and the acquisition of new professional skills by those who are going to take over.

2. Demographic and educational pressures and the stagnation of employment in the 1978-80 period

In addition to the migratory movements, Côte d'Ivoire, like most other developing countries, is experiencing demographic pressure and an expansion of education. The boom in world coffee and cocoa prices in 1976-77, together with the discovery of oil, stimulated governmental optimism, managerial confidence and an influx of workers to urban areas. An examination of the demographic and schooling impacts on the one hand and employment indicators and unsatisfied demand for work on the other will furnish the basis for undersanding the labour market's problems.

In the general context, demographic pressure forms the basis of labour supply. This pressure results from lower mortality rates and a continuing fairly high birth rate. In this transitional stage before arriving at a "modern" condition with low death and birth rates, Côte d'Ivoire's population is increasing by about 4 per cent a year (including net immigration). This is one of the highest rates of increase in the region.

Furthermore, the urban population increases by 8 per cent a year due to combined demographic effects of natural increase, immigration and the rural exodus. At this rate, urban employment would have to double every 9 years simply to maintain 1980 conditions. In the city of Abidjan employment would have to grow at a rate of 10 per cent a year to keep pace with the increase in labour supply (see Table I-9). It is estimated that the excess of urban labour in 1980 was already 223 000 people and this number was increasing at the rate of 14.1 per cent a year (see Table IV-2).

Thus a difficult demographic transition is being aggravated by high immigration and the influx to the cities. This creates a dual complex imbalance. There is a growing excess of labour in urban areas while there is a serious shortage in rural areas. Along side the more or less apparent unemployment of adults, the employment of children creates a social problem difficult to resolve[5].

One particular economic indicator highlights the unfavourable labour market for job-seekers. According to a survey by the *Office National de la Formation Professionnelle*, the number of persons with technical education diplomas who found work was continually falling: from 22 per cent in 1978-79 to 7 per cent in 1980-81. Although faring better than persons who took commercial courses, job-seekers with industrial training who found work never exceeded 16 per cent. In absolute and percentage terms, those who found jobs from both educational streams fell between 1978 and 1981[6]. The potential supply of labour with secondary education dilomas also exceeded the corresponding demand.

On all three markets, the competition between demanders and suppliers is imperfect. Besides the opacity of the markets, supply and demand have difficulty in adjusting to one another automatically because of the long delay between decisions and their effects. There is still need to improve data collection and organisation for the labour market[7]. Greater market transparency would make it easier to achieve a certain balance.

The expansion of education increased demographic pressures (natural and migratory) on the cities. These phenomena contributed to a reduction in the profitability of investment in human resources at both household and state levels. The differences between the labour markets became ever greater. The civil service remained very rigid, maintaining security of employment and a fixed pay structure. The enterprise sector and services to households had minimum wages indexed to the cost of living at a time when the international economic situation was unfavourable for Côte d'Ivoire. The fall in world coffee and cocoa prices together with the increase in prices of imports led to a considerable deterioration in the terms of trade in the years 1978-80 (see Table I-6). The output of modern enterprises started to decline as from 1979 while employment in entreprises stagnated. While over-employment was limited due to the timid Ivorianisation of the labour force, the extra wage cost discouraged recruitment. Although unemployment was partly disguised by occupational mobility towards the traditional sector, it was generally classical or structural[8]. In other words, the legally imposed high wages reduced recruitment as well as sales and output. What is more, the rigidity of the minimum wages fixed for each precise level of qualification prevented any downward adjustment of wages.

45

Conversely, in the traditional sector where wages are low due to free competition, inflation is contained and full employment is assumed. Despite the cheapness of the goods produced, the development of this sector is hampered by the existence of bottlenecks. Thus, in the rural sector, productivity remains low due to inappropriate technology, rudimentary equipment, insufficient inputs and a poor infrastructure. The urban informal sector suffers from the effect of imports associated with conspicuous consumption and the disadvantages of undeclared and family economic activity. Unless they are strongly motivated and encouraged, producers in this sector will be reluctant to legalise their activity because they have too many competitors who do not comply with the labour law. What is more, the wages in the modern sector are so high that moving into it constitutes a real risk for informal sector enterprises.

In the context of the segmentation into three labour markets (public, private formal and private informal), which are more or less opaque, the effects of structural adjustment measures examined below are sometimes difficult to measure. Generally speaking, the overall labour surplus is aggravated by its being concentrated in urban areas, the great qualitative imbalance, the legally imposed wage rigidity and the fragmentation of the market in favour of expatriates.

C. Adjustment measures on the labour markets

The emergence of serious macroeconomic imbalances, resulted in a calling into question of simultaneous expansion of investment, domestic demand, immigration, rural exodus and education, and the government introduced a series of measures (see Chapter III), including some concerning the structure of the labour markets.

Before the structural adjustment programme, there were three outstanding features:

i)   The disproportional growth of expenditures for personnel in the civil service as compared with the expansion of the state budget: in real terms, the state budget increased at an annual rate of 4.2 per cent between 1977 and 1980, while civil service personnel expenditures increased by 6.1 per cent a year.

ii) Wage indexation in the enterprise and services sector: during the 1970s, the SMIG was indexed closely to the general price index. In fact, inflation was 12.1 per cent and the increase in the SMIG was 11.5 per cent between 1970 and 1980[9]. The annual revision of this SMIG generally took place at the beginning of the month of January.

iii) The large expansion of educational personnel.

To try to deal with this situation, three types of adjustment measures were introduced: a freeze on nominal remuneration employment preference in favour of Ivorians and reorientation of the supply of human resources.

The measures introduced under these three headings can be summarised as follows:

Remuneration	Defence of employment	Human resources

1981

Alignment of public entity pay on those of the civil service. No increase in public service wages	Decree of the Abidjan Court of Appeal: legalising dismissal of an expatriate without professional cause if necessary for the reorganisation of an enterprise suffering from the recession and replacement by an Ivorian	Economies in the field of education

1982

Increase of 10 per cent in all minimum wages in the private and semi-public sectors	Tighter control of mass redundancies	Economies in the field of education
Base ceiling for calculating social security charges frozen at the 1980 level (FDFA 70 000)	Suspension of the authorisation of overtime work (more than 40 hours a week)	
	Greater payroll tax discrimination against expatriates: 16 per cent as against 10 per cent for local staff	

1983

Freeze on civil service pay		Limitation of public service recruitment
Limitation on moving to higher pay categories		Economies in the field of education
Modification of housing arrangements for public servants		Reduction in the number of foreign technical assistants
		Limitation of entries to colleges and universities

First of all, unlike the 1970s when wage indexation to the cost of living was normal practice, wage freezes became the rule in the modern sector. In the civil service, promotions in grade and level to compensate for losses of purchasing power were prohibited in 1985. The 10 per cent pay rise in 1982 for employees of enterprises was accompanied by a relative easing of social security charges.

There were two sets of measures concerning employment: one aimed at maintaining employment and the other at increasing the wages of nationals. In 1982, the authorities suspended the authorisation to exceed the normal legal working hours (40 hours a week) and tightened control over mass redundancies.

Measures to promote the employment of "local personnel" consisted of encouragement to fill jobs with Ivorian nationals, higher income tax on the pay of expatriates and increased tax deductions for priority enterprises based on their total payroll for Ivorian personnel.

Lastly, because of the growing mismatch between the educational system and the country's needs, together with the considerable burden of the education system, human resources policy was subjected to three constraints: strict containment of the expansion of the education system; reduction of investment in schools and a reduction in use of foreign resources. Apart from this last measure, this restructuring policy was defined by the objectives of the 1981-1985 Plan (see also the Chronology of measures annexed to Chapter III).

D. The effects on employment

The adjustment programme, which reduced public expenditure and domestic demand and included structural measures concerning the labour markets, affected both the modern and traditional sectors. Because of the lack of data and delayed effects, our quantitative analysis is limited to the civil service and employees in modern enterprises (78 000 and 237 000 people respectively in 1980), and excludes activities where there is no standardised accounting, such as domestic service (51 300 people) and the traditional sector. Thus, in comparison with the Plan data, our analysis covers approximately 80 per cent of the modern sector[11].

1. Increased predominance of education and continuing increase of managerial and supervisory personnel in the civil service

As in most countries, the civil service in Côte d'Ivoire constitutes a very stable element of the labour market. The trend in employment in this segment of the labour market is analysed on three levels: global, functional and professional.

a) Overall growth of the number of Ivorians and gradual reduction of the proportion of technical assistants

Globally, there are two categories of personnel, Ivorian personnel and the technical assistants. By and large the Ivorian work force increased at the same rate as current expenditures between 1981 and 1984. This increase reached 23 per cent at the end of three years, the total volume of employment rising from 74 109 to 91 195 jobs. In 1985 an abrupt reduction of 4 010 jobs was followed by another 543 in 1986. The 1984 level was reached again in 1987 as a result of an increase of 4 210 (see Table IV-3). Over the six years 1981-87, the annual rate of increase was only 3.5 per cent on average, which is quite reasonable as the national population was increasing at about the same rate. However, it is too low when compared with the expansion of the urban population, estimated at 7.8 per cent, and with the surplus labour force which was growing 14.1 per cent a year.

In fact, the government seems to have been hampered by two constraints, the relative youth of civil servants and the system of training maintained by the "technical" ministries. There were not enough people retiring to allow any significant budget savings through eliminating vacated jobs. Conversely, the virtually automatic recruitment of students emerging from schools specialising in administration involved a training period of several years. For example, all the graduates of these schools were taken into the civil service in 1984. As a result of tardy decisions to limit entries to the colleges and universities (1983) and the specialist schools (1985), recruitment by the civil service remained at the level of about 4 000 a year, except for three years. The limitation of recruitment adopted in 1983 led to a reduction of only 10 per cent as compared with the previous year. The loss of 4 026 jobs in the civil service in 1985 is partly explained by the transfer of 1 468 jobs to public institutions. With the easing of the financial constraints (due to higher world prices for coffee and cocoa in 1985), recruitment in 1986 even exceeded the 1980 level. The rate of increase of Ivorian personnel was fairly regular except for the years 1985-86, when the upward trend was not maintained.

The proportion of technical assistants fell continually between 1981 and 1984, from 5.29 to 3.65 per cent. However, in 1986 there was a sharp rise to 4.83 per cent. While the substantial fall in the number of jobs in 1983 can be linked with the objective of "reducing the number of technical assistants" announced by the government, the major factor determining their numbers was financial constraints.

On the whole, instead of the departure of technical assistants being compensated by the creation of jobs for Ivorians, the numbers of personnel of the two categories moved more or less in parallel. In fact, the biggest reduction in recruitment (437 jobs) and in the number of technical assistants (486) coincided in 1983. Again, it was in 1986 that both categories surpassed their 1981 numbers, by 7 per cent for the creation of jobs for nationals and by 6.2 per cent for technical assistants. As we pointed out above, this upsurge in job creation was the result of the budget surplus created by the increase in world coffee and cocoa prices.

Apart from the parallel fluctuations in civil service recruitment and the number of technical assistants, there was a slow overall increase and a gradual rise in the proportion of Ivorian nationals.

b) Continued expansion of education and economic services

While the civil service grew modestly during the adjustment programme (1981-87), one may ask how its structure was evolving according to ministerial function. Five groups can be distinguished:

i)   National representation and general administration;

ii)   Law and order;

iii)   Economic services;

iv)   Education and scientific research;

v)   Social affairs and assimilated.

In 1981, the Ministry of Education alone employed almost half of the civil service personnel, while each of the other four groups accounted for 10 to 14.6 per cent of the total.

The number of personnel in the first two groups, "representation and administration" and public order fell between 1981 and 1987, from 10.5 to 9.1 per cent and from 14.6 to 9.6 per cent respectively. The work force in "law and order" fell by a fifth in absolute terms between these two dates. Over the same period, the "social affairs" share returned to its 1981 level (14.8 per cent). "Economic services" and "education" grew the most: the former from 11.5 to 13.5 per cent and the latter 49.1 to 53 per cent (see Table IV-4).

On the whole, there was a slight restructuring of the civil service with a reduction of public order personnel and an increase for social affairs. Education and economic services were the two beneficiaries of the period, probably because of the rigidity of the teaching system and the urgency of promoting economic development. Neither budget cuts nor the reallocation of training resources prevented the regular growth of personnel employed by the Ministry of National Education and Scientific Research.

c) Swelling of the management and supervisory levels through shifts up the pay scale

During the 1981-87 period, the professional structure of the civil service changed a great deal. It can be analysed by tracing trends in the management and supervisory levels or by the changes in number of personnel for each occupational category. The increase in the proportion of managerial personnel stems from two sources: shifts upwards on the pay scale and promotion of civil servants already employed on the one hand and the higher level of the newly created posts on the other. Before the adjustment programme, the proportion of managerial personnel (middle, senior and unclassified) grew continually between 1976 and 1979. This growth continued at roughly the same rhythm until 1983, then accelerated between 1984 and 1987. The tendency for the skills and responsibilities of public servants to be increased could explain the rise from 30 to 53 per cent in the proportion of supervisory personnel in 11 years (1976-87) (see Table IV-5), but the increase from 37 to 53 per cent between 1983 and 1987 is probably more due to changes of category and promotions, and this despite government measures of 1983 and 1985. The first limited upward movements and the second blocked them. But another factor that regularly contributed to an increase in the proportion of supervisory personnel was the increase in the number of jobs in education (see Table IV-4). A majority of the personnel of this sector which accounts for an increasing proportion of the civil service are supervisory personnel. These various factors resulted in a continued vigorous increase in the proportion of senior and seconded managerial personnel, steady growth in that of middle managers and a fall in the number of skilled and unskilled employees. Compared with 1981, skilled jobs had declined by 13 per cent by 1987 while unskilled jobs had declined by 8 per cent. This decline took place mainly in 1986 and 1987 and resulted in a reduction of 5 313 unskilled jobs and 3 783 skilled jobs. Conversely, during the same period middle management jobs increased by 12 589 and senior and unclassified jobs by 9 465. Thus in six years (1981-87), middle management jobs increased by 65 per cent, or 9 per cent a year, and senior and seconded managerial personnel more than doubled.

Thus long-term trends in employment in the civil service were: increase in the number of Ivorian nationals, reduction in the proportion of technical assistants, and growth of the ministries responsible for economic production and education. Skill categories and the proportion of supervisory personnel increased sharply between 1983 and 1987, despite the measures to limit and then block upward movements on the pay scale. However, the quantitative increase in the proportion of supervisory personnel apears to conceal qualitative problems that we are unable to analyse due to lack of data, namely: namely the relative youth and lack of experience of certain managerial personnel on the one hand and a lack of qualifications and motivation of certain older managerial personnel on the other.

2. Sharp fall in and major restructuring of employment in enterprises

Given the rigidity of civil service employment, it may be asked if labour flexibility in the enterprise sector provided a means of adapting to the economic situation and structural measures. After a general analysis of employment in the context of economic productivity, we shall look at the sectoral variation and then at the trends in its demographic and occupational structure.

a) Recessionary technical progress and heavy losses for enterprises

During the period 1980-85, the volume of production fell by 13 per cent, largely in 1980-82. In the same period, the decline in employment was almost three times greater, a drop of 35.5 per cent, which led to an apparent increase of 45 per cent in the productivity of labour compared with 1980 (see Figure 1). The question that arises is whether this technical "progress", clearly recessionary because of the reduction in employment, should continue in the name of the liberalisation of the factors of production, or, on the contrary, the decline should be halted in order to prevent social conflict?

Two remarks are called for here. First, three measures were introduced to safeguard employment: tighter control over mass redundancies, suspension of the authorisation for working overtime (1982) and reduction of taxes in favour of the employment of Ivorians (1984). Second, the decline in the terms of trade, the increase in interest rates until 1982, and the decline in economic activity, notably due to the drastic reduction of public investment, caused losses to enterprises up to 1985. According to the *Centrale de Bilans*, the average losses in the 1981-84 period amounted to three times the profits in the years 1977-80. Even if the authorities required enterprises to adjust their work force strictly proportionally to their production, the closure of bankrupt enterprises would also increase the apparent productivity of the remaining enterprises.

On the domestic level, the effect of the 1983 drought reduced both government and household consumption for two consecutive years. Conversely, Ivorian exports, 70 per cent of which were agricultural products, increased in volume by 20 per cent between 1980 and 1985, or by 3.7 per cent a year. However, this was not enough to lead to an increase in the gross domestic product, which stagnated over the period as a whole, and even fell slightly in 1982-84[12]. As compared with this aggregate, according to the *Centrale de Bilans*, the output of enterprises experienced a steeper decline and still had not reached their 1980 level by 1985. This indicates that the crisis had a greater impact on modern sector enterprises than on economic activity as a whole.

The institutional balance between safeguarding employment and the liberalisation of the factors of production was not able to prevent a sharp fall in employment due to the heavy losses suffered by enterprises.

b) Loss of jobs in state enterprises and crisis in the building industry

The sectoral level can be analysed either in terms of the financial control of the enterprises or the branch of economic activity. A breakdown into three categories, state enterprises (public capital only) mixed enterprises (majority public capital) and private enterprises (majority private capital) makes it possible to assess the trend specific to each. There was a sharp fall in employment in state enterprises, affecting almost half the work force (down 42.5 per cent) between 1980 and 1985, as against a slight fall in the mixed enterprise category (down 14 per cent). The fall in employment in private enterprises, which accounted for over 62 per cent of total production, approximated the general average (down 35.6 per cent). The differences in these employment trends resulted in a continuing increase in the share of mixed enterprises, which rose from 16.2 per cent of the total in 1980 to 21.7 per cent in 1985, no doubt at the expense of state enterprises, which declined from 21 per cent in 1980 to 18.8 per cent in 1985 (see Table IV-6). Although the state was traditionally a defender of employment, this heavy loss of jobs was due to its policy of privatisation and the closure of a certain number of enterprises. These closures lead to the dismissal of more than some 10 000 people[13].

Overall, after a decline labour productivity in all categories was higher in 1985 than in 1980. In decreasing order, productivity in majority private capital enterprises increased by 41 per cent, that of mixed enterprises by 18 per cent and that of the state by 27 per cent. In 1980, the productivity in state enterprises was only about half that in each of the other two categories.

An analysis of employment by sector of economic activity shows that all branches were affected by the recession of 1980-85. Among those least affected were labour-intensive manufacturing industries (down 18.7 per cent) and capital-intensive manufacturing industries (down 2.0 per cent). Conversely, the "primary product exports" and "formal non-tradeable" branches lost respectively 45.2 and 52.1 per cent of their labour force over this period. In particular, the construction-public works branch retained only 15.2 per cent of its work force (see Figure 2 and Table IV-7). This resulted in a significant change in the structure of employment: the manufacturing branch had 40 per cent of the total enterprise labour force in 1980 and 54 per cent in 1985. Conversely, the "formal non-tradeable" branch which had 52 per cent in 1980, had no more than 39 per cent in 1985. In particular, employment in construction and public works had fallen to 3.5 per cent of the total in 1985, as against 15 per cent in 1980.

c) Increase in supervisory levels in the tertiary sector, growing proportion of Ivorian
nationals and growing female employment in enterprises

The recession did not effect all occupational categories or all sections of the population equally. There were losses in all major occupational categories, but administrative and commercial (tertiary) employment declined by only 20 per cent compared with 33 per cent for employment in production (secondary). This observation is also true for supervisory and management jobs, the tertiary sector losing 6 per cent as against 12 per cent for the secondary sector. This relative increase in employment in the tertiary sector and of the proportion of supervisory personnel in general simply continues a trend that had been evident since 1975. In fact, tertiary employment increased from 21.3 per cent of total employment in 1975 to 24.5 per cent in 1980 and 28.0 per cent in 1985. Similarly, supervisory and management jobs increased from 9.4 per cent of the total in 1975 to 11.3 per cent in 1980 and 14.6 per cent in 1985 (see Table IV-8).

However, there is an apparent contradiction between the relative growth of supervisory jobs in the tertiary sector and the lack of job opportunities for young people emerging from commercial education. There are two reasons for this. First, the number of applicants for commercial jobs was about four times as great as those interested in the industrial sector. Second, the legal minimum wage was fixed for each occupational level, which did not allow automatic adjustment between supply and demand.

In general, the proportion of Ivorian nationals employed increased more slowly during the period of structural adjustment (1980-85) than in the preceding period (1975-80). The proportion of Ivorians in technical production jobs even fell during the period 1980-85. In this sector it was the management levels that grew fastest. In management and supervisory levels as a whole, the proportion of jobs held by Ivorian nationals increased more slowly in the second period than in the first. These fairly complex trends reflect the following restructuring: the relative growth of the industrial sector resulted in a greater proportion of Ivorian nationals in supervisory levels in production at the expense of expatriates, while there was a relative decline in the number of Ivorians to the benefit of immigrants in blue collar jobs.

The slowed rate of increase in the proportion of Ivorian nationals in supervisory and in management jobs in general is because what is involved is higher management levels, whose numbers are relatively small compared with those at lower supervisory levels. In other words, Ivorian nationals were taking over jobs at increasingly high levels, the first period concerning supervisory jobs, the second being the turn of managers and senior managers (see Table IV-9).

Overall, the growth of female employment accelerated during the structural adjustment period as compared with the preceding period. The proportion of women in supervisory and management jobs, higher than that in total employment, increased further during this second period, from 9.85 per cent in 1975 to 11.49 per cent in 1980 and 13.89 per cent in 1985 (see Table IV-10).

Because of the high enrolment of girls in schools after independence and their increasing education attainment, this increase in the proportion of female employment is due not so much to the structural adjustment programme as to the pressure of supply. At the same time, the increasing proportion of Ivorian nationals in higher level jobs was largely due to the growth in the number of young Ivorians being educated either at home or abroad.

A detailed examination of the figures shows where jobs were being created and eliminated (see Table IV-11). The adjustment period resulted in a higher management ratio because the balance between job creations (1975-80) and suppressions (1980-85) was positive for supervisory and management jobs and negative for the others. The relative growth of tertiary sector jobs continued the existing trend but did not result in net recruitment.

Although a certain balance between the social safeguards for employment and the relative liberalisation of the factors of production was maintained (for example greater control over mass redundancies on the one hand and abolition of wage indexation on the other), the heavy losses suffered by enterprises caused a drastic fall in employment while at the same time increasing productivity. While the losses in employment wiped out the gains during the 1975-80 period, they were not equally serious in all categories of enterprise, branches of economic activity or occupational and demographic categories.

The sharp fall in employment in state enterprises was due to privatisation and the crisis in construction and public works was the result of the cuts in public investment spending. Conversely, Ivorian industry appears to have benefited from the adjustment programme. The growth of supervisory and management jobs and the increase in female employment were greater than the medium-term trend.

At the same time, the slowing of the increase in Ivorianisation of posts was due to the upward movement of Ivorian nationals which benefited many unskilled African immigrants and was at the expense of very highly qualified and well paid non-Africans.

On the whole, the adjustment programme probably did not have any major effects on labour supply. Its real or apparent impact on employment was very uneven. The total enterprise sector labour force rose sharply during the 1975-80 period, but then fell sharply during the structural adjustment period (1980-85). The balance over the ten years (1975-85) remained slightly positive (an increase of 2 110 jobs). This overall figure conceals a substantial restructuring to the detriment of non-Africans and immigrants, which benefited supervisors, managers and women.

Non-Africans had a net loss of 1 875 jobs, 1 243 of them management positions, while the African immigrants lost 6 903 jobs. On the other hand, the successive rises and falls ended with a net gain for managers and comparable personnel, 5 011 jobs in the tertiary sector and 3 619 in the secondary. While the gain of 4 954 jobs for women was also the result of compensation, the rate of increase in supervisory and management jobs for women declined during the adjustment period as compared with the preceding period.

The higher proportion of Ivorian nationals and women employed was the result of pressure of the large numbers of educated people and also of greater equality of opportunity for women, who still represented only 7.11 per cent of those employed in enterprises in 1985. The increase in the percentage of managers and supervisors which continued in enterprises and accelerated in the civil service hides a loss of purchasing power due to the wage freeze.

E. Wage policies and their consequences

The modern sector labour force, an active minority, is very sensitive to variations in its pay. Part of this pay, that of civil servants, is a considerable burden on the state budget. The wage level also influences the demand for labour by enterprises. As we have shown above, payroll austerity was part of the adjustment measures from the very outset in 1981 and was effectively practised to differing degrees in the different subsectors as from 1983 (see Table I-11).

1. Slight fall in total payroll and substantial loss of purchasing power for civil servants

Overall, in the general operating budget the share of expenditures for personnel increased rapidly between 1979 and 1983 from 50.6 to 60.7 per cent. This was a maximum and later there was a slight downward trend.

In real terms, this aggregate increased between 1981 and 1983 and subsequently fell. This trend was due to the combination of moderate growth in numbers (up 3.3 per cent a year) and a slightly greater decline in civil servants' purchasing power (down 4 per cent a year) (see Table IV-12). With an inflation of 5.6 per cent a year between 1981 and 1987 and the maintenance of a freeze on wages between 1981 and 1985, it can be assumed that there was a certain compensation through upward movements on the pay scales and professional promotions. We estimate the impact of this compensation to have been about 1.6 per cent of the yearly remuneration. The policy of partial pay indexation to the cost of living was not enough to prevent opposition from the teaching corps, the biggest and best organised group in Côte d'Ivoire. In 1983, there was a big secondary teachers' strike for higher wages[14]. This was no doubt due to the feeling of injustice in view of the increase of 10 per cent in minimum wages in the enterprise and domestic service sectors. Despite the scale of the movement the teachers' wage claim was unsuccessful.

Thus, despite disguised compensation by promotion in grade, the average purchasing power of civil service pesonnel fell substantially by 20 per cent during a six-year period (1981-87). Great rigidity was a common feature of employment and pay policies for the civil service though this was less marked with respect to wages than to the numbers employed.

2. Considerable fall in payroll and stabilisation of the average real wage in enterprises

Unlike the trend in the civil service, in which the overall payroll remained the same and purchasing power fell, in the enterprise sector there was a very sharp reduction in total payroll but stability in the average real pay. These two factors are analysed in turn according to the sectoral dimension (see Figures 3 and 4).

Overall, the real payroll fell by almost 8 per cent a year, or by one-third over five years (1980-85). Only capital-intensive manufacturing industries maintained their total payroll. Despite the freeze on minimum wages as from 1983, labour-intensive manufacturing industries reduced their payroll by a fifth over the adjustment period. The two other branches of economic activity, i.e. "primary exports" and "formal non-tradeable", reduced their total payroll by 40 to 50 per cent over the period. In particular, construction and public works retained only one-fifth of its payroll, which means it was reduced by over one-fourth every year (26.7 per cent, see Table IV-13).

Since the numbers of employees were reduced in similar proportions, average real wages remained stable[15], except in the "formal non-tradeable" branch and, in particular construction-public works branch. In fact a greater reduction in the work force than in the payroll permitted an increase of 3.8 and 5.6 per cent respectively for these two branches. This stability in the average real wage was achieved as a result of two measures: the official increase of 10 per cent in minimum wages in 1982 and promotions as in the civil service. This was true for the branches where job losses were modest. In construction, the mass dismissal of low paid workers no doubt permitted an increase in the average wage of the remaining workers (except for the least skilled who received the minimum wage). In general, inflation was higher than the increase in minimum wages, for example, the SMIG and SMAG (see Table V-3). This meant a loss of purchasing power for persons receiving these wages of 3.4 per cent a year, or 16 per cent during 5 years.

This policy penalised low wage earners, while stabilising the average real pay of those employed in enterprises. This contrasts with the policy in the public service where there was a reduction in real pay for all personnel.

3. Fall in labour intensity: a temporary phenomenon?

In addition to analysing the trends in employment and wages, an examination of the effects of the structural measures on the use of labour is useful for deciding between the arguments for social protection on the one hand and for the liberalisation of labour on the other. By and large, the former defend wage indexation to the cost of living and oppose large-scale redundancies, while the latter are for free competition of the factors of production and flexibility of labour. Given disguised structural unemployment in the traditional sector, the structural adjustment programme appeared to try to find a delicate balance between these two positions.

The wage freeze in the civil service in 1981 was followed by that in enterprises and domestic services in 1983. At the same time, increasing the proportion of Ivorian nationals in employment and mass redundancies were made possible. This liberalisation of the market should have favoured the more intensive use of labour, a factor very abundant in Côte d'Ivoire, but labour intensity, the percentage of the remuneration of labour with respect to the remuneration of all the factors of production (labour + capital + reconstitution of capital) generally fell as compared with the preceding period, with the exception of the formal non-tradeable sector (see Table IV-14).

Thus abolishing wage indexation by freezing nominal minimum wages did not in itself result either in intensifying the use of labour or even stabilising it. In order to better understand this lack of elasticity in the demand for labour it would be necessary to also take into account the other components of the cost structure of enterprises.

Regarding this development which runs counter to liberal logic, two remarks can be made. First, the structural adjustment was in a transitional stage during the 1980-85 period. The fact is that at the beginning of liberalisation, enterprises all try to adjust their work force to their "desired level of employment". As this level is estimated on the basis of pessimistic prospects (contraction of domestic demand), it is scarcely surprising that there were sharp reductions in the work force. Second, in the case of enterprises controlled by foreigners, which have markets available, a probability of political and economic stability constitutes the essential precondition for investing and recruiting. But the general climate in the business world was one of "wait and see".

4. Consequences for the traditional sector

Because of the opacity of the traditional sector and of the delayed effects of adjustment on employment in this sector, our analysis will be limited to a reasoned review of the broad trends projected before the adjustment programmes. It is possible to identify three main elements affecting the labour market: the economically active urban population, urban employment and the equilibrium between labour supply and demand.

In the first place, the total population of Côte d'Ivoire and the number of urban workers are assumed to correspond with the forecasts, because neither migrations nor the economically active population can have changed in such a short time in the absence of any constraining intervention. Thus of the 10 million people living in Côte d'Ivoire in 1985, the estimate of an active urban population of 1.6 million seems to us perfectly correct (see Table IV-15).

Unlike the continuing increase in the labour supply, urban employment had every reason to decline with the recession. In urban employment a distinction can be made between employment in the modern and traditional (informal) sectors and urban agricultural activities. In the modern sector, interpolation of the 1984 and 1986 data gives 92 000 civil servants for 1985, and the *Centrale des Bilans* gives a figure of 164 000 jobs for the enterprise sector. We assume that other enterprises and domestic service reduced their work forces at the same rate.

Thus, in the modern sector, instead of the projected 467 000 jobs, there were in reality only 307 000. As a result, the slight increase in employment in the civil service was not able to prevent the number of job-seekers from rising to 160 000. Assuming that half these job-seekers were able to find an occupation in the urban informal sector (80 000) and one-fourth in urban agricultural activities (40 000), there were still some 40 000 additional persons in the excess urban labour force.

We lack reliable and comprehensive data required to correctly analyse the consequences of adjustment on employment and wages in the traditional sector. In fact there are various differing estimates for informal sector employment, perhaps because the definitions used and/or the methods of estimation differ. Thus for the year 1980, Oudin (1986) estimates modern employment at 318 000 people, as against 382 000 in the 1981-85 Plan estimate. But Oudin also distinguishes an intermediate sector (202 000) and a non-structured urban sector (445 000) that should be compared with the traditional urban jobs in the Plan (330 000). It would be very risky to try to derive any adjustment effects by using these figures. What is more, because many people engage in several activities, it would be incorrect to add the different jobs to arrive at the number of persons employed. We shall nevertheless attempt some additional analyses in Chapter V, on the basis of data concerning expenditure and incomes as revealed by the household surveys. Lastly, we shall evaluate the impact of adjustment on employment and real wages with the aid of simulations produced by a macro-micro general equilibrium model (see Chapter VI).

F. Conclusion

We have seen that the different segments of the labour market were more or less directly affected by the adjustment measures but in different ways. Thus civil servants suffered substantial wage losses but were able to preserve their jobs. By contrast, in the formal enterprise sector it was average real wages that were preserved, but at the price of very substantial job losses.

Of course, within the enterprise sector there were very considerable differences. Construction and transport lost most jobs as a result of the reduction in economic activity in general and the cuts in public investment in particular. It was thus indirect effects rather then measures aimed directly at employment that most affected employees in enterprises. In fact, the freezing of the nominal SMIG in 1983 and hence its reduction in real terms in the subsequent years is not reflected in the average wages recorded by the *Centrale des Bilans.*

The workers who were hardest hit were those who lost their jobs in the formal enterprise sector without receiving any unemployment benefits. They frequently had no other choice but to try their luck in the informal sector. In addition, there were young people who because of the reductions in the number of education grants and in recruitment found themselves excluded from a system to which they would otherwise have had access.

On the other hand, certain workers remaining in the system benefited from the effects of the structural changes in employment that corresponded to broad trends which persisted even when the overall economic situation was unfavourable. Thus the increased proportion of supervisory and management jobs and of Ivorian nationals employed, together with the growth in female employment enabled some persons to improve their situation. Similarly, promotions in the civil service enabled some personnel to cushion the impact of the wage freezes.

There were significant repercussions of the adjustment on immigrant workers from other African countries. While there was overt discrimination vis-à-vis foreigners in certain measures (for example, the differential income tax rates), these affected mostly non-Africans and despite the crisis there were no large-scale measures to discourage or reverse African immigration as was the case in other countries. The loss of unskilled jobs no doubt affected a good number of immigrant workers, but at the same time because they often held jobs that were by nature unpleasant and poorly paid, their employment was often "protected" to a certain extent.

Figure IV.1. Employment and productivity in formal sector enterprises
Index: 1980 = 100

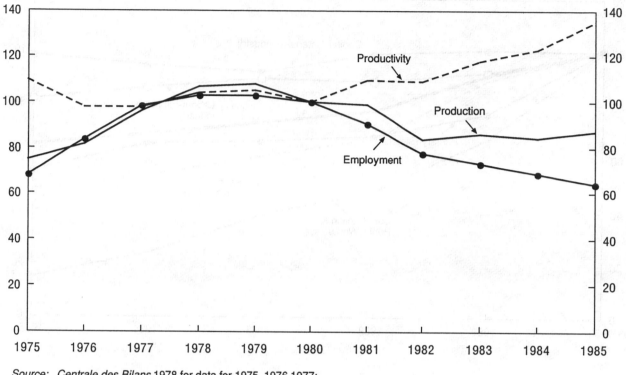

Source: *Centrale des Bilans* 1978 for data for 1975, 1976 1977;
Centrale des Bilans 1981 for data for 1978, 1979 1981;
Centrale des Bilans 1985 for data for de 1982, 1983 1984, 1985.

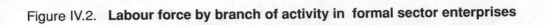

Figure IV.2. **Labour force by branch of activity in formal sector enterprises**

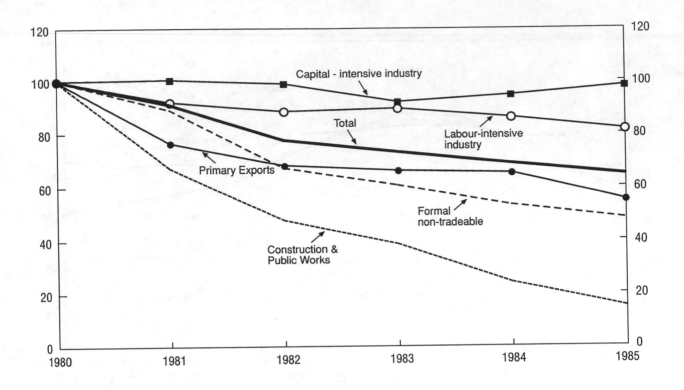

Figure IV.3. Wages and real payroll in all formal sector enterprises
Index: 1980 = 100

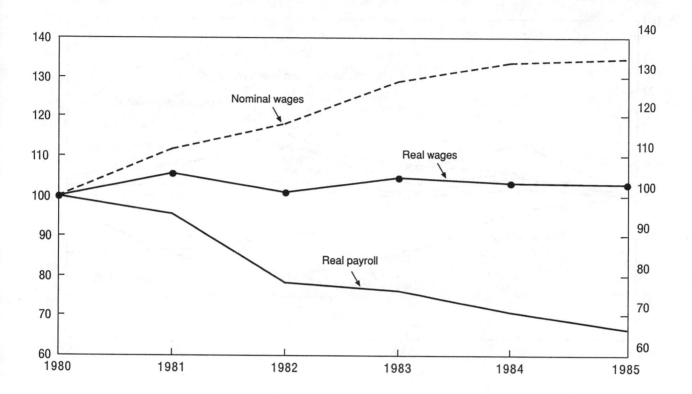

Figure IV.4. **Real wages by sector of activity**
Index: 1980 = 100

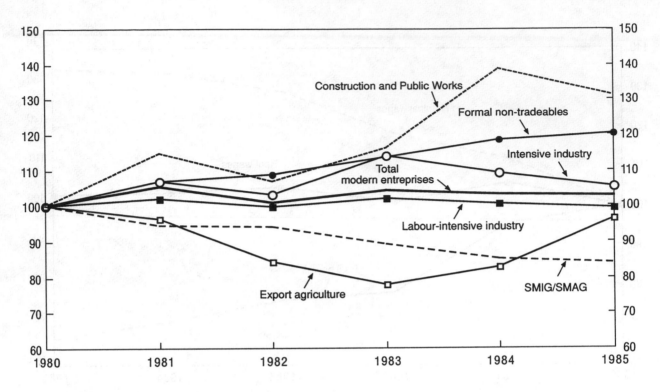

Notes and References

1. Chapter based on an internal report by Nghia Nguyen Tinh.
2. Ministère de l'Enseignement Technique et de la Formation Professionnelle, 1982.
3. Ministère des Relations Exterieures, 1982.
4. Ministère de l'Enseignement Technique et de la Formation Professionnelle, 1982.
5. According to Kurian, 34 per cent of the workers were children, as against 18 per cent for Africa as a whole.
6. Office National de Formation Professionnelle, 1985,p.17.
7. Turnham, 1971, p. 167.
8. Ministère du Plan et de l'Industrie (MPI), 1981-1985, p. 63.
9. International Labour Organisation (yearbooks) and Chambre d'Industrie de Côte d'Ivoire.
10. Ministère du Plan et de l'Industrie (MPI), 1981-1985, p. 63.
11. Ministère du Plan et de l'Industrie (MPI), 1981-1985.
12. Ministère de la Coopération, 1986, Chapter I, p. 74.
13. UNICEF, 1987, p. 12 and Lachaud, J.P. (1988b), p. 5: 29 poorly managed enterprises have been privatised since 1980.
14. Lacoste, 1983.
15. Lachaud, J.P. (1988b), p. 136. According to Lachaud's analysis, the weighted average real wage of the modern sector appears to have fallen by almost 20 per cent from 1978 to 1986.

Annex to Chapter IV

Available Data on Employment in Côte D'ivoire

Ministère de l'Économie et des Finances (MEF), *Centrale des Bilans*, 1973,...,1985.

MEF, *Population de la Côte d'Ivoire, Analyse des données démographiques disponibles*, Abidjan, 1984.

Ministère des Relations Extérieures, B*ilan national de l'emploi en Côte d'Ivoire*, Paris, 1982.

Oudin, Xavier, "Le recensement des activités en milieu urbain de Côte d'Ivoire", in *Séminaire sur les statistiques de l'emploi et du secteur non structuré*, Ministère du Plan, Rabat, 1984.

Koffi Koffo, Paul, "Analyse comparative des sources de données sur l'emploi en Côte d'Ivoire, in *Séminaire sur les statistiques de l'emploi et du secteur non structuré*, Ministère du Plan, Rabat, 1984.

Office Nationale de la Formation Professionelle (ONEP), *Enquête main-d'oeuvre 1984*, Abidjan, 1984.

ONEP, *Le secteur privé et semi-privé en Côte d'Ivoire*, 1979, 1981.

Chapter V

Standards of Living in a Period of Adjustment

A. Overview

1. Introduction

Like many countries, Côte d'Ivoire is experiencing rapid urbanisation. The urban population increased from 32 per cent of the total population in 1975 to almost 50 per cent in 1985. In rural areas, a distinction is generally made between the Forest zone (South) and the Savanna (North). In 1985, about 20 per cent of the total population lived in the savanna zone and 31 per cent in the forest zone. The relative decline in the rural population was greater in the Savanna than in the Forest and the forecasts indicate a continuation of this trend. Table V-1 gives a more detailed overview of the geographical distribution of the population and trends during the years preceding the adjustment (1975-81).

In our analysis, we make a further distinction in the rural zones between Eastern Forest and Western Forest. Farms in the Eastern Forest are different from those in the Western Forest, the latter being often bigger, more recently established and more oriented towards export crops.

The main export crops in the Forest zone are coffee and cocoa, whereas in the Savanna it is cotton. The situation of these crops in the development and adjustment process is highly significant for the main economic activity and household incomes. However, virtually all rural households are also engaged in food growing, either for their own consumption or to produce a surplus to sell on the local market. While the data concerning food crops, and in particular prices, are less complete than those for export crops, food crops are worthy of attention for several reasons. First, for households, they constitute an essential part of subsistence income and they are mainly produced by the women under their own responsibility. In terms of access to land and the use of labour (notably women), food crops are often at a disadvantage as compared with the others because the value added of the day's labour is lower (see Table V-9). However, the government now recognises the importance of re-establishing a balance between food crops and export crops, even if only because of the pressure of increasing food imports at a time when the prospects for the export crop market are poor. The "Food Crop Plan" (*Plan Vivrier*) drawn up by a ministerial commission in 1983 reflects this concern with re-establishing a balance between the different types of crop, but it was still clear in 1988 that this plan had not yet provided sufficient incentives to local food crop growers.

Another aspect of population distribution and type of economic activity is the rural labour shortage and urban labour surplus. This situation reflected the scale of internal and international migration, but was paradoxical because these migratory flows continued while unemployment was rising.

There were significant differences between the educational levels of the rural and urban populations on the one hand and between men and women on the other. The *Demographic Survey* of 1978/79 found 79 per cent of the rural population to be illiterate, as against 62 per cent of the urban population (excluding Abidjan) and 47 per cent in Abidjan. For women, the corresponding figures were 86, 72 and 57 per cent respectively while for men they were 71, 52, and 39 per cent (see *op. cit.* p. 252). This educational inequality has to be born in mind when considering the orientation of the adjustment measures.

It is not easy to compare the economic situation of rural and urban households in terms of incomes because of the absence of any systematic published data. Nevertheless, a first global approximation can be based on the prices paid to producers for the main cash crops, prices fixed by the government (Table V-2), the minimum wages (SMIG and SMAG) and the various price indicators (Table V-3). A more realistic comparison would have to include the incomes derived from crops rather than just their prices. For this it is necessary to take account of production. This calculation is made in Section 2 below. However, to the extent that minimum wages and prices of the main crops are both fixed by the government, it does make sense to compare them.

The indices for the 1980-86 period indicate that households deriving their incomes from the main cash crops were on the whole advantaged as compared with those (mainly in the urban formal sector) relying on the SMIG. The former received prices that had fallen in real terms by between 10 and 18 per cent by the end of the period, while the real SMIG (deflated by the consumer price index) fell by over 21 per cent during the same period. On the other hand, if we consider the rural population receiving the SMAG, we see that their real wage fell between 17 and 27 per cent, depending on the deflator used. Assuming that they had a semi-subsistence way of life and bought mainly manufactured goods, the fall amounted to 27 per cent. This shows that the comparison between rural and urban populations has to take account of the differences existing within these categories. Apart from the differences in the relative changes in incomes, it is also necessary to stress the very low absolute level of the SMAG as compared with the SMIG. A further factor is involved when we extend the analysis a little further in time, for we know that prices on the world cocoa market obliged the government (after long hesitation) drastically to reduce (by 50 per cent) the price paid to cocoa producers in 1989.

Since we also know that the numbers employed in the formal sector fell considerably over this period (see Chapter IV), it is clear that the overall trend was less unfavourable for rural than for urban households. A World Bank report sums up this evolution in terms of a fall in the inequality of incomes. Thus between 1980 and 1984 the ratio between urban and rural incomes is estimated to have fallen from 3.5:1 to about 2.5:1 and perhaps declined further after this. However, this reduction in inequality did not bring about any reduction in poverty, because according to this same source real incomes fell in both urban and rural areas, though in different proportions (10.8 per cent a year for the former as against 1.1 per cent for the latter).

However, the fall in the real income of the urban population was not uniform and certain categories even saw their real wages increase. Thus the SMIG and the average wage in the civil service fell in real terms by about 15 per cent between 1980 and 1985, while in the formal non-tradeable sector, and notably in construction, there were real wage increases exceeding 5 per cent during the same period (see Tables IV-12 and I-11).

Analysis of data from the *Centrale des Bilans* (see Figure 3, Chapter IV) indicates that in enterprises of a certain size (more than 10 employees) the workers were generally able to maintain their real wage.

This analysis of the wage trend has to be seen against the background of a fairly broad range of wages, in the enterprises surveyed by the *Centrale des Bilans* which paid on average three times the SMIG, which itself amounted to four times the SMAG.

Furthermore, a substantial proportion of urban households did not receive any formal sector wages, deriving their revenues from the informal sector and often from several sources. While these incomes are poorly documented, we know that they were generally low and were falling further during the adjustment (see simulations in Chapter VI).

It should also be pointed out that the extent to which households (and thus their real incomes) are affected by price increases depends on their expenditures. The more manufactured or imported goods they buy, the more they are exposed to price increases that generally exceed the consumer price index for African households (see Table V-3). It was the relatively well-off urban households that were most affected by this phenomenon. In fact, their expenditures in absolute terms, and sometimes even in relative terms, on these goods was generally higher than that of poor households (see also Revel, 1988). We shall see in the following sections how the different adjustment measures aimed at specific products actually affected the different categories of households.

2. Adjustment measures and the situation of households

The stabilisation and adjustment measures were formulated and implemented in different contexts over a long period that started in 1978. It is difficult to retrace the implementation of these measures in detail, because there was often a time lag between adoption and implementation. We summarised these measures in Chapter III above, and those concerned more specifically with employment and wages were discussed in Chapter IV. It thus remains for us to focus in this Chapter on the measures directly affecting the expenditure, living conditions and activities of households.

Of course, the more macroeconomic measures — such as monetary restrictions and those concerning foreign trade — can also affect certain households directly but, since they are difficult to take into account in our analysis of rural and urban households, we would refer the reader to the preceding chapters and the macroeconomic simulations (Chapter VI).

In this chapter we first describe certain measures at a general level and then examine what types of households were particularly affected. Analysis of the Household Survey will therefore be used to obtain a more detailed picture of the impacts.

Official documents of Côte d'Ivoire from before the granting of structural adjustment loans by the World Bank rarely make any mention of the poor segments of the population (for example the cotton growers in the Savanna or low income households targeted by the new housing policy), but many of the measures seem to have been oriented to improve the condition of rural households with respect to those of the city. However, the adjustment programmes did not include any measures explicitly aimed at reducing poverty.

Among the first measures felt directly by households, were the **tax increases** that were introduced on several occasions as from 1978: VAT and TPS (a tax on services) and taxes on specific products such as **tobacco and fuels** in 1982 (see the Chronology annexed to Chapter III). We shall try to identify the consumers of the products subject to these measures and the impact these tax increases may have had.

Similarly, we can try to determine the impact of the increases of the government controlled **prices and tariffs**, even though the aim of these increases was not (or not mainly) to increase tax revenue, but to make prices more realistic. As from 1981, the prices for electricity, water and transport were all increased. We shall analyse the impact of the first two on the different groups of households.

Among food prices, the official consumer price of rice was increased by 10 per cent in 1981, 18 per cent in 1982 and 23 per cent in 1984. These increases followed the trend of the rice price on the free market, but without ever actually reaching this price. Thus there was an implicit subsidy (which amounted to almost 30 per cent between 1981 and 1983) for households that bought their rice on the official market. Who benefited from this? We shall see below (Section III) that it was mainly the poor, but it is also necessary to take account of the difference in quality between the free market rice and that on the official market: the latter generally being considered of poor quality. The price of bread was increased in 1984. This measure mainly affected urban households, for according to the 1979 consumption budget survey, 80 per cent of the wheat was consumed in cities.

Another category of price increases adopted in the context of adjustment measures concerned the producer prices for the main export crops and for rice (see Table V-2). While for rice there was first a fall and then a rise, the prices for coffee, cocoa and cotton were all increased as from 1983.

Among the adjustment measures announced in 1983 in the context of the second World Bank adjustment loan were changes in housing policy. More specifically, the operating and maintenance costs of the dwellings owned by the SOGEFIHA and the SICOGI (*Société de Gestion Financière de l'Habitat et Société Ivoirienne de Construction et de Gestion Immobilière*) were to be at the tenants' expense by not later than the end of 1984 and rents were to be increased before the end of June 1985. It is thus necessary to identify the social categories of the tenants of these companies in order to appreciate the impacts of the measures (see Section III below). It can already be deduced from the announcement of this policy that the categories concerned were not exclusively the poorest, for it says that future public investment in this field should give greater priority to low-income households. In addition, the housing advantages of civil servants were to be substantially reduced (abolition of administrative leases and compensation limited to a housing allowance).

In general, the austerity measures having the greatest impact on the households of civil servants and employees of the parastatal sector were the wage policies analysed in Chapter IV. That chapter also analysed the job losses in the private formal sector which were particularly heavy in construction and public works because of the cuts in public investment.

For another group of households, those of farmers, besides the measures concerning the prices of the main cash crops mentioned above (see Table V-2), there were measures that can be considered to support or promote agriculture. These were of a general nature, such as for research or administrative and institutional reform, or were more specifically aimed at particular crops.

In 1981, the promotion of both food crops and export crops was announced, but the measures in favour of rice, sugar and soybeans were limited; the main accent's being on increasing the yield of coffee and cocoa, further expanding the production of cotton and rehabilitating the oil palm, coconut and rubber plantations at the village level. In particular, price increases for palm oil (up 50 per cent) and copra were announced. This contrasts sharply with the cut in the producer price for rice from FCFA 65 to 50/per kg of paddy, accompanied by an increase in the consumer price for rice from FCFA 100 to 110/per kg.

In 1983, the agricultural investment policies favouring export crops were renewed, accompanied by certain producer price increases. Similarly, it was decided to increase the price of fertilizers for cotton (1985) and abolish the subsidies for domestic fertilizer production and for the local processing of cotton and palm oil.

In 1986 it was decided to increase the real prices of coffee and cocoa gradually, with a differential in favour of the former, and to introduce measures to improve quality (Table V-2 shows that these increases were in practice effective only temporarily in 1986 and 1987). Customs duties and export subsidies were to give a minimum effective protection of 20 per cent for palm oil, cotton, rubber, coconuts and pineapples. In addition, the export taxes were to be abolished for palm oil and its derivatives, sugar, cotton and its derivatives, latex and natural rubber, coconuts, copra and its derivatives and fresh pineapples. On the level of investment, the government continued to favour the expansion of cotton growing in the Savanna and envisaged a series of studies for other possible crops.

Food crops retain an important place in the definition of the adjustment policy. International prices are to be taken into account in fixing the prices for rice, wheat flour and other products, but efforts are be made to avoid price increases that would severely affect consumer purchasing power. While new investments are planned to increase rice production, it also was proposed to introduce improved varieties for other food crops such as yam, plantain, cassava, maize and sorghum.

In conclusion, the agricultural adjustment measures had two objectives: the promotion of export crop production and improving their international competitiveness, and the satisfaction of the food needs of the Ivorian population. These measures were not specifically aimed at any precise socio-economic groups.

In reality, apart from the increases in nominal prices (see Table V-2), and improvements in the agricultural advisory system and the reorganisation of big public enterprises (SODESUCRE, PALMINDUSTRIE), few measures were effectively implemented. In particular, incentives for the producers of food crops remained inadequate.

On the whole, the producers of cash crops saw their real incomes increase during the 1980-86 period (except for coffee, down 12 per cent) and this despite the reduction in real producer prices indicated above (Table V-2). The fact is that during this period they increased their output by between 33 and 39 per cent, which led to an increase in real income (by the end of the period and disregarding the climatic fluctuations during the period) of 15 per cent for rice paddy, 19 per cent for cotton and 27 per cent for cocoa growers.

A series of adjustment measures of quite a different nature was announced in 1981 which involved economies in the field of education and took such forms as:

i)   limitation of entries to colleges and universities;

ii) limitation of entries to specialist schools;

iii) reduction of the number of secondary education grants;

iv) reduction of the number of technical assistants.

If we analyse the education budget, we see that between 1980 and 1985 the economies were mainly in the investment budget. The education share fell from 12 to 6 per cent, and this in a budget which itself fell from FCFA 313 billion to 88 billion. On the other hand, the share of education in the operating budget remained fairly high (42 per cent). In terms of expenditure per student at constant prices, however, Tibi finds a fall of over 40 per cent between 1980 and 1985[1]. It can therefore be assumed that there was both a cut in investment and a deterioration in services, at least in qualitative terms.

The greater part of the education investment budget went to higher education (between 52 and 86 per cent), while the primary and secondary education shares were low and at first falling (each getting about 4 per cent in 1982, then 10 per cent in 1985).

It may be assumed that these increases reflected a reaction of the authorities to the dramatic fall in enrolments in primary and, to a lesser extent secondary education between 1981 and 1984 as compared with the preceding five years. In fact, the annual average rate of increase in enrolment in the first year of primary school fell from 9.6 per cent in 1976-8 to 0.5 per cent in 1981. In first cycle of secondary education, the corresponding rates were 14 and 4.2 per cent.

However, the fall in enrolments was not exclusively due to a lack of infrastructure and decline in teaching. There was no doubt also a decline in the demand for education services, due to the reduced employment opportunities for young people leaving school in the situation of "compression" (to adopt the term used in Côte d'Ivoire). What is more, the fall in household incomes must have prevented certain families from sending their children to primary school. We shall see below (Section IV) different types of households were affected and whether there was any discrimination between boys and girls.

3. Different measurements of poverty in Côte d'Ivoire

There are essentially two ways of defining poverty. The first is based on essential physical needs (food, clothing, housing, health, education etc.) translated into a monetary value for a given year and locality and stipulates that any person incapable of satisfying these needs is in a situation of **absolute poverty**. This definition makes it possible to situate a population in time with respect to a fixed line adjusted only for price changes.

Another approach is to use a **relative definition of poverty**. This consists of identifying the people or households in a population with their incomes (or expenditures) and classifying them according to income, for example by deciles. Thus the same proportion of the population is kept in these classes for which, in fact, welfare can very well change.

It is not easy to define a line of absolute poverty, because there are a certain number of (more or less arbitrary) judgments to be made with respect to the composition of the consumption "basket". As far as we are aware, such a definition (which would require regional variants to take account of the differences in physical and social conditions and consumer habits) does not exist for Côte d'Ivoire. On the other hand, on the basis of the data in the 1985 permanent household survey[2] relative poverty lines have been defined, first by Glewwe (LSMS Working Paper no. 29) and then by Kanbur. In what follows we summarise some of the findings of their analyses before presenting our own (based on the same survey together with other information). Glewwe defined several poverty lines on the basis of annual household expenditure (per capita, adjusted for food grown by the household itself and in terms of "adult equivalents"), selecting as the income limits the poorest 10 and 30 per cent of the population:

The very relative nature of this definition of the poverty threshold should be stressed. It classifies as poor (i.e. below the 10 per cent line) households in Abidjan and "other towns" that would be above the 30 per cent line in two of the three rural zones.

The different levels of these lines give a first impression of the localisation of the poverty in Côte d'Ivoire, though they need to be adjusted for regional price differences (Table V-5) and type of expenditures. The latter obviously varies between town and country for housing and transport, for example.

At the **national level**, Glewwe found the majority of the poor in rural areas, notably in the Eastern Forest and the Savanna. They were working mainly in agriculture for their own account, had a very low educational and school enrolment level, lived in households slightly larger than the average, in which the proportion of children in the household was lower than the average and that of working members was substantially higher. The sex of the head of household did not seem to be a determining factor in the situation of the poor.

At the **urban level**, some of the characteristics of the poor mentioned at the national level reappear, but there are also differences concerning the distinction between Abidjan and "other towns". Thus the poor in the other towns were working mainly in agriculture for their own account, while in Abidjan they were working for their own account in the informal sector, in retail trade and services. Similarly, while the school enrolment rate among the poorest 10 per cent was relatively very low in Abidjan this was not the case in the other towns. There was also a certain comfort in the housing of the poorest in Abidjan, indicated by the presence of electricity and WCs, but this was not so often found in the other towns.

Lastly, for the **rural areas**, Glewwe finds the poorest households not so very different from the others (with certain exceptions) and also shows certain characteristics of the poor already seen at the national level. What is more, he points out the over-representation of the Voltaic ethnic group among the poor of the Savanna. Another exceptional feature is that in the Western Forest the poorest did not have a lower educational level than the others.

Kanbur, while using data from the same survey as Glewwe in his analysis of poverty in Côte d'Ivoire defines poverty lines at the national level rather different from Glewwe's, notably FCFA 53 000 per capita for the poorest 10 per cent and FCFA 96 560 for the poorest 30 per cent. It must be assumed that this is mainly due to different evaluations of non-monetary expenditures. Kanbur also differs in the way he distinguishes between urban and rural households. He does not rely on the place of residence, but first of all separates households that own land from the others. Among the first, he classifies as agricultural those whose main income is from agriculture. Then among these households he separates out producers for export, i.e. those who used the greater part of their land to grow one of the main export crops (coffee, cocoa, oil palm, rubber and cotton), the other agricultural households being classified as food producers. The non-agricultural households are classified according to the main activity of the head of household, as:

   i)   civil sector employees;

   ii)   private formal sector employees;

   iii)   "informal", a category that covers all the rest, including the unemployed.

This approach creates artificial categories among the farmers, as we know that the very great majority of farmers grow both export and food crops and there are some crops which belong to both categories (for example plantain and cocoa) and that the attribution of land to a single type of crop may be arbitrary. However, this classification does have the advantage of facilitating reasoning in terms of economic policies.

While Kanbur's analysis provides more detail about the distribution of poverty and may be more useful for planning the policies in favour of the poorest (we shall return to these conclusions in the last chapter), it broadly confirms Glewwe's findings. Farmers are the largest category among the poor and are at the lowest poverty level, and among these it is the food growers who are the most numerous and the poorest. Regionally the Savanna and Western Forest have the greatest numbers of poor people and the greatest degree of poverty.

Given the above-mentioned analyses of the 1985 Survey data and in views of the objective of our research, we have attempted to constitute fairly homogenous groups of households. For the rural areas this involved defining typical agro-ecological zones and excluding from our analysis households outside these zones, i.e. those in Basse-Côte and the Forest-Savanna contact region[3]. Elsewhere, we have adopted the distinction between town and country as defined in the design of the survey (see Ainsworth and Munoz, 1986).

In order to describe the economic level of households better, we have grouped them according to their monetary non-food expenditure per equivalent member in the categories "poor", "medium" and "rich" as indicated in Table V-6. This classification avoids problems of comparability between households with different levels of food self-sufficiency and the difficulty of evaluating the impact of other non-monetary factors on the standard of living. The expenditure brackets for the different categories were fixed by taking into account the information available in the literature and that obtained during two visits to Côte d'Ivoire in 1988. They well reflect the reality of the different categories of households. Thus, for example, the difference in expenditures in the Table V-6 classification between the poor in Abidjan and the poor in the Savanna roughly corresponds to the difference between the SMIG and SMAG (see Table V-3). Similarly, Glewwe's analysis (Table V-4) finds relative differences of the same order of magnitude as in Table V-6 for the different zones and the different socio-economic categories.

Of course, the adoption of a single poverty line (or with slight regional adjustments) for the whole of Côte d'Ivoire would have been preferable if we had wanted to study absolute poverty defined using a "basket" of basic needs. But there is no such basket and we were more interested in studying relative poverty within the different zones. This reflects our objective of identifying poverty that may have been aggravated by the adjustment policies or which should be taken into account for making policies more effective in the future. An analysis using a single poverty line would make these situations less clearly perceptible because they would be "hidden" in more heterogeneous groups.

Applying the brackets of Table V-6 to the sample adjusted as indicated above, we obtain a breakdown of households by region and by economic level presented in Table V-7. The high proportion of poor families (about 46 per cent of the total) suggests that an analysis using the first three deciles does not measure the full extent of poverty in Côte d'Ivoire. Otherwise, Table V-7 confirms that the proportion of poor within the different regions is greatest in the Savanna (62 per cent) and least in Abidjan (34 per cent).

In trying to identify the characteristics of rural and urban households better, above all with respect to the adjustment period and the policy measures actually implemented (or potentially applicable), we analyse separately urban and rural households in the following two sections. However, we subsequently make town-country comparisons wherever possible.

B. The situation of rural populations[4]

We saw at the beginning of this chapter that, overall, the rural populations were rather better placed than the urban populations with respect to the adjustment measures. Among these measures, the most restrictive such as the cuts in public investment and the wage freeze for public servants affected above all the urban populations, while the farmers benefited from several increases in the prices of coffee, cocoa and cotton as from 1983 (though with a cut in the price of cocoa in 1989, see Table V-2).

However, to understand the situation of the rural populations in the adjustment period fully it is necessary to go beyond this type of sectoral analysis and look at the agrarian systems and the expenditures that are the main determinants of the welfare of rural households. We shall therefore briefly analyse the agrarian systems in the Forest zone and the Savanna from the historical standpoint before going on to compare the situation of these populations through the findings of different surveys and field research.

1. Agrarian systems: historical survey

In both zones (Forest and Savanna) itinerant cultivation using the "slash and burn" method is practised, but the sequence and type of crops varies[5]. In the Forest zone, food crops open the cycle and are followed by perennial export crops (mainly coffee and cocoa) for many years, while in the Savanna food crops (mainly maize, rice, sorghum-millet, yams and groundnuts) are grown, often two or three together, alternating with cotton, an export crop grown on over 80 per cent of the farms. The area devoted to cotton has increased greatly since the introduction of this crop at the beginning of the 1960s, but in 1985 it still amounted to only about 5 per cent of the areas under coffee and cocoa.

Over the past two decades coffee and cocoa yields have stagnated and sometimes fallen. Thus producers have been able to increase their real incomes only by expanding the area. On the other hand, the introduction of improved seed for cotton has made it possible to increase yields by about 34 per cent since 1966/67, the year in which Allen cotton growing began. Rice yields are almost 50 per cent higher in the Forest than in the Savanna zone (1.3 t/ha as against 0.9 t/ha). There are also differences between the Forest and Savanna zones in terms of implements (and hence capital-intensity). While small hand implements are found everywhere (machetes, axes etc.) the bigger planters in the south have barrows and sprayers while those in the north use draft animals (10-12 per cent in the late 1970s).

The availability of labour constitutes a major problem in both zones, but in different ways. In the Forest zone, there are bottlenecks during land clearing and at harvest time that are beyond the labour capacity of individual households. They therefore use wage labour, but under different conditions depending on the size of the farm. Access to land in fact determines access to labour, because the big growers who have forest reserves can obtain labour at a relatively low money wage by promising a plot of forest land after a few years' work. Chaléard has shown that this means that small farmers pay a higher price for their (contract) labour than the big farmers who employ a greater proportion of monthly labour. This advantage of the big farmers (who also have access to credit) is perpetuated to the extent that the release of state forests favours the big farmers (see Pillet-Schwartz). Furthermore, some of them who are polygamous can have large areas under food crops (an activity "reserved" to women) and, at the same time satisfy customary law which says that the land should go to those who work it. However, these advantages cannot prevent big farmers from being confronted with an increasingly serious shortage of land which leads them to invest in non-agricultural activities (frequently more profitable), notably real estate and transport.

In the Savanna zone access to labour is also determined by access to land but differently than in the Forest zone. This results in a different distribution of farm sizes as shown in Table V-8 (rural). The fact is that the good land, notably developed marsh land, is as increasingly rare as labour, which is typically family labour because of the migration of young people. Cotton and low-land rice is grown using draft animals or small mechanised implements on the big farms with abundant family labour. However, the overlapping of the periods when much labour is needed for food crops and cotton has led to the stagnation of food growing which is less profitable.

Another aspect of the increasing scarcity of cultivable land that affects both zones is the shortening of the fallow periods which reduces the fertility of the soil. Fertility is greater in the Forest zone, but the exhaustion of the soils in the area of former colonisation in the zone gives a considerable advantage to the western part, where the average yields for coffee and cocoa are 50 to 100 per cent higher than in the Eastern Forest. In the Savanna, the fertility of the cotton land is maintained by the use of chemical fertilizers (200-300 kg/ha). Thus in this zone the increase in the fertilizer prices (in the context of the adjustment measures) was felt the most. The Savanna is relatively sparsely populated, apart from the "dense" area of Korhogo, and its mainly ferrous soils are considered good for traditional agriculture, but it would appear that only a limited part of this area is suited for cultivation using draft animals. Despite the differences between the Forest and Savanna zones just outlined, it can be seen that the occupation and use of the agricultural area follows the same logic in both zones. This logic can be summed up in two principles, the one economic and the other concerned with security of food supply, which have to be taken into account when analysing the impact of the adjustment policies and defining possible alternative policies. The economic principle aims at deriving the maximum value from the day's labour, which is achieved by growing export crops (see Table V-9). The second principle involves seeking food security at the local level. This requires staggering the growing of food crops in time and space to minimise the effects of bad climatic conditions. To the extent that the two types of crop do not use the same land and the periods of maximum labour requirements do not coincide, these two principles are complementary. But we have seen that this is not always the case, and where there is conflict, it would appear that the economic principle prevails.

This choice is made increasingly to the detriment of the women because traditionally growing food crops is largely their domain. They derive a monetary income from selling the surplus and this gives them a certain autonomy, whereas otherwise they are generally used as unpaid family labour in cash crop growing, which is the domain of the men who appropriate the income to themselves.

This overview of the agricultural systems leads to the conclusion that adjustment measures which are most desirable make it possible to reduce the potential conflict between the economic and food security principles, and this for two reasons: the safeguard of food security and a more equitable place for women in the agrarian system, while maintaining or even increasing the production of export crops.

2. Evolution of the condition of rural households

It is not easy to retrace the evolution of the condition of households throughout the adjustment period with any precision. Very often the data available for the different periods do not cover the same questions and the same places (in the case of surveys) and are therefore not directly comparable. However, we have brought together the data from different sources of field research, generally very limited in space, covering the 1979 Consumption Budget Survey, and the 1985 Permanent Household Survey). The result does not enable us to claim perfect comparability (and in fact brings out some contradictions) but it does give us a basis for systematic analysis relevant to our research concerned in particular with the most disadvantaged social groups.

In order to distinguish between the situations of poor households better, we have created three categories of rural household, i.e. "big", "medium" and "small". This classification refers to the size of the farm, but not in a rigid fashion because the data on land are unreliable[6]. The main criterion for classification is annual non-food monetary expenditure per equivalent member of the household. These categories thus become comparable historically and with those used elsewhere in this study, i.e. "rich", "middle" and "poor" (see Table V-6) while maintaining their rural specificity.

The sample of rural households in the 1985 survey was adjusted to increase comparability with the field research of the late 1970s and to concentrate the analysis on typical agro-ecological zones[7]. The result is the sample shown in Table V-7. The 1985 survey data and more recent observations in the field (1988) make it possible to assert that the use of the ecosystem changed little during the adjustment years. However, the fallow periods seem to have been shortened in the Forest zone and (rice) cultivation in the Savanna marshlands increased. This confirms the historic trend for land to become scarce, leading to increased cultivation pressure.

Table V-10 shows that the areas being farmed vary according to the zone. It is confirmed that the small farmers have little fallow land. What is more, there is much more available uncultivated land in the Western Forest which, locally, is still an agricultural frontier area. As regards the Savanna, it should be pointed out that the apparently egalitarian distribution of fallow land is misleading, because in this zone the problem of the availability of land is more one of quality than of quantity.

Table V-10 also shows that there are several important differences in the main crops in different zones as well as within them; Thus the Eastern Forest is distinguished by a relatively small percentage under food crops. This is to be interpreted as a sign of the increasing scarcity of land, given the position of these crops at the beginning of the cultivation cycle. The high proportion of export crops grown by big farmers (notably in the Eastern Forest) reflects differences in access to labour.

From the way the agricultural area is divided among the different crops it can be seen that an adjustment policy giving priority to the main export crops favours the Forest zones and the biggest farmers, depending on the degree of their concentration on these crops and the size of their farms. The Savanna zone seems to suffer from an additional handicap because, apart from the low percentage of the main export crops, it cannot produce other export crops. Particular attention needs to be paid to these structural characteristics in the formulation of any adjustment measures.

The 1985 survey also makes it possible to see the use of non-family labour for the different crops. Here again, there are substantial differences between the regions. Thus in the Savanna zone less than 5 per cent of this labour works on export crops while in the Western and Eastern Forests, the figures are 64 and 50 per cent respectively for the big farmers and almost 20 per cent for the small (see Table V-11).

The type of non-family labour varies according to the same pattern between the zones, i.e. the big farmers employ a much lower portion of sharecroppers than the small (between 10 and 17 per cent for the former as against 36 to 44 per cent for the latter) as the sole form of non-family labour. Conversely, the big farmers more frequently tend to employ both sharecroppers and wage labourers. This leads to the conclusion that the big farmers have a more flexible employment policy, which contributes to a better economic result.

This breakdown of the labour force between the different crops and different types of employment determines the impact of adjustment measures. Thus, for example, better cotton prices affect non-family labour less than would be the case with an equivalent increase in the prices of coffee and cocoa.

3. Structure and level of household expenditure

Analysis of the monetary spending of rural households according to the socio-economic category and the region makes it possible in the first place to obtain a picture of the differences and to evaluate the impact of the adjustment measures on some categories of expenditure (see Table V-12). Engel's law is confirmed in the three zones because the proportion of spending on food tends to fall as we go from "small" to "middle" and "big". In the few households where the head of household is a woman (3 per cent) spending on food is on average considerably higher than in households where the head is a man, regardless of the economic category.

However, if we look at the food products whose prices were increased by the adjustment measures (bread and rice) relative expenditure on them did not change (Eastern Forest) or moved erratically with the socio-economic level. On the other hand, there is a very clear distinction between the zones, with the share of expenditure on rice increasing from south to north and from east to west (from 5 to 18 per cent). Thus the poorest zone, the Savanna, spends relatively more on rice. As a result, the increase in the consumer price for rice aggravated the regional inequality of incomes. Between the two forest zones, the impact on income distribution is less clear cut, and tends towards a balance because two of the three groups (the middle and small) in the Western Forest who consume more rice than those in the Eastern Forest, also have slightly higher total expenditure.

There is no regional trend for expenditure on bread, which is always much lower than that on rice (between 3 and 5 per cent of the total). This last characteristic is also found in the majority of cases in the expenditure of urban households. It can thus be concluded that for both environments (rural and urban) rice is in general a more sensitive commodity than bread because an increase in its price has a greater impact on the population. However, the government directly controls only a limited part of the consumer rice market. In fact, the controlled consumer price applies only to the "official" market which handles only about 10 per cent of total sales. Although our survey data do not enable us to identify the sources of supply for households, it is clear that it tends to be the poor who buy their rice (considered to be of inferior quality) on the official market (see also Section III below concerning urban populations).

Expenditure on transport was another category affected by the adjustment measures (increases in fuel taxes and in rail fares) whose impact on households can be identified. While expenditure on transport clearly increases with economic level in the Western Forest, this tendency is less marked in the other zones. However, it can be said that the share of transport expenditure in "small" budgets is lower everywhere than that of the other categories (varying between 4 and 6 per cent as against 6 and 8 per cent). The result is that in both relative and absolute terms an increase in the price of transport weighs more heavily on the rich and middle households than on the poor ones in rural areas. Although our data concern only direct expenditures, it can be assumed that this conclusion is also valid for indirect expenditures (incorporated in the prices of the goods bought by households) in view of the differences in the levels of total spending. Comparing total spending in the rural and urban environments, it is clear that the rural areas are more homogenous.

Two trends can be seen in spending on education. First, the average proportion is higher in the Forest zones than in the Savanna, and in the Forest it is higher in the East than in the West. This reflects the lower school enrolment rate in the Savanna and the more recent colonisation of the Western Forest. Furthermore, in the Forest zone the education expenditures of the poor households takes a share of their budget higher than the average for all households, while the contrary is true in the Savanna. This difference may be interpreted as the reflection of schooling in the Savanna's being "from the top down" from the economic standpoint.

A comparison of the relative spending on education between the rural and urban environments (see Table V-12 and V-15) strikingly reveals the greater share of these expenditures in urban areas (often double and sometimes triple). This primarily reflects higher enrolment rates in urban than in rural areas. Thus in the Savanna, the enrolment rate for girls is one-third that of Abidjan, while for boys it is 40 per cent. In the other rural areas the differences are less marked but still very clear (see Table V-21). A further explanatory factor is no doubt that in towns there are more secondary and private schools which entail relatively high spending. It is obvious that in these circumstances, austerity measures affecting education will be felt more in the urban than in the rural areas. It should be noted that measures aimed at making families pay more and more for education would have a fairly serious effect on poor urban households, for about 65 per cent of their children are at school.

In order to evaluate the changes that took place in rural households during the adjustment period in the first half of the 1980s, we compare the consumption expenditures according to the 1985 Survey with that of the 1979 Consumption Budget Survey (EBC). While these two surveys are the only ones concerning household spending for the whole country, they are not perfectly comparable because of differences in definitions. However, comparisons of the findings of these surveys (see Table V-13) can indicate the direction of the changes and perhaps, to a lesser extent, their order of magnitude.

A first correction that is required concerns spending on food. With increasing monetisation of the economy (and hence a fall in food self-sufficiency, which also corresponds to the fact that the land available for food crops is becoming scarcer) there is a tendency to overestimate spending on food. For this reason, and also because expenditures on food were not measured in the same way in the two surveys, it is necessary to consider non-food expenditures as being a better indicator of the trend.

Non-food expenditures per equivalent member increased over the period by 28 per cent in the Forest and 11 per cent in the Savanna. This may be explained by increases in real incomes due to certain cash crops (see above, Section I). These increases amounted to 15 per cent for rice and 27 per cent for cocoa over the period 1980-86 as a result of increases in production which more than compensated for the fall in real prices (except for coffee). These increases were thus of a comparable order of magnitude if we do not take into account population growth. If the growth in the agricultural population is estimated at 2 per cent a year (Table V-1 shows substantial regional differences for the period 1975-81) the increases in real per capita incomes turn out to be much lower than the increases in expenditures given by the surveys. Thus there is an apparent contradiction between the two sources.

The global data from the national accounts also suggest that there was only a very small increase in real incomes of agricultural households in the 1980-85 period (about 0.6 per cent). The year 1986 in fact was a peak (up 1 per cent in a year) which was immediately followed by a fall in 1987 (down 4 per cent). During the 1980-87 period, the World Bank indicates an annual average rate of increase in the agricultural sector of 1.6 per cent (see Table I-1). Taking into account the growth of the agricultural population we find a growth rate of about zero and perhaps even negative, thus incompatible with the comparisons of the two surveys. Lacking other more detailed information, it is impossible for us to decide which of the two trends, one which is relatively positive and one which indicates stagnation, is correct.

Elsewhere, the survey data (which remain our only systematic and detailed points of reference) confirm the more favourable situation in the Forest with respect to the Savanna. They are also compatible with the observation of a more favourable trend in rural than in urban areas.

Despite the contradictions observed, it can be concluded that to the extent that rural households were able to increase production so as to more than compensate for the fall in real prices for the main crops (or find other sources of income), they were able to increase or maintain their real income during the first half of the 1980s. The agricultural system favoured farmers who had access to relatively cheap labour and to additional land for cash crops. The main impact of the adjustment measures on the rural populations was thus determined by the agricultural system. This did not change, but rather perpetuated the "broad trends" of the existing system, closely linked to land ownership. In addition, it appears that measures aimed at food crops (other than rice) that would potentially have had a more egalitarian impact were implemented only to a very limited extent. The rural sector thus remains very vulnerable because of its dependence on export crops, something that the country became very aware of in 1986/87 due to a fall of over 50 per cent in the unit value of coffee exports expressed in FCFA.

C. The situation of urban populations

To the extent that urban populations tend to be more in the formal sector, public or private, and thus more integrated in the market economy than the rural populations, they are potentially more exposed to adjustment policies. Wage and employment policies and also the housing policy directly affect civil servants and public sector employees who mainly live in urban areas. The increases in certain taxes such as VAT and TPS (tax on services) also have more impact in urban than in rural areas. We shall now examine the household consumption for certain categories of goods affected by specific tax increases or by price controls.

Indirectly, the reduction of public expenditures — notably investment expenditure — reduced employment in the private formal sector (notably in construction) and hence, as a secondary effect, the demand for goods and services supplied by the informal sector. This reduction in demand caused a fall in informal sector incomes additional to that caused by the above-mentioned measures which reduced real incomes and hence consumer demand.

On the basis of the 1985 survey data concerning the principal activity of heads of households and the size of the enterprise in which they worked, we have constituted a group of non-agricultural informal sector households. This group is made up of households whose head has an activity that meets two criteria:

a)   is in one of the crafts, commerce or certain other fields (chosen from a list of 72 occupations); and

b)   is in an enterprise employing fewer than 5 people.

In Table V-14 we have also included in this category heads of households who did not declare their occupation. The other categories of households by sector have been established exclusively on the basis of the declared occupation.

It can be seen from Table V-14 that among the poor households, those that depend on the informal sector are the most numerous in both absolute and relative terms (between 75 and 80 per cent, a proportion far higher than their share in the sample which is from 50 to 64 per cent respectively. By contrast, among the "rich", it is private formal sector households which are the most numerous and over-represented. However, the proportion of "rich" among the informal sector in Abidjan is far from negligible (33 per cent). This goes to show the great diversity of the informal sector. It should also be noted that among the "middle" in the "other towns", the three categories of household (according to their sector) are found in proportions roughly corresponding to their share of the sample. The inequalities are thus greater in Abidjan than in the smaller towns. Any adjustment policy that intends to reduce inequalities should take account of the differences within the two urban environments as well as those between them.

In trying to trace the impact of certain adjustment measures on the categories of household identified in Table V-14, we examined their average relative spending on goods whose consumer prices were increased by the adjustment programme: **bread, rice, cigarettes** and **petrol**. This analysis reveals that the average urban household in all categories consumes both bread and rice but in proportions which vary greatly without any very clear tendencies. However, if the categories are grouped according to their economic level some very clear trends emerge (see Table V-15). Thus in Abidjan the share spent on bread increases from "poor" to "rich" while the exact opposite is seen for rice. In the "other towns" the trend is less clear for bread if spending on it is taken as a percentage of total monetary expenditures. However, except for the "rich" in Abidjan bread is never as important as rice. Thus the latter is clearly a food of the poor and is particularly important in the other towns where the relative expenditure on rice is about twice (and sometimes more) that in Abidjan at all economic levels. As the level of expenditure does not vary so much between Abidjan and the "other towns" the latter are also more severely affected in absolute terms. Similarly, when comparing rich and poor, total spending on food varies less between rich and poor than the percentage spent on rice. Thus the poor are more affected than the rich in absolute terms. To give an example close to the proportions found in the "other towns": in spending FCFA 90 000 on food (30 per cent of total income) of which one-sixth or FCFA 15 000 on rice, a rich family spends less on rice than a poor family for which the corresponding figures are FCFA 80 000 (50 per cent of total income) and 20 000 or one-fourth of food expenditures on rice. Conversely, the corresponding example for expenditures on bread would show that the rich household spends about twice as much as the poor (FCFA 5 400 as against 2 600).

As we have seen (Section I above) the official consumer price for rice was increased three times during the period 1981-84 — a cumulative increase of about 60 per cent. While it is obvious that virtually all consumers were affected by these price increases, it was the poorest urban households that were hardest hit. The increases in the price of rice thus had regressive effects. These effects cannot be attributed solely to the adjustment programmes because the official price only followed the trend of the free market price, even if the latter applied to a better quality of rice. The survey data do not indicate the source of supply (official or free market) to enable us to establish who were the beneficiaries of the "rent" that the official market provided in the form of a price lower than the free market price.

Two articles affected by the tax adjustment without the problem of the two-tier market were cigarettes and petrol. However, their share of total monetary expenditures is very low (see Table V-15). Spending on cigarettes in most cases is less than 0.05 per cent, while for petrol it is in the order of 0.1 per cent.

In 1981 there were price increases for electricity (up 7.5 per cent) and water (up 14 per cent in two stages). While these increases brought in only about 60 per cent of the revenue resulting from the increase of 10 per cent in petrol tax (according to IMF estimates), it is obvious from the 1985 survey that the direct impact of these measures on households was much greater (see Table V-15). The share spent on these two items seems to exceed that for education. In Abidjan electricity weighed particularly heavily on the "poor" (15.1 per cent). For both items the relative share was higher for the poor than for the rich. These price increases thus had a regressive effect on equity in the urban areas, whatever their micro and macroeconomic justification may have been.

Relative spending on electricity is on average higher in Abidjan than in the other towns, which are much less well equipped. For water the contrary is true (except for the "rich"), but the difference in percentages between Abidjan and the other towns is less than in the case of electricity. Given the definition of the groups at regional level (see Table V-6), absolute expenditure on water is nevertheless higher in Abidjan than in the other towns.

Spending on **education** (see Table V-15) on average weighs heavier on the budgets of rich households than on those of other categories. What is more, the percentages are higher in Abidjan than in the other towns. This is partly explained by a higher enrolment rate (see Table V-21), but also partly by differences in the cost and type of education (according to the level and type of establishment, i.e. public or private).

While the table of relative spending on education may reflect the effect of certain adjustment measures, for example, the limitation of grants in 1984/85 for secondary (down 30 per cent) and higher education (down 50 per cent), the data do not make it possible to establish any formal link. At best we can put forward some hypotheses. Thus it can be assumed that certain households stopped sending their child (or children) to secondary school because they did not receive a grant. Similarly, the limitation of entries to higher education reduced the expenditures of some households. But such a reduction may result also from another phenomenon, that is the deterioration of the labour market for young people emerging from the education system, both secondary and higher. In addition, a substantial part of the education expenditures may reflect a greater sacrifice on the part of some households in response to the limitation of grants. It would require more detailed surveys to show the extent to which each of these hypotheses is valid.

The social origin of pupils and students is treated in the analysis of educational enrolments in Section IV below. Actually, the rich in urban areas (Abidjan and other towns) have an average school enrolment level about 40 per cent higher than that of the poor (see Table V-21). For this reason and because of the high proportion of rich households in urban areas, this was the category most affected in real terms by the increased cost of education.

Housing was another item significant for urban households affected by the adjustment. First, it is necessary to identify those who originally had more or less subsidised housing and who would therefore have been affected by the increases in rents and running costs.

While only a small percentage of our sample benefited from SOGEFIHA and SICOGI housing (approximately 5 per cent in Abidjan and 9 per cent in the other towns), the great majority of these were "rich" households, among them civil servants and comparable personnel.

In 1986, the government finally decided to offer SOGEFIHA dwellings for sale to their tenants instead of increasing rents. This measure made it possible to eliminate a source of losses to the state budget. Its impact in terms of equity was rather regressive because although the conditions of sale were relatively favourable, the less advantaged categories could not finance the purchase of their apartments and were forced to leave them.

It should be pointed out, however, that in the context of the second World Bank structural adjustment loan, the government also stated its intention to promote the social housing sector, though without increasing public expenditure. To this end the *Crédit Immobilier Social* (CIS) was to be set up in 1983 and other institutional measures were to be taken, including the establishment of a development programme for enterprises in the building materials and construction sector. The system finally set up to develop building sites and mobilise savings for housing under the responsibility of the DCGTX was considered to be a success, but we do not have the information necessary for evaluating the social impact of these measures.

Taking in members of the extended family is generally considered a sign of traditional solidarity, which according to some commentators (see Mahieu) is usual for the wealthier classes and notably civil servants. In fact, over half the households in our urban sample included members of the extended family (the figures being slightly higher in other towns than in Abidjan), but the proportion of these households was slightly higher among the "poor" than among the "rich".

Distinguishing between the socio-professional categories within the three economic levels, we find that among the "rich" the households of civil servants and comparable personnel had the highest proportion of extended households (61 per cent in Abidjan and 71 per cent in the other towns). However, in the "middle" and "poor" categories, it was the private formal sector households which had the highest proportion, as much as 80 and 74 per cent respectively in the "other towns". It can therefore be said that on the whole, it was primarily formal sector households in the broad sense which fulfilled this solidarity function of housing members of the extended family. Their economic level and stability of employment apparently allowed these households to fulfil this role better, even though they too were affected by the cuts in employment and other adjustment measures.

The other form of family solidarity is transfers and gifts, which we examined for all households. While no clear pattern emerges for these transfers by type of household, the difference between regions and between urban and rural areas are striking (see Table V-16). The most remarkable feature is that the Abidjan households appear as the only net beneficiaries of money transfers. Our data do not enable us to say to what extent this situation results from the crisis that hit Abidjan particularly hard, the good harvests of 1984 and 1985 or the services rendered by the city dwellers to their rural relatives, for example, housing some of their children. However, these proportions underline the fact that regional differences are not only economic but also socio-cultural, for among the rural zones it was the poorest, the Savanna, that showed the highest transfers. For Abidjan these proportions can only be seen as an indication of the dependence of the capital on the rest of the country.

Besides analysing the spending of urban households, there is a particular aspect of urban employment that merits our attention. We have seen in Table V-14 that over half of the urban households belong to the informal sector and that this proportion exceeds three-fourths in the case of the poor. It is therefore desirable to examine this sector further to situate the impact of the adjustment measures better and suggest alternative measures that would benefit the poorest populations.

The literature on the informal sector often stresses the preponderance of women in this sector. This is confirmed by the findings of the 1985 survey (see Table V-17) which also reveals a new factor for Abidjan: the "richer" the household, the greater the proportion of men. This means that the highest paid occupations in the informal sector are in practice more difficult for women to attain, whether for reasons of education, availability or simply power of appropriation. While our data show the range of households represented in the informal sector they suggest at the same time the existence of a phenomenon also known in the rural areas: as soon as an economic activity turns out to be more profitable the men tend to appropriate it for themselves. It is necessary to bear this phenomenon in mind when envisaging measures for the informal sector intended to improve the situation of women. The women often find themselves at bottom of the scale of activities and in the potentially most vulnerable situations.

The informal sector to a large extent escaped from the adjustment measures affecting taxation, public spending and public employment. Although this is confirmed by our simulations, the sector suffered repercussions from all the austerity measures, either through fiercer competition from persons made redundant or not finding employment in the formal sector, or because of reduced spending by urban and rural households that normally bought goods and services from this sector.

Our analysis of the survey data do not allow us to say to what extent participation in the informal sector was a response to specific adjustment measures or rather due to other causes that may have been cumulative. However, we have identified and quantified the poverty linked with the informal sector in Abidjan in two different ways. First, a greater proportion of the poor work in this sector (Table V-17). Second, households running a business are classified as follows: 65 per cent among the poor, 45 per cent among the middle and 29 per among the rich. The informal sector is thus made up of a good number of poor entrepreneurs, not just poor workers. While the majority of household enterprises are run by women (in both rural and urban areas) there is once again a differentiation according to economic level in Abidjan. Among the rich households, 51 per cent of these enterprises are run by a man and 38 per cent by a women, while for poor households these figures are 25 and 55 per cent respectively (the remaining percentage in each case being enterprises run jointly by men and women).

D. Socio-cultural variables in a period of adjustment[8]

The aim of this section is to clarify the conditions of individuals, particularly women and children, in different situations in Ivorian society. The emphasis is firstly on education, because this was affected by the adjustment measures and because it partly determines access to employment. Moreover, this field in which the government made a considerable effort right from independence, enables us to see, through the different age groups, both the major (long-term) trends and recent deviations.

Second, emphasis is placed on the family structures that determine the behaviour of individuals and hence the way in which certain adjustment measures affect them. Even though it is not possible to determine the impact of past adjustment measures on individuals or groups, identification of their particular situations may be useful through making forgotten dimensions of poverty visible. This identification can also help in the formulation of measures aimed at particular groups, because any global measure not taking account of socio-cultural differences tends to reinforce existing inequalities. This is one of our underlying general hypotheses.

The emphasis is also on the women in this analysis for two main reasons: first, they play an important role in the main activity of the country, agriculture, whether growing food or export crops. It is generally asserted in the literature on agriculture development, that many development efforts have failed because not enough attention was paid to the different roles and behaviours of men and women (see U. Lele). The Côte d'Ivoire food crop plan (*Plan Vivrier*) provides an example of this. It proposed improved cultivation practices that it wanted to make available to the mass of small farmers, but made no distinction between men and women. The question here is to know how such programmes and projects can effectively reach the women in different types of household.

Second, putting the accent on women makes it possible to go beyond the myth of the integrated household, showing solidarity and completely common interests, which is implicit in many analyses and policies. We use the sociological and anthropological literature to describe the context and formulate hypotheses that we examine with aid of the 1985 survey data.

In this field, research has to go beyond determining the consequences of adjustment policy and consider the way in which the identification of the key socio-economic groups can contribute to the success of adjustment programmes in the medium and longer terms. It is also necessary to identify the obstacles and the nature of the constraints that prevent the effective implementation of such programmes.

1. Education

Côte d'Ivoire's efforts to promotion education since independence place the country in the forefront in this domain in Africa. Major objectives included universal primary education for the 6-11 age group in 1986, in a system of free public schools that also tried to increase the enrolment rate of girls[9]. The result of this effort in terms of enrolments in primary, secondary and higher education is presented in Tables V-18 and V-19.

This effort made it possible to considerably increase enrolments in all levels of education. During the 1977-86 period, the numbers in secondary and higher education almost doubled, while they increased by almost 55 per cent in primary education. However, the growth trend weakened during the first half of the 1980s. This may be interpreted as an impact of the crisis and of the adjustment measures which made themselves felt in various ways and perhaps in a cumulative fashion for certain households. Thus the fall in household incomes made the financial burden of sending children to school greater in relative terms, perhaps too great for certain families. This effect was aggravated to the extent that families also lost grants as part of the adjustment measures. Furthermore, with the reduction of employment in the formal sector and growing unemployment among young people with educational qualifications, the demand for education was discouraged because a better education was no longer perceived as a guarantee of a better economic future. What is more, certain families may have been forced to send their children to earn money in the informal sector to compensate for the loss of income suffered by others in the household. This also resulted in a reduction in enrolment rates.

In primary education, the combined effects of all these factors (except that concerning study grants) can be seen in the rate of growth in enrolments which, as from 1983, was between 2 and 3 per cent a year and thus lower than the population increase (4.2 per cent). In secondary and higher education the rate of growth fell more sharply (and even became negative in 1986 in secondary education and in 1981 in higher education). But these rates reached the same level as population growth in 1984 in higher education and exceeded it in secondary education (with an interruption in 1986). While total enrolments increased continually, the numbers in private education fell as from 1982. The shift in the trend was no doubt associated with the higher cost for parents with children in this sector, which became beyond the means of certain families. However, it is possible that at the same time this represented a structural change in the education system.

Concerning the proportion of girls in enrolments at the different levels, the long term trend was a significant increase and this continued without interruption at the primary level. In secondary education there seems to have been a break in 1982 and 1983, while in higher education there was a sudden increase in 1984 to over 20 per cent after a long period of virtual stagnation at around 17.5 per cent (1976-83). Thus there was very little specific negative impact for girls (secondary education) and their share of total enrolments seems to reflect long-term cultural factors more than the effects of crisis and adjustment. The proportion of girls had reached 41 per cent in primary schools, 30 per cent in secondary and 20 per cent in higher education by 1985/86. Thus discrimination against girls persists, but is becoming less with time.

Studies carried out in the 1960s and 1970s agree that there is an educational bias in favour of better-off urban families, and, in the rural zones, in favour of the Forest area and of boys[10]. The national data indicate that the latter bias is being reduced, but still persists. We can examine the nature of this bias in more detail by using to the 1985 survey data which incorporate the effects of long-term efforts as well as of the crisis.

As a result of the major trends we have just analysed at national level, the age group at school just after independence (born between 1956 and 1960 and aged between 25 and 29 in 1985) should have a higher level of education than the preceding generation. This is the case for several categories of persons, notably male heads of family in Abidjan and the Western Forest (see Table V-20). Of course, the regional distribution of people with at least a CEPE results both from the localisation of the educational facilities and the migration of some of the former pupils. Furthermore, in rural areas there was a very low rate of response to the survey question concerning educational level.

In trying to detect the effects of the crisis (but not necessarily of the adjustment measures) using the educational attainment data, it is necessary to consider the youngest age groups. If the "major trend" had continued, the youngest age groups should show the highest level of educational attainment. This is not the case for five of the seven youngest age groups (under 35) in Table V-20. These data then generally confirm the hypothesis that the crisis had a negative impact on education.

Another view of the impact of the crisis can be obtained from the data concerning the secondary education certificates held by male heads of household in Abidjan. Among the 20-24 age group, only 20 per cent had such a certificate, as against 42 per cent for the 25-29 age group. It is therefore possible that many young people were discouraged by the crisis (and/or the cuts in grants) from starting or completing secondary studies. The same trend is visible for young wives in Abidjan.

The educational level by age group shows only one of the dimensions of the impact of the crisis. Another dimension is the economic level of individuals; since education varies with the economic level, the crisis also adversely affects education. This reasoning is confirmed by the survey for Abidjan and the "other towns". Thus, in Abidjan, 42 per cent of the male and female heads of household and the wives of the heads of household among the "rich" have a secondary education certificate, as against only 15 per cent of the "poor".

If we compare the educational level of male heads of household and their wives (Table V-20) we see another striking difference. Among the under 30 age-groups, two to four times as many men as their wives have at least the CEPE. These differences can certainly be explained by socio-cultural factors but they indicate greater differences than the analysis of national data which do not distinguish success at school at the primary level, which must be in favour of boys.

Table V-21 shows a fairly clear discrimination in favour of boys among the "poor", while among the urban "rich" there is no such discrimination. There is not simply discrimination between boys and girls as demonstrated in the enrolment figures at national level, but also, and perhaps greater, discrimination between rich and poor. By making the poor more numerous, the crisis reduced the educational chances of girls. However, the differences in enrolment rates between boys and girls that we observe for all households in Table V-21 are very much less than those that we found in Table V-20 between male heads of household and their wives. This may partly reflect the fact that girls leave school before the CEPE in greater proportions than the boys. But since Table V-22 includes age groups younger than even the youngest in Table V-21, there is also a difference in school generations which may partly explain the differences between these two tables.

Otherwise, Table V-21 confirms the preponderance in enrolment of children from rich families and urban areas. Certain adjustment measures, such at cuts in grants, therefore affect these categories more than rural and poor categories in absolute terms. But as we saw above in the analysis of education expenditures, such spending often weighs more heavily on the "poor" in relative terms than on the "rich". This potential impact of the adjustment measures for reducing enrolment rates among the "poor", and notably of the girls, is something that should be taken into account in adopting selective compensatory measures.

Table V-21 also confirms particularly strong discrimination against the Savanna zone. Enrolment rates for both boys and girls, and at all economic levels, are significantly lower here than in the other rural zones. The low enrolment rate calls for a more detailed analysis to identify the causes and define measures likely to increase it. A better educational level in this zone could be one of the preconditions for economic diversification whose absence was noted above (see Table V-10).

2. Family structure and socio-cultural behaviour

The basic hypothesis of this section is that the poor do not constitute a homogenous group but that their situation and behaviour vary, notably according to the family structures in which they find themselves. The aim here is to identify and define the characteristics that may on the one hand explain the way in which certain groups are affected by adjustment measures and on the other provide the information necessary for formulating possible compensatory measures or alternative policies.

Among the great variety of ethnic and linguistic groups in Côte d'Ivoire, we find family systems and rules of descendants of three types, patrilinear, matrilinear and bilinear. The *matrilinear* systems concern the majority of the Côte d'Ivoire population. In this system, as in the bilinear system, there is not a single family or household budget, but several sources of income and budgets existing in parallel in the same household. The household therefore does not constitute a co-operative production and consumption unit. Each partner is responsible for certain expenditures. By contrast, in the *patrilinear* systems the head of household has greater control over all the incomes of the family. This distinction between matrilinear and patrilinear systems is important for policies aimed at increasing incomes by providing access to additional resources, because typically women have a spending pattern differing from men, having a preference for improving the family's nutrition. This behaviour is verified by the 1985 survey findings (see Table V-12).

The equilibrium of the family structure is not determined only by the rules of transmission of kinship, but also by the possible combinations between these rules of transmission and those that determine the exercise of authority by the men. Kinship on the other hand, is recognised according to one sex or the other.

The **patrilinear** societies thus tend to be not very conflictual and are fairly stable because the exercise of authority and the transmission of kinship are both male functions. The rights and duties of each of the spouses are well defined. The wife is integrated into the group of her husband's relatives (at least during his lifetime) and there is close conjugal solidarity.

In the **matrilinear** societies, the exercise of authority and the transmission of kinship are "disharmonic", kinship's being transmitted by the women while authority is always exercised by the men (of the female lineage); the wives are therefore not integrated into their husband's group, but remain under the authority of their brothers. These societies are characterised by continual conflict between husbands and their wives' brothers. This always limits conjugal solidarity to the benefit of the brother-sister bond and limits the social role of the father to the benefit of the maternal uncle. The father-child link is generally an affective one, while the uncle-nephew link is marked by authority and obligation. In the matrilinear tradition, the goods that a man may accumulate through his work (livestock, for example) are not inherited by his own sons (who work for him in their youth), but by his sister's sons, his uterine nephews.

The matrilinear system is a fragile one, charged with tensions, and does not stand up well to changes in the socio-economic environment (notably the spatial dispersion of the members of the matrilineage), tending to evolve towards patrilinearity or bilinearity. In these societies the men are now able to hand down to their sons modern objects, not covered by customary law, or money.

In the **current evolution of family structures** in Côte d'Ivoire, the following general trends are seen:

— the bilinearisation of matrilinear societies and handing down goods by both lines, feminine and masculine, except for land which is always transmitted to the "legitimate" heir (generally a uterine nephew in the case of matrilinear systems);

— the breaking up of traditional lineages and networks of solidarity and the "nuclearisation" of families. This is caused by the substantial migratory movements (notably due to the rural exodus), the development of the plantation economy and of monetarisation, which has weakened the systems of rights and obligations governing the traditional lineage links. The lineage land holding system is gradually tending to disappear, with restricted families being able to own land;

— the weakening of the hierarchical relationship between the elders and the young: the development of wage labour and of "small trading" in the urban areas is making it increasingly possible for the young to acquire a relative economic autonomy vis-à-vis elders and with the "nuclearisation" of the family favouring the father-son relationship, the fathers can give their children the support that was formerly provided by the elders of the line. But the elders have not lost their supremacy for all this: they still control the matrimonial unions in the patrilinear societies, generally participating in the payment of matrimonial compensation, in return for which they still claim labour services from their dependants. The elders thus manage to accumulate wealth and to extend the size of their farms, which is not the case with the young;

— evolution of the system of matrimonial compensation towards a simple monetary payment in the patrilinear society;

— greater instability of households. Women are most often responsible for this: they try to assure a personal income because they sometimes find it difficult to accept the employer-employee relationship towards which the conjugal link is moving in rural areas. Furthermore, the loosening of the lineage links is resulting in the weakening of family and social pressures on the behaviour of individuals.

In rural areas, the workload is becoming increasingly hard for women to accept, for they no longer benefit from the same compensation as in the past resulting from the principles of exchange and the complementarity of roles. In particular, they are suffering from the effects of changes in the landholding system: when land is privatised it is monopolised by the men, so that women's access to land depends on the contractual relationship they can establish with their husbands and no longer on customary law. Similarly, the wage they receive for the work they do in their husband's fields depends entirely on his good will. At the same time, the obligation to work on her husband's plantation reduces the time that a woman can devote to her own crops.

While the division of agricultural labour between men and women varies by ethnic group and the crop, Table V-22 shows that virtually no crops are grown without the help of women, but that it is most often the men who have the right to the harvest. The exceptions are the lineage crops (for example millet in the case of the Senufo) and certain cash crops (cotton and tomatoes in the case of the Senufo) where the man is at the same time the cultivator and the sole beneficiary.

In any event, according to the economic logic of the traditional societies of Côte d'Ivoire, when a crop becomes commercially profitable, and thus a vector of the social prestige associated with wealth, the men appropriate it to themselves. The men are in fact the owners of the land and can thus easily retain control over its produce. The process of the appropriation of cassava (and attieke production) by the men has already begun in certain parts of the Adioukrou country[11].

The family structure (nuclear, polygamous or otherwise enlarged) determines the woman's position in many ways, in relations with other members of the family and with respect to productive activities. Thus there is a hypothesis that in accord with traditional behaviour in households where one man is with several adult women (who serve as the labour force), the proportion of land used for cash crops will be higher than that used for food crops. Analysis of the survey data does not confirm this hypothesis. In fact, all types of households reserve a greater proportion of their land for food crops than for cash crops. This change in the behaviour of polygamous households may be due to the greater independence of women, who opt for food crops and food security because of the repeated crises they have experienced with cash crops.

No longer obtaining traditional compensation for their labour, women are calling into question their role, notably in the plantation economy zone[12]. This is one of the causes of the substantial female rural exodus, which is contributing to the greater economic isolation of women, notably in the matrilinear societies. In parallel with this isolation, women's responsibilities are increasing, again mainly in the matrilinear societies, where the women who have little solidarity with their husbands also get less and less aid from their brothers.

To conclude this section, we recall that among the socio-cultural variables, it is clearly education that was the most hard hit, both directly by the adjustment measures and more indirectly through the effects of the crisis that brought a fall in the demand for education because the prospects of skilled employment deteriorated and because families had less money to finance the education of their children, even at the primary level. While the crisis did not cause additional discrimination against girls in primary and higher education (besides that which always existed but is gradually being whittled away) a slight temporary aggravation of discrimination can be detected in secondary education.

As regards the family structures and socio-cultural behaviour, we have not been able to identify any direct effects of the crisis or the adjustment measures. However, even a brief analysis of these characteristics suggests that any adjustment policy intended to be socially responsible has to take account of them in order to prevent perverse effects and derive the greatest benefit from the role of women.

Notes and References

1. See C. Tibi, "The Financing of Education: The Impact of the Crisis and the Adjustment Process", in F. Caillods, *The Prospects for Educational Planning,*

2. This survey covered 1 600 households, broken down according to representative criteria into 100 clusters, of which 43 are urban and 57 rural. For further details, see LSMS Working Paper No. 26, *Côte d'Ivoire Living Standard Survey: Design and Implementation.*

3. Thus in Basse-Côte, clusters 44 and 46-49 were excluded and in the Forest/Savanna contact region clusters 53, 73, 74, 77, 78, 83 and 85.

4. Section based on an internal report by Paolo Groppo.

5. Of course this presentation is somewhat schematic, as is in fact the distinction between the zones, whose frontiers are in reality much less clear-cut than may appear here.

6. Several problems arise: the 1985 Survey gives ambiguous results for areas with different crops in association, on the subject of the allocation of land to sharecroppers and on the subject of forest reserves, which play an important role as regards access to labour, but are included under the heading "fallow".

7. The Basse-Côte and Forest/Savanna contact regions (12 survey clusters) were excluded. The classification of households according to non-food expenditures per equivalent member was verified for 200 households using other indicators such as provision with capital goods, area in production, expenditure for labour, spending on food and the enrolment rate of the children.

8. Drafted on the basis of Document Technique No. 9, "Analyse des variables socio-culturelles et de l'ajustement en Côte d'Ivoire, by W. Weekes-Vagliani, OECD Development Centre, January 1990.

9. See P.T. Seya, Ivory Coast: System of Education, in: *International Encyclopedia of Education,* Vol. 5, Pergamon Press 1985; and UNESCO, *International Guide to Education Systems,* 1979.

10. See Remi Clignet and Philip Foster, *The Fortunate Few: A Study of Secondary Schools and Students in the Ivory Coast,* Northwestern University Press, 1966 and Marie Eliou, "Scholarisation et promotion féminines en Afrique francophone: (Côte d'Ivoire, Haute-Volta, Sénégal)", in *International Review of Education,* XIX/1973/1, Special number: "The Education of Women".

11. See A. Traoré, *L'accès des femmes ivoiriennes aux ressources de la terre en pays Adioukrou,* ILO, Geneva 1981.

12. See J. Bisilliat and M. Feiloux, *Femmes du Tiers-Monde,* Le Sycomore, Paris 1983

Chapter VI

Application of a Numerical Model 1980-86

by

Sylvie Lambert* and Akiko Suwa**

This chapter is devoted to the application of a numerical model, which is both macro- and microeconomic, to Côte d'Ivoire between 1980 and 1986. This exercise makes it possible to study, within a coherent framework, the effects of different adjustment measures on the principal aggregates and on income distribution. Thus it is possible to compare the policy actually pursued and alternative measures, in order to evaluate the historical experience and to put forward solid arguments for the choice of future policies. The model is first briefly described (Section 1), and the reference simulation is presented (Section 2) and then the different scenarios are discussed (Section 3).

A. The model

The model integrates into a standard computable general equilibrium model a large choice of macroeconomic closures. Its original feature is to take into account the behaviour of agents in the financial sector. The reader will find a complete description of the model in Bourguignon, Branson and de Melo (1989 a and b). We shall limit ourselves here to a brief review of the specifications used to calibrate the reference simulation for the case of Côte d'Ivoire.

The economy has four types of agents: firms, households, government and financial intermediaries. The firms are divided into six sectors: primary exports, composed essentially of coffee and cocoa (15 per cent of total production; food crop production (11 per cent); light industry (18 per cent); heavy industry (11 per cent); services (37 per cent); and the informal sector (8 per cent). The households are divided into six socio-economic categories: capitalists, big farmers, small farmers, modern workers, agricultural workers and informal sector workers.

The agents intervene on four markets: goods and services; labour; money and securities and the external market. The state of the economy during the given year is defined by the equilibrium in all these markets under certain specifications or "closures". A closure defines the type of adjustment on a market: equilibrium may be achieved either by varying prices or changing quantities. The closures used in the Côte d'Ivoire application are summarized in Table VI-1 and discussed in detail in what follows, after the presentation of each market.

*   Institut National de Recherche Agronomique, Paris
** DELTA (combined research group: Centre National de la Recherche Scientifique, ENS, Ecole des Hautes Etudes en Sciences Sociales), Paris

Markets for goods and services

Firms' short-term production decisions stem from their profit maximising behaviour. In the case of imperfect competition, the decision of enterprises is constrained by the application of a minimum margin on the production price, the "mark-up". The technology is defined by a Leontieff function for intermediate goods and a Cobb-Douglas function for the factors of production (capital, labour, land and a factor specific to the primary exports sector).

On the demand side, there is imperfect substitutability between domestic and imported goods. Domestic demand is defined in the form of composite goods, a combination of imported and domestic goods calculated according to the Armington specification. It should be noted that certain composite goods may be made entirely of imports while others may be entirely domestic. The system of consumption functions defined for each group of households is the linear expenditure system (LES). Each production sector invests according to a profitability criterion close to Tobin's q. Imports depend on the relative domestic/foreign price and international demand.

In a given period (one year), the market may achieve equilibrium in two ways:

i)   Competitive adjustment (Walrassian prices): this is the case of all the sectors in Côte d'Ivoire except the modern sector; and

ii) Setting the mark-up price and adjusting by means of variations in the capacity utilisation rate. This is the hypothesis adopted for the modern sector in Côte d'Ivoire, because of the chronic under-employed production capacities and the situation of imperfect competition.

The labour market

Wages can be fixed in different ways:

i)   Complete wage flexibility and full employment, which is the hypothesis adopted for the agricultural sector and the informal sector. In addition, the informal workers are paid at the per capita value of their production; they therefore have no guaranteed minimum wage and are completely dependent on demand; or

ii) Rigidity against downward movements of the nominal wage in the private modern sector. Public sector wages are exogenous and of a fixed nominal value.

Money and financial markets

Once wages, direct and indirect taxes, interest payments and dividends are taken into account, firms determine their financing requirements according to the desired level of investment and of working capital. Given the lack of any equity market in the model, households are assumed to invest directly in physical capital in addition to their financial investments. Enterprises borrow the rest on the domestic or foreign market.

The domestic financial market depends on the government's budget deficit and the way it is financed. Tax revenues come from many types of tax: on production, incomes, payroll imports and primary exports (the CSSPPA). Public expenditure includes pay for personnel and operating expenditures, debt servicing and investment. The deficit may be financed by borrowing from the *Banque Centrale* or abroad, in the absence of a domestic Treasury bond market[1].

The model thus contains three types of financial assets: money, domestic securities and foreign securities. Households arbitrate between these assets according to the anticipated relative rate of return: they first fix their demand for money according to their income and the anticipated real interest rate; then they decide their investment in physical capital according to the relative yield of physical and financial investment. In the absence of Treasury bonds, the remaining wealth is devoted to lending abroad. The savings rate of households depends on the income; it also takes into account a wealth effect of the revaluation of property. Similarly, firms distribute their borrowings between domestic and international markets according to the interest rates and their expectations of devaluations. The macroeconomic closure depends on the financial market hypothesis, taking into account certain constraints inherent in Côte d'Ivoire:

i) Absence of Treasury bonds: the budgetary deficit is financed mainly by the creation of money and borrowing abroad; and

ii) Sterilisation of net entries of foreign capital in the calculation of the volume of money. This hypothesis was introduced to take account of the attempts by the monetary authorities to have an independent policy.

The foreign exchange market

The current account is determined by the balance of trade, interest payments on the external debt and transfers (of wages or profits), notably remittances by non-Ivorian agricultural workers and French technical assistants in Côte d'Ivoire. The market reaches equilibrium in two ways:

i) Fixed exchange rate: this is the case with Côte d'Ivoire as a member of the franc zone. The UMOA countries actually must maintain a fixed parity between the CFA franc, their common currency, and the French franc (FCFA 1 = 0.02). In the reference simulation, the exchange rate was calculated with respect to a basket of currencies of the main trading partners. The parity between the FCFA and the French franc being fixed, the nominal devaluation introduced in the model in fact stems from the nominal devaluation of the French franc with respect to the other currencies, weighted by the structure of Côte d'Ivoire's foreign trade. Thus the chosen closure assumes that the government borrows abroad as much as is necessary to satisfy the external constraint; or

ii) Floating exchange rate: the government's foreign borrowing is fixed in exogenous fashion and the exchange rate adjusts itself accordingly.

Dynamics

The dynamics of the model correspond to a series of temporary equilibria. The periods are connected by variations in capital stocks, demographic movements and technological progress. Capital is fixed for one year. It increases by the amount of investment, taking account of depreciation. The increase in global productivity is exogenous, as are expectations of inflation and devaluation. The demographic growth rate is exogenous, but there may be social mobility — notably rural exodus — through endogenous migrations in line with Harris-Todaro.

B. The reference simulation

The adjustment policies were tested on a reference simulation reproducing the essential features of economic evolution in Côte d'Ivoire between 1980 and 1986.

Adjusting the model to a particular country, calibration, involves two stages. The parameters for the behavioural functions are adjusted to a base year (1980). The structure of the Ivorian economy in 1980 was summarised in a social accounting matrix based on the National Accounts and data from the *Centrale des Bilans* (Table VI-2). In a second stage, the exogenous annual variables concerning economic policy for the international environment determine the dynamics. For these variables we used the statistical annex from Berthélemy and Bourguignon (1989). In particular, the CSSPPA deduction was adjusted in order to reproduce the evolution in the terms of trade (export prices) and the prices received by the producers of traditional exports. The main parameters are summarised in Table VI-3.

The model makes it possible to see the evolution in household incomes. These depend on three factors: wages and income from property, variations in the cost of living, and the composition of the financial portfolio. The breakdown into six social categories makes it possible to distinguish the impact of these different factors. The big and small farmers share with the capitalists the ownership of the factors specific to traditional exports, but hold the greater part of the land used for food crops. The capital of the modern sector is owned, in decreasing order, by the capitalists, foreigners and modern workers. The pattern of consumption also varies according to the social category, those in rural areas devoting a substantial part of their budget to agricultural products, while city dwellers buy more manufactured goods; this has consequences for the cost of living specific to each group. Lastly, as regards the financial portfolio, the capitalists are the only group to hold foreign securities; other households only hold money.

The breakdown makes it possible to monitor certain social indicators, such as the Theil index, the percentage of poor or the relative sum of poverty[2]. In order to calculate these indicators, we chose a threshold of real poverty, held constant during the simulation period and fixed at FCPA 200 000 a year in 1980: 46 per cent of the active population was then below this threshold. For these indicators, the unemployed are considered as being from the modern sectors (agriculture being in a situation of full employment), and also subsidised by workers in the modern sector. This hypothesis must be borne in mind when considering the indicators of relative income: obviously, the impact on income distribution would be different if the unemployed were fed by their families who had remained in rural areas[3]. In particular, it will be seen that devaluation improves the situation of the producers of export crops; this observation would be less true if they had to look after an increasing number of unemployed.

The exchange rate in the reference simulation is, as mentioned above, an effective exchange rate. With parity of the CFA franc and the French franc constant, the variation in exchange rates in the reference simulation comes from movements of the French franc vis-à-vis other currencies. Thus we see a real **devaluation** between 1980 and 1983 (of about 12 per cent a year) and above all a real **appreciation** in 1984-1985. This phenomenon is important to bear in mind: if we keep the same evolution of exogenous variables (economic policy and international environment) as in the reference simulation we still find two contrasting phases. This dichotomy means that it is difficult to make a global judgement for the period as a whole.

The results of the reference simulation are given in Figures VI-1 to VI-3. However there are two divergences with respect to the observed data that should be noted. In reality the volume of investment fell drastically: down 60 per cent between 1980 and 1986. Such a fall could not be found in a model that assumes investment behaviour to be determined by a profitability criterion depending on the market interest rate. In particular, the model does not take account of possible psychological effects connected with the growing uncertainty in a period of crisis, this being increased by the drastic cuts in the investment programmes of the state and public enterprises. Second, according to the time series observed, GDP fell by 4 per cent for two consecutive years (1983 and 1984), while final consumption only remained stagnant. This "disengagement" of consumption with respect to incomes may be explained by reduction in a rate of savings or a return home by non-Ivorians who had lost their jobs. In the model, however, savings are defined as a percentage of income, modulated by the wealth effect: in the case of aN appreciation of property, households save less. Such an appreciation did not occur in 1984 and consumption, which depends on the available income after savings, follows the fall in national income in the reference simulation. Application of the model to Côte d'Ivoire first shows an increase in inequality and in poverty in 1984 which was perhaps not quite so great in reality. In addition, during this year the volume of money (M2) increased by 12 per cent. Where can the corresponding increase in the demand for money come from in a climate of deep recession? We assumed that Côte d'Ivoire is a debtor economy, and thus the main thing was controlling interest rates and their stability, even if to do this means deviating from the M2 growth series published in the national accounts.

C. Simulations of adjustment policies

This study is concerned with two major problems in Côte d'Ivoire during the 1980s: reduction of the budget deficit and the question of the exchange rate necessary to balance the current account.

A first set of simulations studies different budget policy measures all aiming to achieve the same reduction in the deficit: reduction of expenditure first of all, concerning in turn public investment (SI), civil service wages (SW), and operating expenditure (SG); then fiscal reform, concerning the indirect taxes on production (ST) and the CSSPPA levy (SE).

A second set of simulations explores the effects of a variation in the exchange rate: a single devaluation in 1981 (SD) and a switch to a floating exchange rate (SF). The simulation scenarios are summarised in Table VI-4.

The budget deficit

Reduction of the budget deficit and the current account deficit are essential objectives of any adjustment policy. The first set of simulations covers different budgetary measures aimed at reducing the deficit to a given percentage of GDP (Table VI-5). This permits a better comparison of the different methods of reducing this deficit. Three simulations show the effect of reducing one of the items of government expenditures: investment (SI), civil service pay (SW) and operating expenditures (SG); the last two are concerned with increasing tax revenues: taxes on production (ST) and taxes on exports (SE). Furthermore, to take into account the constraints imposed by membership in the UMOA, the aim of the government's monetary policy is keeping fluctuations in interest rates within a narrow range around the interest rate on the French money market[4]. The simulations with a budgetary objective therefore all assume that the government adjusts the growth of the monetary base in order to maintain the series of interest rates of the reference simulation[5].

The first scenario (SI) fixed investment at a much lower level than the reference level in 1981 (FCFA 50 billion instead of 90, or a budget deficit of 10.5 per cent of GDP instead of 11.7 per cent), then to maintain it at this level in the subsequent years. The resulting reduction of the budget deficit, measured as a percentage of GDP, fixes the goal for the other simulations; the disappearance of the budget deficit in 1986, whereas in the reference simulation it amounts to 2.3 per cent of GDP (Figure VI-4).

Reduction of public spending

Two types of effects on the budget deficit are to be expected from a cut in government investment. First, since the State spends less the deficit is directly reduced. Second, since investment has a very high import component, its reduction will bring an improvement in the balance of trade and the current account; the government will then have less need to borrow abroad, which will reduce debt servicing; the budget deficit will be reduced accordingly. On the GDP side, the cut in public investment will cause a recession, due both to the reduction of absorption and the multiplier effect of public investment. However, this multiplier is reduced here because 60 per cent of investment is made up of imported goods. Lastly, reducing public investment should cause a fall in interest rates because of the fall in demand which would favour private investment (the "crowding in" effect). This effect is prohibited here because of the chosen monetary policy of maintaining interest rates at the reference simulation level.

(SI) certainly shows the recessionary effects expected, with even a slight fall in the general price level between 1981 and 1983. Private absorption falls because of the lower level of consumption by households. Private investment sustains the consequences of the recession while being unable to benefit from the crowding in effect: it is from 1.5 to 5 per cent lower than the reference level. This contraction of demand reinforces the improvement in the balance of trade through the sharp reduction in imports (Table VI-5). This improvement in the balance of trade is particularly marked in 1982, a year in which the difference between the level in government investment in the reference simulation and that in (SI) is the greatest (Figures VI-5 and VI-6).

The output of the non-tradeable goods and services sector shrinks considerably in volume (FCFA 624 billion as against 675 billion in the reference in 1982). In fact public investment mainly concerns this sector (74 per cent); the fall in demand results in adjustment of quantities in this sector, where fixed prices have been assumed.

The reduced activity of enterprises explains why unemployment remains at a higher level. Income distribution moves in the direction of the aggravation of inequality and poverty, and this despite an effect in principle favourable to a fall in the cost of living. The shrinking of demand causes a fall in prices in most sectors, particularly significant in the food crop sector of agriculture and the informal sector. Despite this however, the consequences for income distribution are negative. The capitalists and modern workers, who produce goods whose prices are relatively protected, actually see their real incomes improve, while the informal and agricultural workers are hit by the recession; their incomes depend directly on demand, and the fall in the prices of the goods they consume is not enough to compensate for the fall in the value of their production[6].

These developments, favourable to the richest categories and unfavourable to the informal workers, together with the increase in unemployment, explain the deterioration in the Theil indicator and the increase in the relative sum of poverty.

On the face of it, reducing operating expenditures has the advantage of being less risky for the future than reducing investment expenditures. (SG) presents the implementation of such a measure. In addition, reducing operating expenditures causes a corresponding reduction in the number of civil servants, unless there is an improvement in the efficiency of government. Since it is impossible to measure the efficiency of government services, it has been assumed to be constant. (SG) is thus characterised by a cut in operating expenditure together with a proportional fall in public employment, so that the budget deficit measured as a percentage of GDP reaches the same level as in (SI).

The recessionary effect of such a measure is very clear: the volume GDP falls to considerably below the reference level, but also below the level reached in (SI). It should be noted however that the results of (SG) are not directly comparable with the others, to the extent that the reduction in public employment, through the conventions of national accounting, has an automatic effect on GDP. The fact is that government value added, because of its non-tradeable output, includes the wages paid. A fall in civil service wages therefore reduces the national income through the accounting effect. The contraction of government demand explains more than half of the recession. On top of this accounting effect there are derived effects: diminished public sector recruitment and the fall in incomes affect consumption.

This fall in domestic demand leads to a reduction of imports. On the export side, the deflation of the initial years increases price competitiveness: foreign demand, very price elastic, increases rapidly, tending to push prices up again. At the equilibrium point, the price level will be very close to that of the reference simulation, but exports will have increased. The balance of trade therefore improves, which through the process described in (SI), favours the re-establishment of the budget. It must be asked, however, whether the high price elasticity of traditional exports (twice that of goods in the modern sector) is realistic. Actually, coffee exports during this period were governed by the International Coffee Agreement which fixed prices on the international market and set quotas for each producer country. In the case of cocoa, Côte d'Ivoire has a virtual monopoly. For these two products, which form the greater part of its exports, the assumption made in these simulations of a strong response of foreign demand to variations in price may be debatable[7].

The effect on inequality of a cut in public expenditures with a freeze in the level of employment is not obvious at first sight. On the one hand, creating unemployment among civil servants affects one of the most advantaged categories (modern workers) so that inequality is reduced. However, the recession caused is likely to hit informal workers particularly hard because they are more dependent on demand; this would lead to increased inequality.

(SG) shows that the income effects for the different categories of household are comparable to those obtained by reducing public investment. The cost of living settles at a lower level than in the reference simulation for all classes. Rural households have a real income unchanged with respect to (BR). Modern sector workers have to take in charge an increasing number of unemployed, so that their real income diminishes. As for the informal sector, it was in fact hit by the recession in 1981-1983, before a social mobility effect (reduced rural exodus towards a now unattractive sector) brought per capita output back to the reference level (BR). All in all, inequality as measured by the Theil index is less than the reference simulation or the case of cuts in public investment (SI). On the other hand, the relative sum of poverty reaches a level close to that of (SI) and higher than that of (BR).

It should be pointed out that the model does not take into account the cost of the cut in expenditure on education and health, items included in the operating budget. Thus the living conditions of the population could be affected more than appears from this simulation.

The last possibility envisaged for cutting government expenditures was to reduce civil service wages (SW). In order to achieve the objective fixed in terms of the budget deficit, it was necessary to reduce the nominal payroll by over 40 per cent in two years (1981-1982) with respect to the reference, or by the same order of magnitude as in the reforms envisaged in the spring of 1990.

It would be expected that a reduction in civil service wages of this magnitude would have a drastic effect at the level of household consumption. The main difference between this and the preceding simulations is that because of the structure of household consumption, the fall in demand is going to affect agricultural products, whose prices are very flexible, more than goods produced by the modern sectors.

This policy first results in a fall in the GDP deflator between 1981 and 1983, automatically induced by the very low level reached by the public expenditure deflator (down 14 per cent over two years). Household consumption is sharply reduced; it reaches a level even lower than that of the reduction of operating (SG). The real effect on GDP is very small. On the one hand, the weakening of domestic consumption is compensated by increased exports, and on the other, the sharp fall in the GDP deflator in the initial years helps to maintain GDP in real terms (Figure VI-4).

The sequence of events described in (SG) are found again here, but this time centred on relatively well-off public sector employees: the reduction in inequality is greater than in (SG). The relative sum of poverty increases.

This simulation gives rise to two sorts of problems. First of all, the reduction of inequality needs to be qualified[8] by two remarks: it is plausible that a fall in the wages paid in public enterprises would have a spin off effect in the private sector; second, it is assumed that a wage provides a living for a single household, whereas it is very probable that certain civil servants send part of their income to members of their family living in rural areas. In this case, these rural families, who are not among the more advantaged categories of the population, would also suffer from a cut in civil service wages. A second problem, to which we return in the conclusion, also arises when we try to model government expenditures: little is known about the efficiency of this expenditure. What is the initial efficiency of the state? What is the effect of wage cuts on the quality of services provided to the population? An evaluation of this economic policy depends on the answers to these questions.

Fiscal reforms

In (ST), the experiment consists of increasing tax revenues by increasing taxes on production, except in the food sector.

The initial increase in all prices causes a contraction of domestic final demand and investment. Household consumption moves to a very low level, even below that reached in simulation (SW), but the weakness of domestic demand is compensated for by increased exports: very clearly in this simulation, foreign demand replaces domestic demand. The producers of coffee and cocoa, whose price is fixed by the state, see their profits increase thanks to the fall in intermediate costs: their production increases.

This measure is the one that causes the worst effects in terms of inequality. The incomes of informal workers are very hard hit by the fall in demand. The other categories do not see their real incomes change, except those modern sector workers who support an increasing number of unemployed. This more than compensates for the improvements that might be expected from a fall in the cost of living for all groups, and is particularly marked in the case of the poorest (small farmers, agricultural workers and informal workers). The relative sum of poverty is greater than in any other simulation: in 1982 it is almost 50 per cent higher than the reference level.

Lastly, simulation (SE) shows the effects of increasing the CSSPPA levy. Increasing this levy brings a substantial fall in the producer price (10 per cent or more with respect to the reference level)[9]. In fact, the fiscal objective is not achieved (Tables VI-4 and VI-5), for a Laffer curve is attained if the levy is increased too greatly, the planters produce less and the tax take falls. The increase in the levy has conflicting effects on the level of exports. The reduced profit in the traditional exports sector is a disincentive for production[10], while modern exports whose price is not controlled are stimulated through increased price competitiveness. Overall exports are lower than (BR) until 1984, the year in which the revival of modern exports begins.

The deflation of the initial years (until 1983) reduces the cost of living. The capitalists and the big farmers, the two groups that derive part of their income from exports, see their real income diminish. The price of agricultural goods also having been affected by a substitution effect between the export and food growing sectors of agriculture, agricultural workers and small farmers also suffer a reduction in their incomes. The modern workers, whose prices are not affected, see their income improved, whether they have to share it with the unemployed or not. Overall inequality is increased, as is the relative sum of poverty, similarly to case (ST).

If a choice has to be made between these different budget deficit reduction policies, several points have to be considered. All the simulations in this group show good results for the target values of the adjustment policies (budget deficit, current account deficit, balance of trade), a reform of the CSSPPA levy (SE) being the least effective. They lead to a total external indebtedness (public and private) 5 to 10 per cent lower than the reference simulation, except again for (SE). which on the contrary leads to slightly higher overall indebtedness. The average level of investment is always a little higher than that of (BR), except in (SI).

As for poverty, the tax increases are the most disastrous in the absence of any redistributive transfer. It would appear that the expenditure reductions are less painful. However, it is necessary to bear in mind the remarks made earlier about the limits to this set of simulations. In particular, a variation in the level of public expenditure acts directly through demand, whereas a change in the *rate* of taxation results in induced effects from its impact on the tax base itself. What is more, operating expenditures have in reality a long-term effect making such expenditures a sort of investment in human capital. In this model, however, they are seen as having an effect only on a given period. The asymmetry between the effects of a cut in operating expenditures and those of an increase in taxes calls for caution here.

Among the expenditure reduction simulations, cutting civil service wages (SW) and reducing operating expenditure (SG) lead to the best results in terms of poverty and inequality. It should be noted, however, that poverty increases with respect to the reference, while inequality is reduced. (SG) nevertheless has the disadvantage of leading to the biggest reduction in national income in this group of simulations. As a result, simulation (SW) seems to be preferable to any of the others.

Devaluation

The second set of simulations (SD,SF) are concerned with external equilibrium. The aim is to reduce the external debt by means of a depreciation of the exchange rate, either through devaluing once and for all or by allowing the exchange rate to float. The effects of a devaluation act in two ways: the first is the price effect on exports and imports; the second concerns the reallocation of the financial portfolio according to the changes in the relative yields of investments (in particular, depending on whether the devaluation is anticipated or not). In order to see the second effect better, the assumption that interest rates are kept at their reference level was abandoned. Furthermore, as noted above, the closure of the model when there is a fixed rate of exchange assumes that equilibrium of the foreign exchange is assured by public borrowing abroad, by the government's borrowing enough to finance the deficit in the balance of payment (current account and private capital movements). In order to clearly see the endogenous effects of the devaluation, exogenous debt rescheduling were eliminated. As before, the detailed content of the simulations is presented in Table VI-4 and the results are shown in Table VI-5.

Simulation (SD) deals with the case of a sharp, non-anticipated devaluation in 1981 (22 per cent in real terms). This devaluation is with respect to a basket of currencies representing the principal trading partners; in practice it amounts to a devaluation vis-à-vis the French franc. After the initial shock of 1981, the exchange rate varies in the same way as in the reference simulation (BR). The devaluation has the desired effect on the balance of trade (export boom and fall in imports): the current account becomes positive beginning in 1985; in accord with the model's closure hypotheses the government can reduce its borrowing and the total debt (public and private) represents no more than 98 per cent of GDP in 1986 as against 110 per cent in (BR). The devaluation results in greater growth (stimulated by foreign demand) than any other simulation (BR and the budget policy simulations); the unemployment rate is thus lower in (SD) than in all the other simulations (see Figure VI-8). The budget deficit decreases as a result of growth-induced receipts and a smaller public foreign debt.

The economic upturn is accompanied by an increase in prices. The growth in demand and the high price of imports increase the demand for money and cause a rise in the interest rate. Firms respond to the increased differential in interest rates by borrowing more abroad than on the domestic market. In addition, the decision to reallocate their loans is not subject to the constraint of exchange rate control or by any lack of liquidity on the international capital markets: thus the private component of the external debt increases (67 per cent as against 57 per cent in the reference simulation). Thus the nature of the external debt changes.

Beginning in 1984, the exchange rate follows the evolution of the reference simulation and appreciates. Domestic demand (consumption and investment) improves, resulting in a slight increase in imports (Table VI-6).

A devaluation can have two effects on income distribution: it increases the cost of living, above all for households consuming a high proportion of imported goods; it increases the incomes of modern sector exporters and also of those in the primary sector if the CSSPPA levy remains unchanged. As a result, modern sector employees, whose nominal incomes are fixed, see their purchasing power diminish with inflation, while the rural populations (farmers and agricultural workers) benefit from an increase in their nominal incomes. The nominal incomes of capitalists certainly increase, but less than the increase in the cost of living; in fact, the CSSPPA takes part of the export gain thus reducing the purchasing power of the capitalists. The incomes of informal workers increase with the demand boom. All this leads to a reduction of inequality (Figure VI-9). The improvement in the condition of the poorest and the lower unemployment rate results in a reduction in the relative sum of poverty (Figure VI-10).

Simulation (SF) represents another way of balancing the external account, this time adopting a floating exchange rate. The rate floats in such a way that the current account is compatible with a predetermined level of public foreign indebtedness. Here the annual increase in the government's external debt is fixed at a rate half that of the reference. In 1986, the public external debt thus represents 37 per cent of GDP as against 47 per cent in (BR). This brings a sharp real devaluation in 1981 (26.4 per cent as against 15 per cent in the reference), which subsequently slows down, finally giving way in 1984 to a substantial revaluation (18 and 15 per cent in 1984 and 1986 respectively, while the real rate of exchange in the reference appreciates by 10 per cent on average). The magnitude of the revaluation stems from the choice of the objective itself: in fact, the initial series of the rate of growth of the government foreign debt was in the form of an inverted U-shaped curve, while simulation (SF) assumes that the debt grows at the uniform rate of 4 per cent a year, i.e. half the reference rate. By choosing a *linear* objective for the growth of the debt, the economy is subject to fewer constraints in later years and a greater rise in the exchange rate is permitted. Thus a crucial role is played by the profile of external public debt, exogenous in a closure under a flexible exchange rate.

After a strong revival in 1981 (up 4 per cent), growth slows due to the sharp increase in the domestic interest rate; in 1986, GDP is again close to the (BR) level. In 1984, at the end of the period of real devaluation, the fiscal deficit is virtually zero, as against 7 per cent of GDP in (BR) while the current account deficit is 6 per cent of GDP, as against 8.5 per cent. In 1986 however, the budget deficit is 5 per cent of GDP, or more than in the reference and more than in (SD), because of the fall in the tax take. The balance of trade deteriorates with the revaluation and the current account deficit in 1986 amounts to 7.5 per cent of GDP, or twice that of (BR). Similarly, the devaluation favours the take off of the industrial sectors, but they are hit by the later revaluation and end up at levels slightly lower than those of the reference.

Income distribution follows the same contrasting movements. In 1981, the increase in the cost of living due to the increase in the price of imported goods, particularly felt in the agricultural sector (about 40 per cent) and the informal sector (75 per cent), makes the capitalists and modern workers worse off, but leaves the farmers at a similar level (this is the effect already noted in the previous case: the farmers benefit directly from the devaluation), while the informal sector workers see their situation improve: inequality is reduced. The reverse happens as from 1984. In 1985-1986, inequality as measured by the Theil index is greater than its level in (BR) and in the case of a single devaluation (SD), while the relative volume of poverty is comparable to that of (SD).

The two devaluation simulations give rise to a fundamental problem. It would appear that in practice, Côte d'Ivoire firms would have difficulty in finding foreign creditors. The next stage, in this type of simulation, would then be to consider several cases according to the actual possibilities for foreign loans. Let us return for example to the simulation of a single, non-anticipated devaluation (SD). If it had been assumed here that there was exchange control and that firms could not borrow any more but they could repay their debt, the results would have been very different with respect to those of (SD) where there is perfect mobility of capital. The state would have taken the place of the enterprises prevented from borrowing abroad as principal debtor, which would have aggravated the budget deficit. Firms would turn to the domestic capital market and domestic interest rates would increase, slowing capital formation.

D. Conclusion

Having completed this exercise, the adjustment measures can be judged by different criteria despite the instability of Côte d'Ivoire's economy during the 1980s[11], which makes an appraisal difficult.

A first criterion is GDP growth. As regards the budget policies, all affect the national income. Foreign demand takes over from domestic demand, except in (ST) where the increase in taxes makes exports less competitive. The devaluation simulations are beneficial or neutral with respect to growth. The sectoral distribution of growth is also important: the budget measures lead to a slower rate of growth in food crops and the modern formal sector, while the primary exports sector is less affected than in the reference. The devaluation simulations have a less clear cut effect on the sectoral breakdown: a single devaluation brings a boom in primary exports, whereas a floating exchange rate with the assumptions of (SF) gives rise at the end of the period to a resumption of absorption that favours the sectors oriented towards the domestic market. In addition, today's growth determines the future: in this respect (SI) and the devaluation simulations, because they affect investment, compromise the future if the productivity of capital remains unchanged.

The second criterion concerns income distribution. If we take as indicator the number of poor below the poverty threshold, this figure is minimised by the devaluation simulations, (SF) and, above all, (SD). The more marked growth makes it possible to increase employment; the maintenance of demand gives informal sector workers the resources to cover their needs. Among the budget measures, public expenditure reductions increase the number of poor less than do fiscal reforms.

Two vital issues are raised by the results that go far beyond the scope of a numerical model, i.e., the efficiency of the civil service and the credibility accorded to the economic policy. A better knowledge of the efficiency of the civil service would be useful at two stages: before any reform, then during a change in budget policy. A measure of efficiency should take account of the fact that certain state expenditures are in the nature of an investment in human resources (health and education). Regarding the dynamics, if for example, a cut in wages in public enterprises does not influence either the quantity or the quality of production, then it can only be beneficial. However, it is more likely that the cut in pay will cause a fall in efficiency.

The devaluation simulations led to the question of the credibility of the economic authorities and underlines the sensitivity of the results to the assumptions made regarding the degree of effective access to new international loans.

Finally, the major finding is that Côte d'Ivoire's authorities had very little room for manoeuvre: the key budget policy instrument, the CSSPPA imposition, seems to have reached its limits (Laffer curve); monetary policy and exchange rate policy depend on the UMOA; and the financing of the economy depends on access to the international financial market. For these reasons, the only really credible policies are those aimed at reducing budget expenditures; and among these, the reduction of public wages or operating expenditures, which are more neutral in terms of growth and poverty, without penalising investment. The credibility of these measures within the country and the degree to which they can be sustained have still to be studied.

Notes and References

1. The budget deficit referred to in what follows is therefore not the primary deficit (tax revenues less debt servicing and operating expenditure in the broad sense, i.e. wages and current expenditure). It is a secondary deficit, including the government's capital account expenditure.

2. Inequality is measured by the Theil index. This is the sum of the intra-group inequality (Theil, T_i) and the inter-group inequality of real per capita incomes. It takes the form:

$$T = \frac{\Sigma \, y_i \, n_i \, Ln(y_i/n_i) \; + \; T_i \, y_i \, n_i}{Y_0 \, N}$$

where:

y_i: real *per capita* income of social group i;

n_i: population of group i;

Y: real average income;

N: total population.

The population of the group of modern workers includes the unemployed: it is thus assumed that they are supported by employees of the modern formal sector (industry and public service).

The second indicator concerns the relative volume of poverty (poverty gap). It is a function of the number of persons below the poverty threshold and the amount of transfers they need to receive in order to reach this threshold.

3. This seems to be the case: the Savanna is in fact the region that transfers the most to Abidjan, despite its relative poverty (see Chapter V).

4. The room for manoeuvre of the Côte d'Ivoire monetary authorities is limited. Their main concern is to prevent the domestic rate falling below the foreign rate, with the attendant risk of capital flight. However, any policy that reduces public expenditure should normally entail a reduction of interest rates: the government, requiring less financing, reduces its demand for money. Thus in the case when economic policy includes reducing the budget deficit, the monetary authorities have a tendency to adopt a contractionist policy.

5. In what follows, unless otherwise stated, the terms "improvement", "aggravation", "reduction", "increase" mean with respect to the reference simulation.

6. In the longer term, however, a readjustment is possible through the phenomenon of migration: the income of informal workers falling with respect to those of other classes, the share of this group shrinks (fewer new arrivals, plus departures). At a given level of demand, this causes an increase in the incomes of the remaining informal workers.

7. The high elasticity of traditional exports was introduced to take account of Côte d'Ivoire's growing dependance on the outside world and the decisive role of the external constraint on growth.

8. This is also true in the case of (SG).

9. The price is endogenous in the model; it thus increases with the CSSPPA deduction, but only slightly (1 to 2 per cent).

10. The extent of the disincentive remains to be studied (Table V-9).

11. The imbalances are such that no measure manages to improve the situation durably on all fronts. This is aggravated, in the case of the devaluation simulations, by the twofold movement of exchange rates. After a real devaluation, there begins from 1984 a revaluation and there are two sharply contrasting phases.

Figure VI.1. **Reference simulation: GDP**
Volume: base = 1980

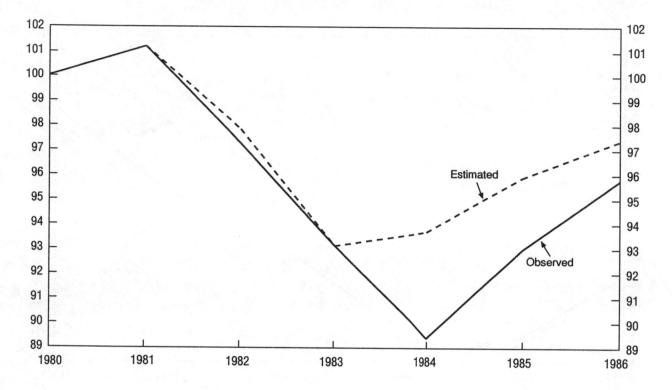

Figure VI.2. **Reference simulation: budget deficit**
(percentage of GDP)

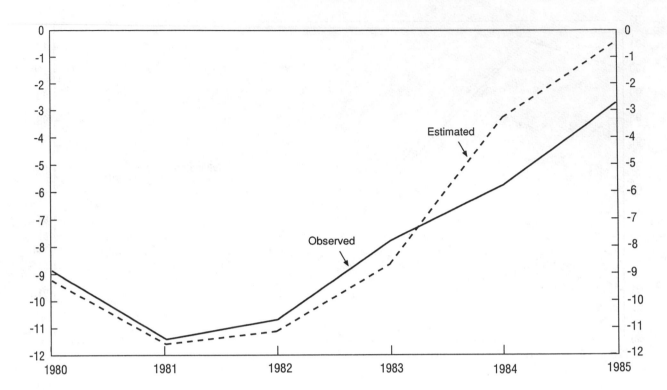

Figure VI.3. **Reference simulation: current account**
Billion FCFA

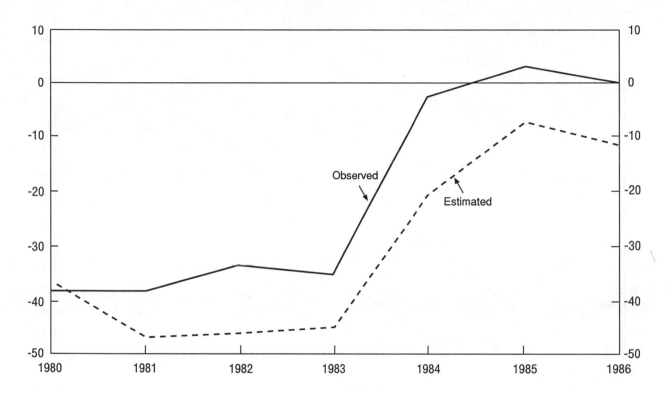

Figure VI.4. **Budget policy simulations: budget deficit**
Percentage of GDP

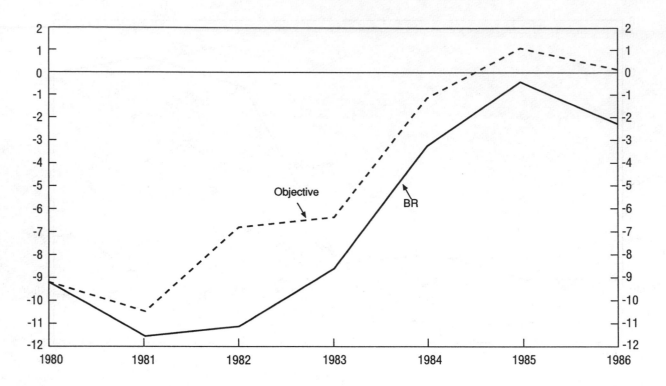

Figure VI.5. **Budget policy simulations: GDP**
Billion FCFA

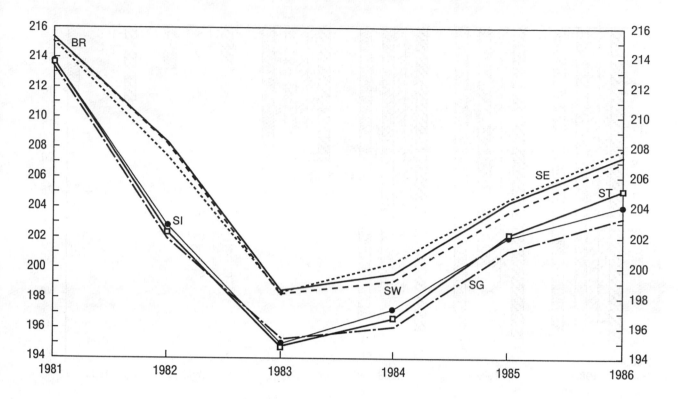

Figure VI.6. **Budget policy simulations: current account**
Billion FCFA

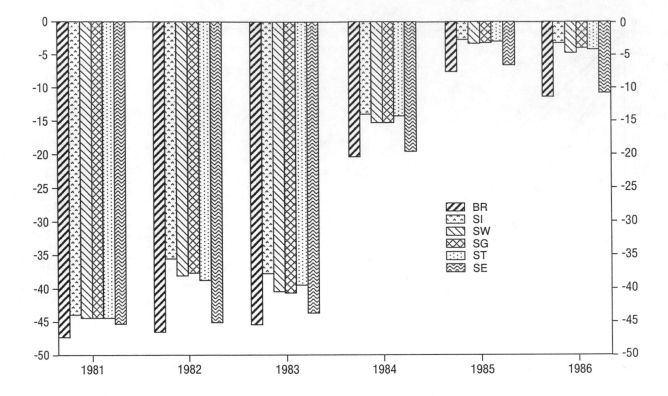

Figure VI.7. **Budget policy simulations: Theil**

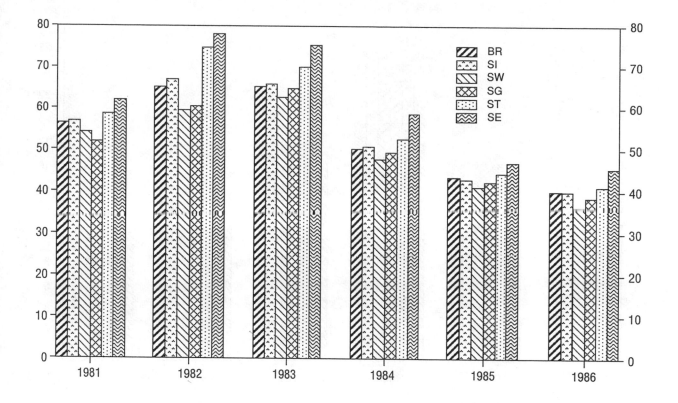

Figure VI.8. **Budget policy simulations: relative sum of poverty (%)**

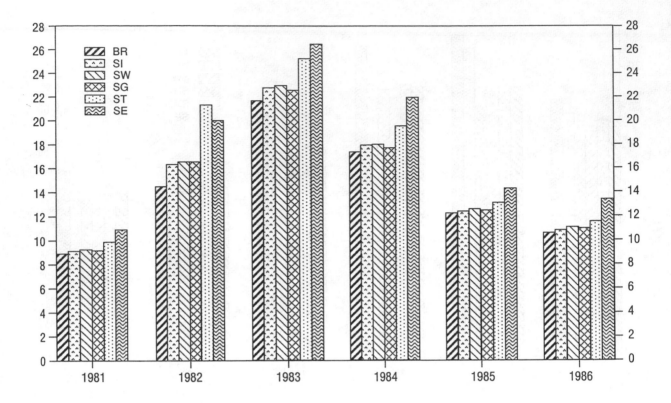

Figure VI.9. **Devaluations: inequality**
Theil index

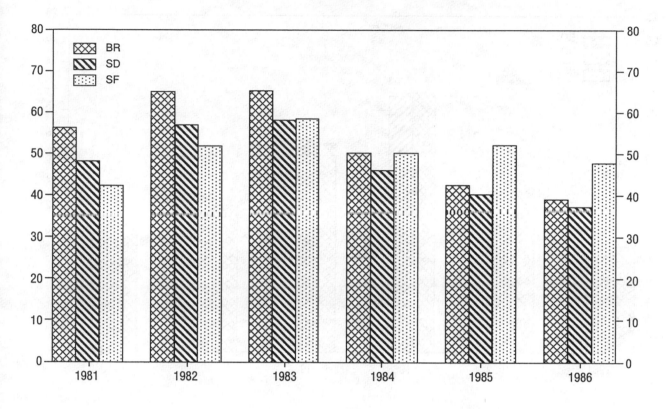

Figure VI.10. **Devaluations: relative sum of poverty (%)**

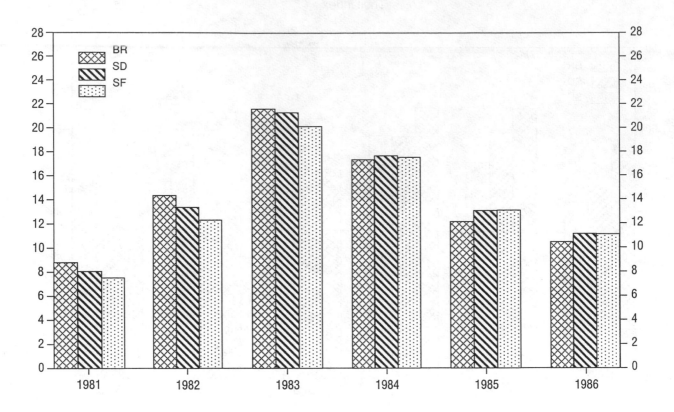

Key to the Model

1. Firms

(A.1) $q^s = u\,F(k,\,p,\,w)$ Production (u is the capacity utilisation rate)

(A.2) $L^d = \lambda(w/p)q^s$ Demand for labour

(A.3) $I = (g + \delta)\,k + I\,(ru/(\delta + \bar{c} - \dot{p}^e)$ Demand for investment

     $où \ \ r \equiv (\partial f / \delta k)/p_k$ Gross marginal income of capital (p_k is the price of capital goods)

(A.4) $\pi \equiv p\,q^s - w\,L^d - e\,i^*_{-1}\,L^*_{w,-1}$ Profits (π)

(A.5) $H_f = H\left[\dfrac{g_o\,i + (1 - g_o)(1 + i^{*e})}{1 + \dot{p}^e}\right]^\gamma pq^s$ Working capital (H_f)

(A.6) $\Delta B = p_k\,I + \Delta H_f - \alpha\,\pi - S_k$ Financing of investment (ΔB)

(A.7) $B = L_{b,-1} + e\,L^*_{w,-1} + \Delta B$ Debt of firms (bonds)

(A.8) $\Delta L_b = g_o\,\Delta B - \rho\,L_b; \quad g_o \equiv \varphi_o\left(\dfrac{1 + \bar{i}}{(1 + i^{*e})}\right)^{\varepsilon_o}$ Breakdown of loan capital between domestic bonds (Lb) and foreign bonds (ρ is the rate of repayment; $\bar{\imath}$ the interest rate)

2. Households

$$(A.9) \quad Y = wL^d + w_G \bar{L}_G + (1 - \alpha)\pi + \tilde{B}_{h,-1} + e \, \tilde{F}_{h,-1}$$

Income constraint

$$(A.10) \quad W = H_h + B_h/i + e \, F_h^*/i^* + p_a E$$

Wealth constraint

$$WG \equiv (H_{h-1} + B_{h,-1}/i + eF_{h,-1}^*/i^* + p_a E_{-1}) - W_{-1}$$

Definition of gain in wealth (WG)

$$(A.11) \quad C = [(1-s) \, Y + \gamma(WG)]/p_c$$

Consumption (p_c is the price of the composite good)

$$(A.12) \quad S = sY - \gamma \, (WG)$$

Savings

$$(A.13) \quad W = W_{-1} + S$$

Increase in wealth

$$(A.14) \quad \ln(H_h/\bar{p}) = a \, \ln(Y/\bar{p}) - z_i \, i - z_p \, \hat{p}^e$$

Demand for money (p is the cost of living)

$$(A.15) \quad p_a \, E = g_1(W_{-1} + S - H_h)$$

Demand for shares

$$g_1 = \psi_1 \left[\frac{1 + r - \delta + \hat{p}^e}{g_2 \, (1 + i) + (1 - g_2)(1 + i^{*e})} \right]^{\varepsilon_1}$$

$$(A.16) \quad B_h/i = g_2(1 - g_1) \, (W_{-1} + S - H_h)$$

Demand for domestic bonds

$$g_2 = \psi_2 \left[\frac{(1 + \bar{i})}{(1 + i^{*e})} \right]^{\varepsilon_2}$$

$$(A.17) \quad e \, F_h^*/i^* = (1 - g_2) \, (1 - g_1) \, (W_{-1} + S - H_h)$$

Demand for foreign bonds

$$(A.18) \quad p_a = [k(p_k(1-\delta) - p_{k,-1}) + \pi + \Delta \, H + E p_{a,-1})/E$$

Price of shares (p_a)

Net increase in capitalisation and in direct financing of investment

$(A.20)$ $p_c = d \, p \, (1 + t_i) + (1 - d) \, e \, \bar{p}_m^* \, (1 + t_m)$

Price of the composite good

3. Government accounts and balance of payments

$(A.21)$ $GR = t_i \, pq^S + e \, \bar{p}_m^* \, t_m M$

Tax revenue

$(A.22)$ $GE = p_c \, \bar{G} + \bar{W}_G \, \bar{L}_G + p_c \, \bar{I}_g + i_{-1} \, B_h + i_{-1}^* \, B_w^*$

Public expenditure

$$GD \equiv GR - GE$$

Budget deficit

$(A.23)$ $GD = B_h / i - (B_h / i)_{-1} + e \, (B_w^* - B_{w,-1}^*) + \Delta \, B_b$

Financing of the deficit

$(A.24)$ $CA = p_e^* \, X - \bar{p}_m^* \, M - i_{-1}^* [B_{w,-1}^* + L_{w,-1}^*]$

Current account

$(A.25)$ $KA_p = \Delta \, L_w^* - \Delta \, F_h^*$

(Private) capital account

4. Market equilibria

$$q^s = q^d$$

Walrassian regime

$(A.26)$ ou

or

$$p = (1 + m) \, \lambda \, W$$

Keynesian regime   **Goods market**

$$\hat{W} = \psi_o + \psi_1 \, \bar{p} + \psi_s (L_u^{-1} - L_{u,o}^{-1})$$

Wage indexation

$$L_u = 1 - (\bar{L}_G + L^d) / \bar{L}^s$$

Labour market

$(A.27)$

or

$$\bar{L}^s = L^d$$

Flexible wages

$$\Delta H_f + \Delta H_h = \Delta MS + (1 - \theta) KA_p \qquad i \leq i_{max}$$

Equilibrium through prices

or

Money and bond market

(A.28) ou

$$\Delta L_b(\bar{i}) = \Delta MS + (1 - \theta) KA_P - \Delta B_b \qquad \bar{i} > max$$

Credit rationing

$$CA + KA_p = -\Delta \bar{B}_W^*$$

Flexible exchange rate

or

(A.29) ou

$$-\Delta B_w^* = CA + KA_p$$

Endogenous government borrowing (fixed exchange rate)

5. Dynamics

Capital accumulation

(A.30) $\Delta k = I + k^S$

Increase in the active population

(A.31) $\Delta L/L = n$

Source : Bourguignon F., W. Branson and J. de Melo, *Journal of Development Economics*, forthcoming.

Note : With the exception of share prices, these equations correspond to those used in the model.

Notations

Firms

q^s	production of a sector
u	capacity utilisation rate
k	capital stock
p	price
w	wage rate
L^d	labour demand
I	investment demand
δ	rate of depreciation
p^e	rate of inflation
p_k	price of capital goods
i	domestic interest rate
$\bar{i}$	reference interest rate
i^*	foreign interest rate
L_b	domestic debt of firms
L^*_w	foreign debt of firms
e	exchange rate
π	profit
H_f	working capital of firms
ρ	repayment

Households

Y	household income
w_g	exogenous public wage
$\bar{L}_g$	public employment
B_h	domestic bonds held by households
F^*_h	foreign assets
E	shares
P_a	share price
s	rate of saving
WG	gain in wealth
H_h	cash in hand
$\bar{p}$	cost of living
S	total savings
S_k	savings in shares
p_c	price of the composite goods

Government and balance of payments

GR	tax revenue
$\overline{p}_m^{\bullet}$	exogenous foreign import price
t_m	customs duty
GE	public expenditure
G	public operating expenditure
$\overline{I}_g$	public investment
$B_w^{\bullet}$	external public debt
B_b	monetary financing
CA	current account
$p_e^{\bullet}$	foreign export price
KA_p	private capital account
m	marginal rate
L_u	unemployment
$\overline{L}_a$	exogenous labour supply
θ	currency sterilisation rate

112

Chapter VII

Conclusions

We have analysed how the structure of the Ivorian economy and the functioning of its public finances have created a "disequilibrating dependence" in this economy. This is a dual dependence: exports are very heavily concentrated on two agricultural products, coffee and cocoa; tax revenue also depends to a large extent on these same two products. This is not an ineluctable dependence stemming entirely from Côte d'Ivoire's natural resource endowment, but rather a dependence strengthened by the development strategy pursued for many years.

It is true that this strategy brought a certain prosperity to Côte d'Ivoire so long as there was a favourable world market for coffee and cocoa. Nonetheless, we found that this economic prosperity was not accompanied by social advances (in education and health) comparable with that of other countries at the same economic level. This difference could perhaps be interpreted as reflecting a social disequilibrium which, in a certain fashion, compounds the economic and fiscal imbalances to which we have referred. During the years of economic prosperity however, this social imbalance attracted little attention.

The fact is that the economic prosperity associated with the boom in export crops caused a certain euphoria and development policy that with hindsight can be considered over-ambitious. This outlook led to other disequilibria: public over-investment (given the financial resources, excessive state involvement in the enterprise sector and given the very limited capability for to ensuring sound economic and financial management), and a lack of strict management of public finances in general.

When the world market conditions for the export crops deteriorated, the government moved rapidly to reduce certain expenditures, notably investment. However, its ability to act effectively was limited, by the lack of instruments for rigorous management and by the sheer weight of its many commitments. The situation was then further aggravated by two factors outside government control: the rise in interest rates on the international financial markets (increasing debt servicing costs) and the drought of 1983.

To understand Cote d'Ivoire's economic and social performance better we briefly recapitulate here the macroeconomic shocks and tensions which it experienced during the period studied.

First of all, it is necessary to keep in mind the large fluctuations in the terms of trade. Taking 1975 as 100, the ratio mounted to 174 in 1977 only to fall back to 84 by 1982. These movements generated hopes and plans for rapid expansion which had to be scaled back or abandoned almost as soon as they were put into practice. To the extent that things were not scaled down, the burden was greater than planned because of the severe deterioration of the terms of trade.

Secondly and more insidiously than the decline in the terms of trade, the debt service (as a percentage of exports) increased from 12 per cent in 1977 to 43 per cent in 1982. This was the result of a positive but falling balance of trade and foreign borrowing which attained 91 per cent of public sector investments in 1980. The public sector savings were 22 per cent of the GDP in 1977 and practically nil in 1981. In that year government investment spending, which had been 19 per cent of the GDP in 1977, was limited to 12 per cent. These outlays continued to fall until they reached the level of interest payments on the public debt (8 per cent). Interest payments had been rising continually since 1977 when they had reached 1 per cent of the GDP. Thus financial tensions were increasing despite major austerity measures, especially in the domain of investments.

The external shocks also had repercussions on government revenues. While tax receipts remained nearly stable at around 20 per cent of the GDP, the returns from the Caisse de Stabilisation (CSSPPA) fell steeply from 17 per cent of the GDP in 1977 to 1 per cent in 1981. This was the origin of the government's inability to save and finance investments from its own resources. A decline in the inflow of foreign capital aggravated the financial situation faced by Cote d'Ivoire.

In 1981 the inflow (official and private) was 50 per cent of the 1980 level and in 1985 it was one-sixth of that level. Official inflows on the whole were maintained and even increased but were far from compensating for the decline in private capital. The increasing share of the public debt at a floating interest rate further aggravated the situation. This share attained 45 per cent in 1981 when the interest rate payable to private creditors reached an average of 17 per cent.

This résumé of economic and social disequilibria is the background for our analysis of the impact of the crisis and the adjustment on employment and wages, and more generally on the population's standard of living.

Employment and Wages

The adjustment programmes acted in "classical" fashion by reducing public expenditures and domestic demand. Furthermore, they included specific labour market measures. These programmes acted on both the modern sector and the traditional sector, though more indirectly on the latter. However, the informal sector labour market is quite opaque due to the lack of data. We therefore had to focus our analysis of employment and wages on the modern sector. Within this sector we found very different results in the enterprise sector and in the civil service.

Thus civil service employment continued to increase during the adjustment period (at an annual average rate of 3.5 per cent between 1981 and 1987), while it fell by over a third in the enterprise sector. The adjustment therefore did not affect the overall employment of cvil servants, but it did substantially reduce their real wages (down 20 per cent over the period). By contrast, the average real wage was maintained in the enterprise sector.

This divergent trend in the two major sectors on one hand reflects the legal constraints on the government with respect to civil service employment, and on the other the greater flexibility of the enterprise sector. It is interesting to note that the state behaved differently depending on whether it was dealing with the civil service or public enterprises. Thus in the latter, employment fell by 43 per cent between 1980 and 1985, or even more than the average for enterprises.

Over and above the legal constraints on civil service employment, however, there were also pressing needs that the state had to try to meet, notably in the field of education. In fact, during the adjustment period the Ministry of Education's share of public service employment increased from 49 to 53 per cent. Teachers thus benefited more than proportionally from the continued growth of civil service employment. Civil servants in the economic services were the only other category to increase its share (from 12 to 14 per cent.

While there is thus a sharp contrast overall between the civil service and the enterprise sector, there are also considerable variations within the latter.

While employment fell in all branches of activity during 1980-85, the fall was less in manufacturing industry than in the "formal non-tradeable" sector and primary product exports (down 52 and 45 per cent respectively for these last two sectors). The "construction and public works" branch lost as many as

85 per cent of its jobs, mainly because of the cuts in public investment. There was thus a significant change in the sectoral breakdown of employment. The share of the "formal non-tradeable" sector fell from 52 to 39 per cent.

Such a restructuring could have been welcomed to the extent that it freed resources that could have been employed in the "tradeable" sector and thus help improve the balance of payments. No such redeployment took place, however, because employment fell everywhere in the enterprise sector. Overall therefore, there was a shift of labour from the formal to the informal sector, because those who lost their jobs in the enterprise sector generally had no other choice (other than being unemployed without any benefits).

A more detailed analysis of employment shows in fact that among those who were able to retain their jobs in the formal sector, some were even able to compensate for any loss of real wages through being promoted. Actually the proportion of supervisors and managers increased during the adjustment period.

As regards wages, besides the fall in the real wages of civil servants already mentioned, we have also observed a great diversity within the enterprise sector. The maintenance of the real average wage between 1980 and 1985 actually conceals a real fall of 16 per cent for those at the bottom of the scale receiving only the SMIG or the SMAG. By contrast, the average real wage increased by over 30 per cent in the sector that experienced the biggest drop in employment, construction. This of course reflects a change in the pattern of employment in the sector due to the large-scale redundancies among the lowest-paid workers.

The fall in average real wage of civil servants corresponds to the "classical" type of adjustment through general austerity. Despite some protests from the persons concerned, notably the teachers, the need for this austerity seems to have been accepted without too many problems. In the private sector, the type of wage adjustment was quite different, the austerity being imposed mainly at the lower end of the wage scale, on unskilled workers. This type of adjustment is unusual (for example, it is the contrary of what happened in Morocco during the adjustment there), and requires explanation, all the more so because it aggravates inequality. Two explanatory hypotheses can be put forward: the first is that among the unskilled workers there was a high proportion of foreign workers from neighbouring countries, not protected by any union organisation and who did not feel their status was secure enough to demand more equitable treatment with any vigour. The second hypothesis concerns the persons at the top of the wage scale: in wage negotiations they were able to make use of their acquired advantages (e.g. social contacts, political influence, skills essential to the enterprise) that enabled them to safeguard or even improve their wages. This type of adjustment at the expense of the poorest categories is reprehensible from the point of view of equity and inefficient economically because it did not permit the competitiveness of enterprises to be increased sufficiently.

Under these conditions, the adjustment measures, notably the disindexation of wages and liberalisation of employment did not lead to the more intensive use of labour in enterprises or even to its stabilisation. At best, they made it possible to reduce enterprise losses and budget deficits. This effort to readjust, while necessary, did not take place in a sufficiently dynamic economic context for it to trigger a departure towards renewed growth in an improved structural context.

Standard of Living

While wages and employment to a large extent determine the standard of living of households deriving their incomes from the modern sector, it must be borne in mind that the vast majority of the active population derive their incomes from the traditional agricultural and non-agricultural sectors. What is more, the government influences the standard of living through its spending, taxation and pricing policies.

We have seen that, overall, the rural populations were rather better placed than the urban populations with respect to the adjustment measures. Among these measures, the most restrictive, such as the reduction of public investment and the freeze on civil service wages, concerned above all the urban populations, while the farmers benefited from several increases in prices of coffee, cocoa and cotton beginning in 1983.

Even though the increases in the nominal producer prices were not able to prevent a fall in real prices due to inflation, the producers of cash crops, as a group, nevertheless saw their real incomes increase over the 1980-86 period, as a result of increasing their production by over 33 per cent. By the end of the period this had resulted in increases in real incomes ranging from 15 per cent for rice growers to 19 per cent for cotton growers and 27 per cent for cocoa growers. Only the real incomes derived from coffee fell, by 12 per cent.

However, a more detailed analysis of the condition of the rural population reveals that an adjustment policy giving priority to the main export crops favours the Forest Zones and the bigger farms. This biased impact is not the result of a deliberate targeting of these measures but of the distribution of the crops and functioning of the agrarian system. To begin with, the proportion of the agricultural area used for cash crops in the Forest Zone is twice (and sometimes three times) that in the Savanna. Moreover, the Forest Zone farms are on average 50 to 100 per cent bigger than in the Savanna. Finally, the fallow land available for expanding export crops is greater in the Forest Zone and among the biggest farmers. Because of their land reserves, it is also the latter who had access to the relatively cheap labour necessary for working the new land.

The main impact of the adjustment measures on the rural populations was thus determined by the pattern of agriculture. This was not changed but, rather, there was a perpetuation of the "main trends" in agriculture closely associated with the question of land ownership. In addition, the measures aimed at food crops other than rice which potentially would have had a more egalitarian impact were only very partially implemented.

In urban areas, the standard of living of the population in the informal sector is more difficult to assess than that in the formal sector. While for the latter the impact of the adjustment measures was relatively direct through employment and wages (see above), the impact was largely indirect for those working in the informal sector. It made itself felt partly through a fall in demand for the goods and services this sector supplies to households and enterprises. However, neither the prices nor the quantities supplied are recorded. Analysis of the Household Survey nevertheless permits us to affirm that the poor are over-represented in the informal sector: while 50 per cent of all the households in Abidjan belong to the informal sector, the proportion rises to 75 per cent in the case of the poor in this city.

Another impact of the adjustment on the informal sector was an increasing number of people working in it after having lost their jobs in the formal sector. This number can be estimated at some 100 000 between 1980 and 1985, in addition to the "natural" growth of the same order of magnitude. Thus it was likely that there was downward pressure on incomes and increased competition between persons active in the sector, but this was not entirely due to the adjustment. We have also seen through the simulations of different possible adjustment measures that informal sector workers are particularly vulnerable to austerity policies, which reduce the demand for this sector's products in various ways.

It must be borne in mind that in the urban areas the adjustment not only affected the standard of living of the relatively well-off populations of the formal sector but also that of a population that was poorer on average and even more numerous, working in the informal sector. The majority of the active persons in this sector are women. In Abidjan, among the poor, 90 per cent of the women are in this sector as against only 56 per cent of the men. Among the rich, these proportions are 29 and 25 per cent respectively.

We also analysed the impact of the adjustment on the standard of living of different population groups through the spending patterns. This varies between town and country on the one hand and between rich and poor households on the other. The increases in the controlled consumer prices for rice and bread under the adjustment measures, are the most striking examples of impacts very much to the disadvantage of the poorest groups.

Thus the price of rice increased much more than that of bread (34 per cent as against 7 per cent). While the poor urban households spend a greater share of their income on rice than on bread, these proportions are reversed for the rich households. Furthermore, in the poorest rural region, the Savanna, the percentage spent on rice is roughly twice that in the Forest Zone (between 15 and 18 per cent as against 5 to 11 per cent).

Electricity and water are two other items that were affected by price increases under adjustment measures. In the poorest urban households, these two items together amount to about 20 per cent of monetary expenditure, as against 12 per cent for the rich households. These price increases thus weighed relatively more heavily on the poor than on the rich.

Spending on transport, which was also affected by the adjustment measures, provides an example of the reverse situation in rural areas. The poor spend 5 per cent of their income on this item as against 8 per cent for the rich.

Educational expenditure weighs a little more heavily in urban than in rural areas (8 per cent as against 7 per cent, all economic levels taken together). In towns, it is the rich households which spend relatively more on this item than the poor.

Lastly, analysis of educational enrolments during 1975-87 throws more light on the overall social effects of the crisis and the adjustment. In fact, the number of children at school, after having increased sharply during the 1970s, grew at a rate below that of the population increase after 1982. In primary education, the annual rate of increase was about 2 per cent in 1983 and 1984 and 3 per cent in the two following years. However, during the 1980-87 period, school enrolment at the primary level rose only from 76 to 78 per cent. While this rate remains low compared with other middle income countries, it is encouraging that this increase is due to a higher enrolment rate among girls (65 per cent as against 60 per cent) while that for boys remained unchanged at 92 per cent.

The trend was more irregular in secondary and higher education, but broadly speaking there was a sharp fall followed by modest increases. There are several factors that may explain this development. First, adjustment measures such as the reduction of grants and cuts in admissions to specialised colleges, and second, the increasing difficulty experienced by households in financing the education of their children. In addition, the deterioration of the employment prospects after completing education must have discouraged some from continuing their studies.

Simulations of alternative policies

A computer model, at the same time both macro- and microeconomic, was applied to the case of Côte d'Ivoire between 1980 and 1986. This made it possible to study, within a coherent framework, the effects of different adjustment measures on the principal aggregates and on income distribution. Thus the effects of actual policies and alternative measures could be compared, permitting an evaluation of past experience and providing a solid basis for choosing future policies.

The simulations concerned the two major problems in Côte d'Ivoire during the 1980s: the reduction of the budget deficit and the question of the exchange rates necessary to balance the current account.

Five different measures to reduce the budget deficit by the same amount were compared: reduction of public investment, reduction of current government expenditures, and reduction of public service wages on one hand, and increases in taxes on production and on primary exports on the other. All these simulations have recessionary effects at first, but show good results for the target parameters of the adjustment policies: budget deficit, current account deficit and balance of trade. From the poverty standpoint, expenditure reduction policies are less painful than tax increase policies. It should be noted, however, that there are some limits to the comparability of these simulations. Thus a variation in the level of public spending has a direct effect through demand, while a change in the rate of tax causes induced effects through its impact on the tax base itself. Furthermore, some of the operating expenditures actually have long-term effects that make them a sort of investment in human capital. In the simulation model, however, these expenditures are treated as having an effect only during a given period.

Among the expenditure reduction simulations, the reduction in civil service wages seems preferable to all the others, but it should be noted that poverty increases with respect to the reference level, even though inequality is diminished.

The second set of simulations was aimed at reducing the external debt by means of depreciating the exchange rate, either by devaluing once and for all, or through letting the exchange rate float. In both cases there is a strong revival of the economy accompanied by a reduction in inequality and in poverty. But inequality increases beginning in 1984 in the case of a floating exchange rate. While the first of these simulations seems very favourable, it should be noted that both make the assumption that firms can obtain foreign loans, which is not very likely in practice. If this assumption is abandoned, the results become much less favourable.

At the end of this simulation exercise, we noted three points. First, the instability of Côte d'Ivoire's economy, which means that no single measure can durably improve the situation in all respects. Second, the question of the credibility of the economic authorities and the sensitivity of the results to assumptions made about access to new foreign loans. Third, the Ivorian authorities lack room for manoeuvre in the short term: the key budget policy instrument, the CSSPPA imposition, seems to have reached its limits (Laffer curve); monetary policy and exchange rate policy depend on the UMOA; and the financing of the economy depends on access to the international financial market. For these reasons, the only really credible policies are those aimed at reducing budget expenditure; and among these, the reduction of public sector wages or operating expenditures, which are more neutral in terms of growth and poverty, without penalising investment.

Towards a durable adjustment

In the light of our analysis and other countries' experience of adjustment, what are the lessons for the formulation of future policies? The most general conclusion of our analysis is that the adjustment process is of a complex nature, with multiple endogenous and exogenous factors that combine and sometimes reinforce one another. Thus we cannot expect simple and rapid solutions. Rather, adjustment should be considered as a lengthy process consisting of redefining and implementing a development strategy made up of a great many components. Furthermore, this task is not just technical, but highly political. The government does not control all the action variables and thus has to be able to incite economic agents to change their behaviour in the desired manner; it also has to be able to anticipate any resistance likely to arise.

We have been able to demonstrate the results of alternative policies by simulations using a computer model. It must be remembered, however, that because of its structure and the values of the parameters selected, this model is not a perfect replica of reality. Thus, for example, the elasticities of supply used are not necessarily a faithful reproduction of microeconomic reality, but they do make it possible to illustrate certain types of reaction. Even with these reservations, it should be stressed that none of the alternative measures manages to improve the situation durably on all fronts. A choice therefore has to be made between different objectives. Furthermore, profound structural and policy changes are needed to obtain better and lasting results.

Based on the analysis of adjustment in many countries, Thomas *et al.* (1989) suggest five general principles of durable reforms:

1. Long-term policies must be "sound" but must also permit rapid adjustment to shocks;

2. It is necessary to limit the negative effects on growth, employment and poverty to a fairly short period;

3. It is necessary to ensure that supply can respond quickly;

4. It is necessary to link the mobilisation of external resources to the costs of the adjustment;

5. Lastly, the measures, adapted to the situation of the country, must be able to rely on strong government commitment.

It must be admitted that in Côte d'Ivoire many good measures were decided upon, but they were not all applied, and some could not produce the desired results because they were implemented too late and only partially. In addition, there are certain structural characteristics that have not been modified and which, as a result, have maintained or aggravated certain existing imbalances.

In the first place, the structural vulnerability of Côte d'Ivoire must be stressed. As we have shown, the heavy concentration of exports on very few primary products remained virtually unchanged throughout the 1980-87 period. The task of export diversification, which was mentioned in the development programmes, for the most part still remains a dead letter. This is a matter of identifying viable and practicable alternatives. Creating or strengthening the structures that could promote this diversification is thus one of the measures that needs to be implemented. Here it is necessary to ensure that the existing price structure, insofar as it is controlled by the government, does not prevent such an adjustment.

Another area where vulnerability must be reduced and some sort of equilibrium re-established is that of food crops. Côte d'Ivoire's authorities recognised this necessity as early as the beginning of the 1980s (food plan) but did not act with sufficient resolve to achieve the desired result. This is certainly a long and complicated task that involves changes in the traditional agrarian system, but it would be well worth undertaking energetically. In this way it would be possible not only to re-establish the balance of production, but also achieve an improvement in the situation of the socially disadvantaged groups in both urban and adjacent areas. Once again this type of adjustment requires attention to the existing level of prices, partly determined by the exchange rate system and by international competition that is sometimes clearly unfair. If a devaluation cannot be carried out under the present monetary regime, thought should perhaps be given to well-targeted protection through import taxes. In this way, it would be possible at the same time to mobilise certain resources to promote productivity in the food crop sector. In addition, if favourable general conditions could be created for this sector, it would probably constitute an example of adjustment based largely on the mobilisation of local resources.

A fiscal system based largely on export taxes is another domain requiring measures to reduce vulnerability. This system has transmitted the fluctuations on the principal export markets to the public budget which needs to be made more stable and more predictable. Furthermore, through the receipts of the *Caisse de Stabilisation et de Soutien des Prix et des Productions Agricoles* (CSSPPA), this system exempts part of the fiscal revenue from any tight management control. By seeking a more stable tax base and more complete control over revenues and their utilisation, it would be possible to reduce this type of vulnerability which is at the same time a source of inefficiency.

A worrying feature of adjustment as it has been seen in Côte d'Ivoire is the very considerable drop in investment, both public and private. Comparing adjustment in the CFA zone countries with other sub-Saharan countries, Devarajan *et al.* (1990) have explained this phenomenon as follows: the impossibility of a nominal devaluation for the member countries of this zone has practically obliged them to adjust more through the reduction of expenditures than through the reallocation of resources that would be induced by the relative price changes following a devaluation. This type of adjustment through reducing investment has serious consequences for the future and cannot go on indefinitely. Even if it is assumed that some of the scrapped investment projects were not economically viable, others will be sadly missed from the stock of real capital on which future growth depends.

The question thus arises once more, though from a different angle, whether a monetary regime that does not allow nominal devaluation should be retained. This is a very controversial question and the answer must, of course, also take account of the stabilising effects of and the confidence inspired by this regime. If the regime is retained, it will be necessary to devise other methods of stimulating a reallocation of the factors of production to make it possible to re-establish the desired balances. Taxes that increase import prices together with export subsidies could possibly play this role. While such measures can change prices in the desired direction, it must nevertheless be stressed that private investment will not react unless the whole set of measures is considered credible and are situated in a general climate favourable to investment including the broader socio-economic and political framework, which must make investors confident that they will not run too high a risk if they go ahead with their investment.

Any measure that makes it possible to increase the efficiency of the production of goods and services is likely to facilitate, directly or indirectly, adjustment in its different forms. For example, enterprises that produce at a lower cost become more competitive on the international market and/or make it possible to reduce the price of intermediates on the domestic market. Administrations that can provide the same service at lower cost help to reduce the budget deficit and the burden that the State imposes on taxpayers, and hence enterprises, and the result is as in the first example. Thus the search for greater efficiency in all fields, already begun in different forms in Côte d'Ivoire, must continue. However, this effort, and hence the resulting adjustment, cannot be durable if it does not take account of the consequences for certain persons or social categories in the short term, and for the future of the society as a whole.

While the austerity practised in Côte d'Ivoire was able to facilitate the restoration of certain balances, it is not necessarily synonymous with increased efficiency and the future has been compromised in various ways. In order for the adjustment to be equitable and durable, it is thus necessary to propose measures that can, for example, find work for those who have lost their jobs and ensure a certain minimum of education and health care provision for those who risk being deprived of it. These measures can cushion the negative impact of adjustment at the individual level and spread the cost more evenly over the society. This is also a field where external aid can be useful (as in the context of the PAMSCAD programme in Ghana) to provide support until the adjustment starts to bear fruit and the country is able to carry the full cost of such redistribution operations on its own.

How can the socio-economic equilibrium be maintained during the process of economic or social adjustment? That requires giving special attention to the distribution of the adjustment costs among the different socio-economic groups. Our analysis revealed that the urban population bore a much greater share of these costs than the rural population. From the standpoint of equity, this was an acceptable burden for certain relatively advantaged urban groups such as civil servants and this was corroborated by our simulations. This distribution of the adjustment costs reflects a political situation in which power is based largely on clients among the coffee and cocoa planters. To the extent possible, these planters were relatively shielded from the adjustment measures.

However, there are reasons for believing that this distribution of the adjustment costs does not correspond to the country's social reality. This was indicated by the protest movements and results of the 1990 elections. The high vote received by the opposition (permitted to run for the first time) in the districts of Abidjan inhabited by persons working in modern sector, in part, reflects new forces which will have to be taken into account in formulating future adjustment policies.

In the same vein, it will be necessary to be more concerned about the less advantaged urban dwellers who derive their incomes from the informal sector. Their numbers have increased as a result of the crisis and also because of demographic and migratory pressures. Although the migration has both domestic and international components, it is noteworthy that up to now the Ivorian authorities have not attempted to send immigrants back to their countries of origin. Such a policy would not be consistent with Ivorian regional policy and, if attempted, would cause acute problems for the immigrants and their countries of origin.

In conclusion, it is important for economic adjustment to take account of the socio-economic readjustments which are occurring. This is not just a matter of new political forces and social justice but it also involves the country's fundamental economic indicators which have become unfavourable to coffee and cocoa.

List of Acronyms

BCEAO	Banque centrale des États de l'Afrique de l'Ouest
BEPC	Brevet d'études de premier cycle
BGF	Budget général de fonctionnement
BSIE	Budget spécial d'investissement et d'équipement
BTS	Brevet de technicien supérieur
CAA	Caisse autonome d'amortissement
CAP	Certificat d'aptitude professionelle
CAPEN	Centre d'assistance et de promotion de l'entreprise nationale
CEPE	Certificat d'études primaires élémentaires
CFA	Communauté financière africaine
CIS	Crédit immobilier social
CM2	Cours moyen, second year
CSSPPA	Caisse de stabilisation et de soutien des prix et des productions agricoles
DCGTX	Direction du contrôle des grands travaux
DUT	Diplôme universitaire de technologie
EBC	Enquête budget consommation
EECI	Energie électrique de la Côte d'Ivoire
FCFA	Franc de la CFA
METFP	Ministère de l'enseignement technique et de la formation professionnelle
ONFP	Office national de formation professionnelle
SICOGI	Société ivoirienne de construction et de gestion immobilière
SIR	Société ivoirienne de raffinage
SMAG	Salaire minimum agricole garanti
SMIG	Salaire minimum interprofessionnel garanti
SOGEFIHA	Société de gestion financière de l'habitat
TPS	Taxe sur la prestation de services
UMOA	Union monétaire ouest-africaine
LSMS	Living Standards Measurement Survey

Bibliography

AINSWORTH, M. and J. MUNOZ (1986), *Côte d'Ivoire Living Standards Survey, Design and Implementation*, LSMS Working Paper No. 26, World Bank, Washington, D.C.

ARRIGADA, A.M. and G. PSACHAROPOULOS (1986), "La composition de la population active par niveaux d'instruction : une comparaison internationale", *Revue internationale du travail*, Vol 125, No. 5, Sept./Oct., Geneva

ASSOCIATION INTERPROFESSIONNELLE DES EMPLOYEURS DE CÔTE D'IVOIRE (ASECO) (1977), *Convention collective interprofessionnelle de la République de Côte d'Ivoire*, Abidjan.

BANQUE CENTRALE DES ÉTATS DE L'AFRIQUE DE L'OUEST (BCEAO), several years, *Notes d'information et statistiques*, Dakar.

BENARD, J. (1987), *Revue de théorie sur les réglementations publiques de l'activité économique*, Paris : CEPREMAP, No. 8702.

BERTHÉLEMY, J.C. and F. BOURGUIGNON (1989), *Growth and crisis in Côte d'Ivoire*, DELTA, Paris, mimeo.

BISILLIAT, J. and M. FIELOUX (1983), *Femmes du Tiers-Monde*, Le Sycomore, Paris.

BOUGEROL, P. (1986), "La crise et la politique d'ajustement en Côte d'Ivoire", in Ministère de la Coopération, *Déséquilibres structurels et programmes d'ajustement en Côte d'Ivoire*, Paris.

BOURGUIGNON, F., W.H. BRANSON and J. DE MELO (1989a), *Macroeconomic Adjustment and Income Distribution: A Macro-Micro Simulation Model*, OECD Development Centre, Technical Papers, No. 1, Paris.

BOURGUIGNON, F., W.H. BRANSON and J. DE MELO (1989b), *Adjustment and Income Distribution: A Counterfactual Analysis*, NBER Working Paper, Cambridge, Mass.

BOURGUIGNON, F., W.H. BRANSON and J. DE MELO, *Journal of Development Economics*, forthcoming.

BROCHET, C. and J. PIERRE (1986), *Industrialisation des pays d'Afrique sub-saharienne: le cas de la Côte d'Ivoire*, ministère de la Coopération, Paris.

BROOKE, J. (1987), "Economic Boom Beckons Immigrants to Ivory Coast" in *Herald Tribune*, January 16.

BUREAU DE DÉVELOPPEMENT INDUSTRIEL (BDI) (1980), *Coûts des facteurs en Côte d'Ivoire*, Abidjan, October.

CENTRE D'ASSISTANCE ET DE PROMOTION DE L'ENTREPRISE NATIONALE (CAPEN) (1983), *Coûts des facteurs en Côte d'Ivoire, Abidjan*.

CHALEARD, J.L. (1979), *Structures agraires et économie de plantation chez les Abe*, Thèse de 3e cycle, Université de Nanterre, Paris.

CHAMBRE D'INDUSTRIE DE CÔTE D'IVOIRE (1978), *L'industrie ivoirienne en 1977 : liste des industries*, Abidjan.

CHESNAIS, J.C. (1986), *La transition démographique*, Paris : PUF, cahier No. 113.

DEVARAJAN, S. and J. DE MELO (1990), *Membership in the CFA Zone: Odyssean Journey or Trojan Horse?* Working Paper, World Bank, Washington, D.C., August.

EDIAFRIC (1980), *L'économie ivoirienne*, Paris.

EDIEMA (1988), *Guide permanent du travail et de l'emploi en Côte d'Ivoire* (Directory), Paris.

GLEWWE, P. (1987), *The Distribution of Welfare in the Republic of Côte d'Ivoire in 1985*, LSMS Working Paper No. 29, World Bank, Washington, D.C.

GLEWWE, P. and DE TRAY D. (1988), *The Poor during Adjustment: A Case Study of Côte d'Ivoire*, LSMS Working Paper No. 47, World Bank, Washington, D.C.

GLEWWE, P. and VAN DER GAAG J. (1988), *Confronting Poverty in Developing Countries: Definitions, Information, and Policies*, LSMS Working Paper No. 48, World Bank, Washington, D.C.

GROOTAERT, C. and R. KANBUR (1990), *Policy-oriented Analysis of Poverty and the Social Dimensions of Structural Adjustment, 1985-1988*, Social Dimensions of Adjustment in Sub-saharan Africa No. 1, World Bank, Washington, D.C.

GROPPO, P. (1989), *La paysannerie en Côte d'Ivoire*, Thèse de doctorat, Institut National Agronomique Paris-Grignon.

HARRE, D. (1989), "Production nationale et approvisionnement extérieur: le cas de la Côte d'Ivoire", *Économie Rurale* No. 190.

KANBUR, R. (1990), *Poverty and the Social Dimensions of Structural Adjustment in Côte d'Ivoire*, SDA Working Paper No. 2, World Bank, Washington, D.C.

KOESTER, U., H. SCHAFER and A. VALDÉS (1989), "External Demand Constraints for Agricultural Exports: An Impediment to Structural Adjustment Policies in Sub-Saharan African Countries?", *Food Policy*, August.

KURIAN, G.T. (1984), *The New Book of World Rankings*, New York: Facts on File Publications.

LACHAUD, J.P. (1988), *Pauvreté et marché du travail urbain : le cas d'Abidjan*, Geneva : ILO/Institut international d'études sociales (French only).

LACOSTE, Y. (1983), "Golfe de Guinée", *l'État du monde*, Annuaire économique et géopolitique mondial, Paris : Éd. La Découverte/Maspéro.

LECAILLON, J., F. PAUKERT, C. MORRISSON and D. GERMIDIS (1984), *Income Distribution and Economic Development, an Analytical Survey*, International Labour Organisation, Geneva

LELE, U. (1988), in T.F. Bassett, "Breaking up the Bottlenecks in Food Crop and Cotton Cultivation in Northern Côte d'Ivoire", *AFRICA* 58 (2).

LEUWAT, G. (1988), "La pratique des codes d'investissement en Afrique noire francophone", Paris : *Rencontres africaines*.

LUNGART, A. (1989), *Etude de cas sur la Côte d'Ivoire,* Atelier régional sur la gestion stratégique du processus d'ajustement du secteur industriel en Afrique, UNIDO, December 11-15, Vienna.

MAHIEU, F.R. (1989), "Principes économiques et société africaine", *Revue Tiers Monde,* t. XXX, No. 120.

MALINVAUD, E. (1980), *Réexamen de la théorie du chômage,* coll. Perspectives de l'Économie, Éd. Calman-Lévy, Paris.

MARCHÉS TROPICAUX ET MÉDITERRANÉENS (1985), *L'industrie ivoirienne, stratégie de son développement,* suppl. du No. 2094, Paris : Moreaux éditeurs.

MARGURAT, Y. (1985), "Les jeunes délinquants d'Abidjan", *Les Cahiers de l'ORSTOM,* vol. XXI, No. 2, 3, pp. 373-379.

MINISTÈRE DE L'AGRICULTURE (1984), *Actualisation du Plan Vivrier 1984-86,* Rapport de synthèse, Abidjan.

MINISTÈRE DE LA COOPÉRATION (1986), *Déséquilibres structurels et programmes d'ajustement en Côte d'Ivoire,* Paris.

MINISTÈRE DE L'ÉCONOMIE ET DES FINANCES (1984), *Budget général de fonctionnement, gestion 1984,* Rapport de présentation, Abidjan.

MINISTÈRE DE L'ÉCONOMIE ET DES FINANCES (1984), *Population de la Côte d'Ivoire : analyse des données démographiques disponibles,* Abidjan.

MINISTÈRE DE L'ÉCONOMIE ET DES FINANCES (1988), *La Côte d'Ivoire en chiffres,* Abidjan, éditions 1980/81 et 1986/87, Abidjan.

MINISTÈRE DE L'ÉCONOMIE ET DES FINANCES (1989), *Memento macro-économique de la Côte d'Ivoire,* Abidjan.

MINISTÈRE DE L'ENSEIGNEMENT TECHNIQUE ET DE LA FORMATION PROFESSIONNELLE (METFP) (1982), *Le secteur privé et semi-public en Côte d'Ivoire.,* Abidjan.

MINISTÈRE DU PLAN ET DE L'INDUSTRIE (1981-1985), *Plan quinquennal de développement économique, social et culturel,* tome 1, Abidjan.

MINISTÈRE DU PLAN ET DE L'INDUSTRIE, several years, *Les Comptes de la nation,* Abidjan.

MINISTÈRE DES RELATIONS EXTÉRIEURES, Coopération et Développement (1982), *Bilan national de l'emploi en Côte d'Ivoire,* Paris.

MINISTÈRE DES RELATIONS EXTÉRIEURES, Coopération et Développement (1982), *Côte d'Ivoire : analyse et conjoncture,* Paris.

OFFICE NATIONAL DE FORMATION PROFESSIONNELLE (ONFP) (1985), *Un diplôme pour l'emploi ?,* Abidjan.

OUDIN, X. (1986), *Population et emploi non structuré en Côte d'Ivoire,* Amira brochure No. 51, Paris.

PILLET-SCHWARTZ, A.M. (1982), *Aghien, un terroir Ebrié : quinze ans de technostructure en Côte d'Ivoire,* ORSTOM, Atlas des structures agraires.

RÉPUBLIQUE DE CÔTE D'IVOIRE, several years, *Centrale des Bilans,* Abidjan.

REVEL, E. (1988), *Effets des mesures des plans de stabilisation du FMI sur la répartition des revenus ; deux exemples : la Côte d'Ivoire et le Sénégal*, Thèse de doctorat, Université Paris I, Paris.

RICHARDS, P. (1986), "Le maintien de l'emploi et les plans de stabilisation économique : peut-on fixer un objectif d'emploi ?", *Revue internationale du travail*, No. 4, July/August.

RIDLER, N.B. (1988), "The Caisse de Stabilisation in the Coffee Sector", *World Development*, vol. 16, No. 12.

RODRIK, D. (1990), "How Should Structural Adjustment Programmes be Designed?", *World Development*, vol. 18, No. 7.

SAUVY, A. (1983), *Théorie générale de la population*, Paris : PUF.

THOMAS, V. and A. CHHIBBER (1989), *Adjustment Lending: How it has Worked, How it can be Improved*, World Bank, Washington, D.C.

THURON, L.E. (1975), *Generating Inequality: Mecanisms of Distribution in the US Economy*, New York, Basic Books Inc. Publishers.

TIBI, C. (1989), "The Financing of Education: the Impact of the Crisis and the Adjustment Process", in F. Caillods, *The Prospects for Educational Planning*, UNESCO, Paris.

ORE, A. (1981), *L'accès des femmes ivoiriennes aux ressources de la terre en pays Adioukrou*, ILO, Geneva.

UNDP (1990), *Human Development Report*, New York, Oxford University Press.

UNESCO (1987), *UNESCO Statistical Digest*.

UNICEF/info (1987), *Doc.*, No. 23, November/December.

UNITED NATIONS (1981), "World Population Prospects as Assessed 1980", *Population Studies*, No. 78, New York (in J.C. Chesnais).

WEEKES-VAGLIANI, W. (1990), *Analyse des variables socio-culturelles et de l'ajustement en Côte d'Ivoire*, Document Technique No. 9, OECD Development Centre, Paris.

WORLD BANK, several years, *World Development Report*, Washington, D.C.

WORLD BANK (1987), *Côte d'Ivoire in Transition: From Structural Adjustment to Self-sustained Growth*, 4 vol., Washington, D.C.

Table I.1. **Comparative profile of the Côte d'Ivoire economy: 1980-87**

	1980	1987	Average for middle income countries[2]
Population (million)	8.3	11.1	
Urbanisation rate (%)	40.0	44.0	
Annual average population growth (80-87)	4.2		
Life expectation	47.0	52.0	
GDP Structure (%)			
Agriculture	34	36	(22)
Industry	22	25	(32)
Services	44	39	(47)
GDP breakdown (%)			
Private consumption	59	65	
Public consumption	18	17	
Gross domestic investment	28	13	
Gross domestic savings	23	19	
Exports	35	39	
Imports	41[1]	28	

	1965-80	1980-87
Average annual growth (%)		
GDP	6.8	2.2
Agriculture	3.3	1.6
Industry	10.4	−2.4
Services	8.6	4.2

1. Based on Berthélemy and Bourguignon (1989).
2. Figures for the lower middle income countries for 1985.
Source: World Bank, *World Development Report*, 1982, 1987 and 1989, except where otherwise indicated.

Table I.2. **Situation of the formal industrial sector***

Index: 1980 = 100

Year	Production[1]	Employment	Productivity
1975	74.5	68.2	109.2
1976	81.7	83.6	97.7
1977	95.7	97.9	97.7
1978	106.8	102.7	104.0
1979	107.5	102.6	104.8
1980	100.0	100.0	100.0
1981	98.8	90.4	109.4
1982	83.9	77.3	108.5
1983	85.8	73.0	117.6
1984	84.0	68.4	122.8
1985	86.9	64.4	135.0
Absolute value for 1980	Billion FCFA 783 980	Number 237 205	Million FCFA 3.30

* Includes public, private and mixed enterprises with 10 or more employees.
1. At constant 1980 prices.
Source: Centrale des Bilans.

Table I.3. **CSSPPA receipts and tax revenues: 1970-88**

GDP %

Year	Tax revenue	CSSPPA receipts	Total	CSSPPA receipts as % of total
1970	19.8	4.2	24.0	17.6
1971	19.9	1.4	21.3	6.2
1972	21.2	0.2	21.4	1.0
1973	20.7	1.8	22.5	8.0
1974	19.2	6.7	25.9	25.9
1975	20.2	2.2	22.4	9.7
1976	21.2	9.7	30.9	20.3
1977	20.5	16.5	37.0	44.7
1978	20.5	10.4	30.9	33.6
1979	20.4	7.4	27.8	27.9
1980	21.4	2.9	24.3	12.4
1981	22.3	1.3	23.6	3.0
1982	21.2	2.6	23.8	11.3
1983	20.6	3.7	24.3	15.3
1984	18.4	8.8	27.2	31.8
1985	20.2	8.1	28.3	28.6
1986	20.7	4.7	25.4	18.5
1987	21.8	−1.4	20.4	−6.8
1988[1]	21.0	−2.8	18.2	−15.4

1. Provisional figures.

Source: Berthélemy and Bourguignon, who base their figures on the *Comptes de la Nation* and the *Memento macro-économique*, ministère de l'Économie et des Finances, Abidjan 1989.

Table I.4. **Value added by industry: 1981-88**

Billion current FCFA and per cent

	1981	%	1983	%	1985	%	1988	%
Mining	37	11.6	59	15.7	56	11.9	11	2.8
Food processing	106	33.2	113	30.1	143	30.5	128	32.3
Textiles	35	11.0	57	15.2	63	13.4	48	12.1
Timber	17	5.3	14	3.7	14	3.0	10	2.5
Miscellaneous industry (including rubber, oil, building materials, chemicals)	42	13.2	46	12.2	100	21.3	93	23.5
Mechanical and electrical engineering	30	9.4	32	8.5	29	6.2	23	5.8
Electricity and water	52	16.3	55	14.6	64	13.6	83	21.0
Total	319	100.0	376	100.0	469	100.0	396	100.0

Source: A. Lungart, *Etude de cas Côte d'Ivoire,* prepared for the Regional Workshop on the Strategic Management of the Adjustment Process in the Industrial Sector in Africa, UNIDO, Vienna, December 1989.

Table I.5. **Structure of foreign trade: 1980-87**

	1980[1]	1987[1]
Exports		
Fuels, minerals, metals	5	4
Other primary products	87	86
of which: Coffee[2]	(21.8)	(20.1)
Cocoa[2]	(29.4)	(39.4)
Building timber	(15.1)	(6.6)
Manufactures	8	9
Imports		
Food products	15	19
Fuels	11	15
Other primary products	2	4
Machinery and transport equipment	35	28
Other manufactures	37	35

1. Or the closest year available.
2. Including intermediate goods and processed products, the share of which increased from 5.5. per cent in 1980 to 8.3 per cent in 1987.

Source: World Bank, *World Development Report, 1982 and 1989, La Côte d'Ivoire en chiffres 1986-87*, Berthélemy and Bourguignon (1989).

Table I.6. **Foreign trade and current account balance: 1975-85**

Billion FCFA

Year	Exports	Imports	X-M	M coverage %	Terms of trade[1]	Current account balance
1975	254.6	241.4	13.2	105.5	100.0	−82.3
1976	392.5	311.6	80.9	126.0	116.4	−59.4
1977	529.2	429.6	99.6	123.2	172.9	−43.2
1978	524.4	522.5	1.9	100.4	142.3	−189.7
1979	534.8	528.9	5.9	101.1	134.6	−293.3
1980	663.9	631.9	32.0	105.1	130.8	−385.7
1981	689.3	653.3	36.0	105.5	94.6	−383.0
1982	747.5	718.6	28.9	104.0	84.1	−333.8
1983	796.8	704.2	92.6	113.1	87.5	−355.6
1984	1 184.3	658.6	525.7	179.8	100.0	−23.7
1985	1 318.1	773.0	545.1	170.5	117.7	−30.3

1. Terms of trade for all exports, based on BCEAO.
Source: BCEAO (1987) and Berthélemy and Bourguignon (1989).

Table I.7. **Public sector consolidated accounts: 1975-85**

Percentage of GDP

	1975	1976	1977	1978	1979	1980	1981	1982	1983	1984	1985
Revenue											
Government	26.4	34.4	39.1	33.4	30.8	26.6	25.7	24.4	25.6	28.6	30.4
of which: Taxes	20.2	21.2	20.5	20.5	20.4	21.4	22.3	21.2	20.6	18.4	20.2
Other	4.0	3.5	2.1	2.5	3.0	2.3	2.1	0.6	1.3	1.4	2.1
CSSPPA	2.2	9.7	16.5	10.4	7.4	2.9	1.3	2.6	3.7	8.8	8.1
Public enterprises net surplus	0.5	-0.2	-0.4	0.4	0.8	-0.5	-0.4	-0.2	-0.3	-1.7	-0.7
Total revenue	26.9	34.2	38.7	33.8	31.6	26.1	25.3	24.2	25.3	26.9	29.7
Current expenditure											
Government	21.3	20.3	17.2	21.4	23.0	21.2	25.2	23.8	23.7	25.1	24.9
of which: Goods and services	7.8	7.1	6.1	7.9	8.5	6.9	6.8	6.2	5.7	5.4	4.5
Wages	9.2	9.1	7.5	8.4	9.7	10.0	10.8	11.2	11.2	9.8	9.4
Subsidies to productive sectors	1.6	1.6	2.0	2.8	2.0	1.6	2.8	3.0	2.6	2.3	2.5
Interest payments	0.9	1.0	1.0	1.4	2.1	2.6	3.6	5.4	6.3	7.2	7.8
Other	1.8	1.5	0.6	0.9	0.7	0.1	1.2	-2.0	-2.1	0.4	0.7
Public sector savings	5.6	13.9	21.5	12.4	8.6	4.9	0.1	0.4	1.6	1.8	4.8
Investment expenditure	15.2	14.9	18.6	21.0	18.9	13.7	11.5	11.1	9.4	7.6	7.6
Government	7.5	8.4	9.3	8.9	7.3	6.5	3.9	8.3	6.1	4.4	5.2
Public enterprises	7.7	6.5	9.3	12.1	11.6	7.2	7.6	2.8	3.3	3.2	2.4
Public sector deficit	9.6	1.0	-2.9	8.6	10.3	8.8	11.4	10.7	7.8	5.8	2.8
Foreign loans	2.8	4.9	9.6	9.0	6.9	7.9	6.6	11.2	1.3	5.0	2.8

Source: Berthélemy and Bourguignon (1989). These figures are estimates based on Treasury operations, as actual expenditure is not published.

Table I.8. **Trend in the Côte d'Ivoire public external debt: 1977-1985**

Billion FCFA

	1977	1978	1979	1980	1981	1982	1983	1984	1985
Debts									
Outstanding	434.8	601.8	745.3	971.6	1 368.9	1 815.8	2 185.8	2 534.9	2 371.8
New loans	492.2	366.8	329.2	293.4	640.9	381.2	440.4	333.9	350.2
Total	927.0	968.6	1 074.5	1 265.1	2 009.8	2 196.52	626.2	2 868.9	2 722.1
GDP	1 539.3	1 783.9	1 944.6	2 149.8	2 291.3	2 486.32	605.7	2 883.5	3 137.4
Debt/GDP (%)	60.2	54.3	55.3	58.8	87.7	88.3	100.1	99.5	86.8
Debt servicing	71.4	90.1	120.8	189.8	248.4	321.3	344.9	257.1	377.2
Exports (X)	592.5	590.3	579.1	663.9	689.3	747.5	796.8	1 184.3	1 318.1
Debt servicing/X (%)	12.0	15.2	20.8	28.6	36.0	42.9	43.3	21.7	28.6

Source: *La Côte d'Ivoire en chiffres* 1986/87, except for 1977-1979 exports (Berthélemy and Bourguignon).

Table I.9. **Urban and rural population by nationality: 1980-85**

	Inhabitants (1 000s) 1980	Percentage of total %	Annual rate of increase %	Inhabitants (1 000s) 1985[1]	Percentage of total %
Total	8 262.3	100.0	4.2	10 180.6	100.0
Ivorians	6 180.2	74.8	3.5	7 340.2	72.1
Rural	4 990.4	60.4	1.5	5 365.2	52.7
Urban	3 271.9	39.6	8.0	4 815.4	47.3
Rural Ivorians	4 081.5	49.4	1.0	4 286.0	42.1
Urban Ivorians	2 098.7	25.4	7.8	3 054.2	30.0
Rural non-Ivorians	908.9	11.0	3.5	1 079.2	10.6
Urban non-Ivorians	1 173.2	14.2	8.5	1 761.2	17.3
Abidjan	1 597.0	19.3	10.0	2 530.2[1]	24.9

1. Plan Projections 1981-85.
Source: ministère de l'Économie et des finances, *Côte d'Ivoire*, 1984.

Table I.10. The active population by sex and by sector: 1980-85

Thousands

	Activity rate		Activity rate	
	1980	%	1985	%
By sex [1]				
Men	2 326	53.8	3 138	59.1
Women	1 418	35.3	1 784	36.2
Total [2]	3 744	44.9	4 922	48.1
By sector				
Primary (agriculture and forestry)	2 380	65.4	2 498	59.0
Modern	333	9.2	209	4.9
Informal	924	25.4	1 527	36.1
Total [2]	3 637	100.0	4 234	100.0

1. The percentages in the first block represent participation rates.
2. The differences in the totals reflect the existence of unemployment, but for 1985 probably also problems of the precise definition and application of statistical concepts (see test).
Source: World Bank (1987), Vol. III.

Table I.11. Average annual real wage by sector: 1980-85

	1980 in '000 FCFA	1981	1982	1983	1984	1985
Primary exports	380					
Index	100	96.5	84.2	78.0	82.7	96.2
Labour-intensive industry	900					
Index	100	101.9	99.9	102.1	100.4	99.4
Capital-intensive industry	740					
Index	100	107.0	103.2	114.1	109.1	105.5
Formal non-tradeable	1 550					
Index	100	106.8	108.8	113.7	118.5	120.4
of which: Construction	1 357					
Index	100	114.8	106.7	116.3	138.9	131.2
Total modern enterprises	1 180					
Index	100	105.5	101.0	104.4	103.3	102.8
SMIG [1]	362					
Index	100	94.8	94.4	89.2	85.4	84.3
SMAG [2]	82.5					
Index	100	94.5	94.0	89.0	85.0	84.0
Public service	n.a.	2 738				
		100.0	100.0	96.0	84.0	81.0

1. Minimum monthly industrial wage multiplied by twelve months.
2. Daily agricultural wage multiplied by 300 days.
Source: Centrale des Bilans and Budgets généraux de fonctionnement.

N.B.: The modern food-crop sector is not representative of agriculture as a whole. The figures are given pro mem.:

	1 350					
Index	100	111.2	79.1	89.5	69.2	64.9

Table I.12. **Wage differentials according to educational attainment and nationality – 1979**

FCFA '000

Attainment:	Illiterate	CM2	CM2 CEPE	3e CAP	3e BEPC CAP	Final Class	DUT/BTS	Higher	Not stated	Total
Ivorians	39.17	47.35	50.71	53.29	75.63	99.62	176.96	273.43	35.06	52.23
Other Africans	33.08	41.91	52.03	63.89	86.17	110.58	167.25	229.64	26.03	35.11
Non-Africans	236.01	299.71	278.41	264.90	331.15	361.36	403.08	469.33	373.28	387.69
Total	36.83	46.83	52.58	55.62	101.78	137.19	251.74	358.28	38.94	59.95
Non-Africans/Ivorians	6.0	6.3	5.5	5.0	4.4	3.6	2.3	1.7	10.6	7.4

Notes: CM2: Cours Moyen second year.
CEPE: Certificat d'Etudes Primaires Elémentaires.
BEPC: Brevet d'Etudes de Premier Cycle.
CAP: Certificat d'Aptitude Professionnelle.
DUT: Diplôme Universitaire de Technologie.
BTS: Brevet de Technicien Supérieur.
The number of non-Africans at the bottom of the education attainment scale is obviously relatively low and the wage ratios calculated for levels lower than the CAP are thus not very significant.

Source: Ministère de l'Enseignement Technique et de l'Enseignement , 1982.

Table I.13. **Comparison of some welfare indicators[1]: 1980-87**

	Côte d'Ivoire		Other middle income countries (lower range)	
	1980	1987	1980	1987
Health				
Life expectation at birth	47	52	57	64
Infant mortality rate:				
Below 1 year	125	105[4]	95	82[4]
1-4 years	25	15[4]	14	11[4]
Number of inhabitants per doctor	21 040	n.a.	7 751	3 330[2]
Number of inhabitants per nurse	1 590	n.a.	2 261	1 070[2]
Daily calorie intake per inhabitant:				
a) Total	2 746	2 562[3]	2 476	2 777[3]
b) As % of nutritional needs	112	10*	106	119
Education* (Enrolments as % of age group)				
Primary School				
Total	76	78[3]	98	104[3]
Boys	92	92[3]	105	108[3]
Girls	60	65[3]	91	100[3]
Secondary School	17	20[3]	33	51[3]
Higher Education	2	3[3]	10	17[3]
Adult literacy rate	35	n.a.	59	n.a.

* The enrolment rates exceeding 100 per cent are explained by late schooling: some young people older than normal primary education age are still in it.
1. Figures for 1980 and 1987 except otherwise indicated.
2. Figures for 1984.
3. Figures for 1986.
4. Figures for 1985.
Source: World Bank, *World Development Report,* various years.

Table II.1. **Foreign trade and main crops: 1975-86**

Year	Terms of trade[2]				Producer price[3] (FCFA/kg)		Domestic production[4] ('000 tonnes)	
	Total exports[1]	Coffee	Cocoa	Timber	Coffee	Cocoa	Coffee	Cocoa
1975	100.0	70.8	94.8	123.2	150.0	175.0	270.0	241.0
1976	116.4	103.0	108.1	139.4	150.0	175.0	308.0	231.0
1977	172.9	198.8	172.7	138.4	180.0	180.0	291.0	223.0
1978	142.3	131.2	173.6	131.1	250.0	250.0	196.0	304.0
1979	134.6	128.8	157.8	134.8	250.0	250.0	277.0	318.0
1980	130.8	119.2	120.5	157.5	300.0	300.0	250.0	401.0
1981	94.6	77.7	74.4	127.1	300.0	300.0	367.0	417.0
1982	84.1	69.5	68.6	102.4	300.0	300.0	248.0	(465.0)
1983	87.5	81.6	71.2	100.9	350.0	350.0	(253.0)	(360.0)
1984	100.0	100.0	100.0	100.0	380.0	375.0	(103.0)	(421.0)
1985	117.7	118.8	108.2	115.0	346.0	375.0		
1986	120.6	127.6	107.0	138.1	370.0	400.0		

1. BCEAO (Banque Centrale des Etats de l'Afrique de l'Ouest) series.
2. Berthélemy and Bourguignon, 1989.
3. Ministère du Plan.
4. World Bank (1987), Vol. IV. The volume of production refers to coffee and cocoa beans.

Table II.2. **Public investment and indebtedness: 1975-81**

Billion FCFA

Year	Public sector investment (1)	Public sector gross external loans (2)	Loan financed Investment in % (2)/(1)
1975	131	71	54.4
1976	165	82	49.7
1977	340	191	56.2
1978	415	210	50.6
1979	343	198	57.7
1980	313	284	90.7
1981	333	280	84.1

Source: ministère de la Coopération (1986).

Table II.3. **Plan figures and actual figures: 1976-80**

Billion constant 1975 FCFA

	Plan	Actual
Total investment	1 591	1 670
Public	826	1 135
Private	765	535
Public financing of investment	1 020	1 433
Foreign loans	534	555
Public	327	438
Private	207	117
Debt service as % of exports	7.5	25.0
Average annual growth rates 1976-1980: GDP	8.7	7.7
Agriculture	6.0	4.7
Industry	14.1	11.0
Export industries	15.9	7.4
Cash crop exports	5.4	3.6
Total exports	7.3	4.2
Construction	9.3	11.1
Services	9.1	8.3

Source: Berthélemy and Bourguignon 1989.

Table II.4. **Public investment by sector: 1976-1980**

	Plan		Actual	
	(Billion FCFA of 1975)	%	(Billion FCFA of 1975)	%
Agriculture	348.5	34.1	418.5	29.2
Industry	59.5	5.8	16.1	1.1
Tertiary sector	11.0	1.0	30.2	2.1
Transport-communications	220.5	21.6	311.2	21.7
Energy	149.5	14.7	241.5	16.9
Housing/sanitation	96.5	9.5	160.0	11.2
Health	19.0	1.9	18.9	1.3
Education	48.5	4.8	122.6	8.6
Other	667.0	6.6	113.6	7.9
Total	1 020.0	100.0	1 432.6	100.0

Source: 1981-1985 Plan.

Table II.5. **Savings and net transfers: 1975-1987**

Percentage of GDP

| Year | Savings | | | | Net transfers |
	Total	Enterprises	Households	Government	+ factor payments
1975	14.1	4.4	4.6	4.5	7.0
1976	19.9	1.7	4.2	13.8	7.4
1977	25.3	0.7	2.0	21.9	6.7
1978	19.7	3.2	4.0	12.0	7.9
1979	14.5	1.6	4.2	7.8	8.7
1980	9.3	0.8	2.4	5.4	9.5
1981	6.4	4.8	0.5	0.5	11.0
1982	6.0	2.7	2.1	0.6	12.9
1983	5.1	2.1	0.6	1.9	13.9
1984	7.5	1.5	1.7	3.5	15.5
1985	10.5	1.8	2.3	5.5	14.0
1986	8.0	0.4	3.5	3.1	10.8
1987	7.5	5.2	1.7	0.2	7.9

Source: Based on Berthélemy and Bourguignon 1989.

Table III.1. GDP at factor cost: 1975-87

Billion constant 1984 FCFA

Year	Agriculture	Forestry	Oil industry	Manufactures	Public services	Construction	Transports	Other services	Total GDP
1975	643.9	36.1	10.5	149.5	25.2	102.3	139.7	588.8	1 696.2
1976	692.2	28.9	6.7	183.7	23.5	118.3	148.7	666.3	1 868.3
1977	657.2	32.5	13.7	172.0	29.3	150.4	151.7	723.4	1 930.2
1978	722.3	33.1	9.8	184.4	36.5	204.5	177.7	753.1	2 121.4
1979	720.7	37.6	9.2	200.0	59.0	201.8	211.8	737.9	2 177.9
1980	825.3	31.0	21.7	251.7	65.2	172.9	230.5	856.3	2 454.5
1981	853.2	20.9	43.0	273.1	71.6	174.7	207.9	828.7	2 473.1
1982	823.2	39.1	68.7	236.0	55.9	117.7	196.3	841.7	2 378.4
1983	741.6	25.5	119.4	203.5	61.9	108.2	204.9	855.3	2 320.2
1984	741.0	26.9	62.8	232.2	27.4	51.7	190.1	823.8	2 155.9
1985	830.7	24.6	54.7	231.5	44.7	46.1	183.4	826.6	2 242.2
1986	838.6	10.6	58.7	213.6	42.8	40.0	192.4	913.5	2 310.3
1987	803.2	14.0	29.4	171.7	34.5	34.9	175.2	996.6	2 259.4

N.B.: These series indicate a deeper depression (notably in agriculture) than that shown by the data in the World Bank *World Development Report 1989,* to which we refer in Table I-1.

Source: Berthélemy and Bourguignon (1989).

Table III.2. GDP at market prices in terms of final use: 1975-87

Billion constant 1984 FCFA

Year	Total GDP	Final consumption	Investment	Changes in stocks	Exports[1]	Imports[1]
1975	2 225.2	1 580.9	443.8	10.1	952.0	761.6
1976	2 481.7	1 802.1	548.4	24.8	1 063.7	957.2
1977	2 574.8	1 977.5	784.4	39.6	979.4	1 206.1
1978	2 822.1	2 210.2	955.9	3.1	1 035.7	1 382.8
1979	2 877.8	2 265.8	863.2	28.6	1 059.3	1 339.1
1980	3 210.3	2 486.7	882.9	65.7	1 188.7	1 413.6
1981	3 248.1	2 296.1	782.4	57.1	1 357.4	1 244.9
1982	3 123.5	2 221.1	670.2	52.5	1 342.4	1 162.6
1983	2 991.0	2 244.7	567.8	3.5	1 189.1	1 014.0
1984	2 869.3	2 224.7	352.6	−38.3	1 311.8	981.5
1985	2 982.1	2 290.3	335.9	37.9	1 348.0	1 030.0
1986	3 072.7	2 500.7	350.6	−34.6	1 281.1	1 025.1
1987	3 005.0	2 532.2	318.6	3.2	1 383.3	1 232.3

1. These two columns, and in particular imports, differ from the foreign trade figures because they include payments and transfers in addition to foreign trade.

N.B.: See Table III-1.

Source: Berthélemy and Bourguignon (1989).

Table IV.1. **Trends in the financial control of enterprises and the labour force by origin: 1975-85**

	1975	1976	1977	1978	1979	1980	1981	1984	1985
A. Value of Ivorian capital in enterprises (Billion FCFA)	62.44	115.94	149.63	168.26	230.26	265.99	299.61	389.33	275.50
B. Ivorian capital as % of capital of all nationalities	39.97	51.35	54.60	53.93	58.23	61.83	61.81	64.28	57.01
C. Ivorian private capital as % of capital of all nationalities	8.28	18.77	6.64	7.34	7.73	7.28	9.28	7.64	10.00
PERCENTAGE – of the total of all nationalities									
D. Ivorian senior managers	19.50	21.22	22.48	22.48	22.97	23.55	24.84	22.54	23.92
E. Non-African senior managers	78.71	76.31	75.76	75.62	75.29	74.41	72.61	74.23	73.00
F. Ivorian middle managers	36.51	40.09	42.65	44.52	44.15	46.78	48.29	60.07	62.52
G. Non-African middle managers	60.05	53.57	52.93	51.17	51.19	48.07	46.74	35.91	32.46
H. Ivorian supervisors	67.80	67.28	65.63	70.27	72.76	74.35	77.90	82.44	84.52
I. Non-African supervisors	22.60	21.90	22.33	19.26	16.50	16.51	13.12	8.68	7.46
J. Total Ivorian labour force	58.43	61.32	61.81	62.53	63.09	63.64	64.60	63.70	64.30
K. Total non-African labour force	4.83	4.72	4.46	4.53	4.22	4.20	4.40	3.75	3.63
Total labour force in absolute figures	94 797	121 597	143 597	149 365	152 177	148 490	138 475	107 523	105 718

A: ministère de la Coopération française, *Déséquilibres structurels et programmes d'ajustement,* Paris, 1986, Annex 1, p. 10 *bis.*
B, C: World Bank, *World Tables,* 1987, Washington, on tape.
D to K: World Bank, *World Tables,* 1987, Washington, Annuaire.
N.B.: Data not available for 1982 and 1983.
Source: G to K Centrale des Bilans.

Table IV.2. **Active population and urban employment: 1980-1985**

	Number 1980 in thousands	Percentage 1980	Annual increase %	Number 1985 in thousands [1]	Number 1985 in thousands [2]
Total population in Côte d'Ivoire	8 262	100.0	4.3	10 181	10 181
Urban Population of working age (15-59 ans)	1 896	22.9	8.0	2 792	2 792
Urban active population available	1 100	13.3	7.7	1 591	1 591
Urban jobs available	977	10.6	5.7	1 159	1 118
Modern jobs	382	4.6	4.1	467	307[3]
Traditional jobs	330	4.0	6.5	452	532[4]
Urban agricultural jobs	165	2.0	7.7	239	279[4]
Excess urban labour force	223	2.6	14.1	432	473

1. 1981-85 Plan figures.
2. Revised figures on the basis of data available in 1989 and estimates.
3. Sum of public service jobs (interpolation), enterprises (Centrale des Bilans) and other activities (projection).
4. Estimate based on assumptions concerning the breakdown between informal agricultural activities and other informal activities.
Sources: ministère de l'Économie et des Finances (1984), and ministère des Relations extérieures (1982).

Table IV.3. Trends in the employment of nationals and technical assistants in the public service: 1981-87

	Recruitments	Nationals Total Number	Nationals Total Index	Technical assistants Number
1981	4 442	74 109	100	4 143
1982	4 160	79 177	107	4 212
1983	3 723	83 112	112	3 726
1984	4 094	91 195	123	3 460
1985	−4 026[2]	87 185	118	3 000[1]
1986	4 775	86 642	117	4 399
1987	4 210	90 850	123	4 399

1. Estimate.
2. Transfers of posts in the enterprise sector.
Source: General operating budgets.

Table IV.4. Personnel employed by ministry: 1981-87

	1981 Number[1]	1981 Index	1985 Number[1]	1985 Index	1987 Number[1]	1987 Index
Representation and general administration	7 805	100	8 587	110	8 306	106
Law and order	10 844	100	13 246	122	8 692	80
Economic services	8 538	100	9 822	115	12 247	143
National education and scientific research	36 409	100	44 805	123	48 178	132
Social affairs and assimilated	10 514	100	10 725	102	13 427	127
TOTAL	74 110	100	87 185	118	90 850	123

1. Excluding technical assistants.
Source: General Operating Budgets.

Table IV.5. Variation in the professional structure
Civil service: 1976-87

Year	Management level posts (as a percentage of all posts) Unclassified and senior	Management level posts (as a percentage of all posts) Middle level	Management ratio[2]
1976[1]	6.9	23.7	30.6
1977[1]	7.3	25.6	32.9
1978[1]	7.9	25.8	33.7
1979[1]	8.8	26.5	35.3
1980[3]	(8.83)	(26.23)	(35.07)
1981	8.87	25.97	34.84
1982	9.43	27.04	36.47
1983	10.25	26.57	36.82
1984	13.53	28.13	41.66
1985	13.62	28.54	42.16
1986	16.35	34.78	51.13
1987	17.65	35.04	52.69

1. Office National de Formation Professionnelle. *Un diplôme pour l'emploi.*
2. Management: unclassified, senior management (A), middle management (B).
3. Estimated by interpolation.
Source: General operating budgets.

Table IV.6. Trend in production[1], employment and productivity according to the type of ownership: 1975-1985

Index 1980 = 100 at 1980 constant prices

Year	Entirely public capital			Majority public capital			Majority private capital			Total[2]		
	Production	Employment	Productivity	Production	Employment	Productivity	Production	Employment	Productivity	Production	Employment	Productivity
1975	47.5	58.2	81.6	87.5	82.8	105.7	87.7	83.4	105.2	74.5	68.2	109.2
1976	53.7	78.3	68.5	77.2	92.8	83.2	99.0	98.1	100.9	81.7	83.6	97.7
1977	91.1	110.7	82.4	31.1	29.1	106.9	113.7	115.0	98.9	95.7	97.9	97.7
1978	111.3	91.1	122.2	90.4	95.9	94.2	109.9	108.3	101.5	106.8	102.7	104.0
1979	127.1	104.1	122.2	91.9	98.0	93.7	107.8	103.3	104.4	107.5	102.6	104.8
1980	100.0	100.0	100.0	100.0	100.0	100.0	100.0	100.0	100.0	100.0	100.0	100.0
1981	103.6	96.6	107.2	99.2	88.8	111.7	97.9	88.7	110.4	98.8	90.4	109.4
1982	55.1	71.8	76.8	88.9	89.1	99.7	87.8	76.3	115.1	83.9	77.3	108.5
1983	55.8	59.0	94.6	102.5	88.6	115.7	87.1	73.7	118.2	85.8	73.0	117.6
1984	69.9	56.1	124.7	87.2	85.2	102.4	85.7	68.2	125.6	84.0	68.4	122.8
1985	73.0	57.5	127.0	101.1	86.0	117.5	86.0	61.1	140.7	86.9	64.4	135.0
1980	Bn FCFA	Number	Mn FCFA	Bn FCFA	Number	Mn FCFA	Bn FCFA	Number	Mn FCFA	Bn FCFA	Number	Mn FCFA
Absolute value	96 060	50 009	1.92	131 965	38 471	3.43	555 955	148 725	3.74	783 980	237 205	3.30

1. General African consumer price index. ILO Yearbooks.
2. The overall total is slightly different from the subtotals according to the source.
Source: Centrale des Bilans 1978, 1981, 1985.

140

Table IV.7. **Employment by branch of activity: 1980-85**

	1980 Number	1980 Index	1981 Index	1982 Index	1983 Index	1984 Index	1985 Index	Annual Average variation 80-85 (%)
Primary exports	18 693	100	76.3	68.2	65.8	65.1	54.8	−11.3
Labour-intensive industry[1]	56 998	100	92.0	88.6	89.3	85.9	81.3	−4.1
Capital-intensive industry[1]	36 700	100	100.5	98.9	92.2	94.4	98.0	0
Formal non-tradeable	123 100	100	88.8	67.0	60.7	52.8	47.9	−13.7
of which: Construction	35 197	100	66.8	47.4	38.3	23.9	15.2	−31.5
TOTAL (excluding food crops)	235 491	100	90.8	77.3	72.9	68.3	64.4	−8.4

1. See Table IV-14. for definition.
Source: Centrale des Bilans 1981 and 1985.
N.B.: "Modern" food crops are not representative of the agricultural sector as a whole. The figures are cited pro mem.

	1980 Number	1980 Index	1981 Index	1982 Index	1983 Index	1984 Index	1985 Index	
Food crops	1 714	100	89.7	85.2	80.9	82.8	69.1	−7.1
TOTAL (including food crops)	237 205	100	90.4	77.3	73.0	68.4	64.4	−8.4

Table IV.8. **The labour force by sector, professional status and sex: 1975-85**
Private and semi-public sectors

	1975		1980		1985	
	Number	% women	Number	% women	Number	% women
Administration and commerce	34 619	21.33	57 154	24.50	45 945	27.95
of whom managers and equivalent	8 292	5.11	14 131	6.06	13 303	8.09
Industry	126 500	77.95	175 484	75.21	117 899	71.72
of whom managers and equivalent	7 006	4.32	12 126	5.20	10 625	6.46
All sectors	162 288	100.00	232 638	100.00	163 844	100.00
of whom managers and equivalent	15 298	9.43	26 257	11.25	23 928	14.55

Source: Centrale des Bilans, 1975, 1980, 1985.

Table IV.9. **Percentage of Ivorians in the labour force by sector and professional status: 1975-85**
Private and semi-public sectors

	1975	1980	1985
Administration and commerce			
Managers and equivalent	49.5	60.1	69.2
White collar workers	74.7	81.1	81.2
Average for the sector	68.7	75.9	77.8
Industry			
Managers and equivalent	52.2	58.8	73.8
Blue collar workers	55.5	59.7	57.7
Average for the sector	55.3	59.6	59.1
Overall average	58.4	63.6	64.3

Source: Centrale des Bilans, 1975, 1980, 1985.

Table IV.10. **Variation in female employment: 1975-85**

Private and semi-public sectors

	1975		1980		1985	
	Number	%	Number	%	Number	%
Administrative and commercial management						
Women	1 210	14.59	2 610	18.47	2 880	21.65
S/Total	8 292	100.00	14 131	100.00	13 303	100.00
Industrial Management						
Women	297	4.24	406	3.35	443	4.17
S/Total	7 006	100.00	12 126	100.00	10 625	100.00
Management all branches						
Women	1 507	9.85	3 016	11.49	3 323	13.89
S/Total	15 298	100.00	26 257	100.00	23 928	100.00
All jobs						
Women	6 733	4.15	11 989	5.14	11 687	7.11
TOTAL	162 288	100.00	233 317	100.00	164 398	100.00

Source: Centrale des Bilans, 1975, 1980, 1985.

Table IV.11. **Creation and suppression of employment: 1975-1985**

Private and semi-public sectors

	1975-1980			1980-1985		
	M	F	Total	M	F	Total
Administration and commerce						
Senior management	527	79	606	−233	3	−230
Middle management	1 513	355	1 868	−546	155	−391
Supervisors	2 399	966	3 365	−319	112	−207
Skilled workers	7 956	1 637	9 593	−4 851	−608	−5 459
Unskilled workers	6 369	734	7 103	−4 914	−8	−4 922
Industry						
Senior management	313	13	326	−228	7	−221
Middle management	1 580	65	1 645	−758	−3	−761
Supervisors	3 118	31	3 149	−552	4	−548
Skilled workers	17 822	411	18 233	−14 179	−333	−14 512
Unskilled workers	13 819	270	14 089	−19 256	353	−18 903
Labourers	10 848	694	11 542	−22 659	−10	−22 669
Apprentices	−491	1	−490	−122	−3	−125
Total	65 773	5 256	71 029	−68 617	−331	−68 948

Source: Centrale des Bilans.

Table IV.12. **Remuneration of personnel**
Civil service: 1977-87

	Payroll at current prices	Share of BGF (%)	General price Index[1]	Payroll at 1981 prices	Number of employees[3]	Average pay at prices	
						Current prices	1981 prices
	Index			Index	Index	Index	Index
1977	49.1	51.1					
1978	59.3	50.3					
1979	71.3	50.6					
1980	84.9	54.0					
1981 base year	100.0	57.2	100.0	100.0	100.0	100.0	100.0
1982	114.9	58.7	107.4	106.9	106.2	108.2	100.7
1983	123.0	60.7	113.7	108.1	110.5	111.2	97.8
1984	122.0	59.1	118.7	103.0	120.5	101.4	85.4
1985	115.1	59.2	120.8	95.3	114.8	100.3	83.0
1986	124.3	58.3	128.8	96.5	115.9	107.3	83.3
1987	131.9	59.0	(139)[2]	(94.9)[2]	121.3	108.8	(78.3)[2]
1981 Absolute value	Bn FCFA 215.1			Bn FCFA 215.1	Number 74 110	'000 FCFA 2 738	'000 FCFA 2 738

1. International Labour Office, *Consumption of African Households.*
2. Estimate.
3. Nationals and technical assistants.
N.B.: For the period 1977-1984 these are recapitulative data.
Source: *Budget général de fonctionnement* (BGF).

Table IV.13. **The real payroll by sector: 1980-85**

	1980 Mn FCFA	1981	1982	1983	1984	1985	Annual average variation 1980-85(%)
Primary exports	7 191						
Index	100	73.6	57.4	51.3	53.9	52.7	−12.0
Labour-intensive industry[1]	51 146						
Index	100	93.7	88.5	91.2	86.2	80.8	−4.2
Capital-intensive industry[1]	27 295						
Index	100	107.5	102.1	105.2	103.0	103.4	+ 0.7
Formal non-tradeable	190 947						
Index	100	94.8	72.8	69.0	62.6	57.7	−10.6
of which: construction	47 770						
Index	100	76.8	56.6	44.5	33.3	21.2	−26.7
TOTAL[1]	276 579						
Index	100	95.3	78.2	76.2	70.8	66.4	−7.9
Increase in nominal *minimum* wages.							

* See Table IV-14. for definition.
1. Not including "modern" food-growing, which is not representative of the agricultural sector: it had a total payroll of FCFA 2.3 billion in 1980.
Source: *Centrale des Bilans.*

Table IV.14. **Labour intensity of production by sector: 1975-85**[1]

	1975	1980	1985
Primary exports	57.31	67.70	65.80
Labour-intensive industry[1]	66.32	65.64	59.01
Capital-intensive industry[1]	60.32	34.67	14.48
Formal non-tradeable	62.17	60.46	70.90
of which: construction	73.68	71.04	57.70
Total enterprises	62.51	57.44	44.93
Public enterprises	–	14.48	43.96
Majority public capital enterprises	–	47.27	41.20
Majority private capital enterprises	–	65.85	46.17

1. Labour intensity is calculated as: remuneration of labour x 100 rem. labour + rem. of capital + reconstitution of capital. Labour-intensive industries are considered to be those where the intensity so calculated exceeded 50 per cent in 1980. All others are classified as capital-intensive.
Source: Centrale des Bilans.

144

Table V.1. **Population, its density and growth by region (1983)**

	Total population	Agricultural population		Area	Population density (inhabitants/km²)		Annual average population growth 1975-81 (%)	
	('000)	('000)	%	('000 ha)	Total	Agricultural	Total	Agricultural
A. *Savanna*								
North	546	406	74	3 936	14	10	1.1	−0.1
North West	385	330	86	5 168	7	6	0.8	0.4
North East	286	236	83	2 988	10	8	0.4	0.2
Centre	1 484	1 129	76	6 003	25	19	2.0	1.7
Bouaké town	335	–	–	–	–	–	n.a.	n.a.
Total Savanna	3 036	2 101	69	18 095	17	12	2.1[1]	1.2
B. *Forest*								
East	927	658	71	2 605	36	25	3.3	3.0
South East	1 006	565	56	2 484	40	23	3.4	3.2
Centre West	878	660	75	2 239	39	29	4.0	4.4
South West	682	502	74	3 711	18	14	4.3	4.5
Centre	1 484	1 129	76	6 003	25	19	2.0	1.7
Abidjan town	2 000	–	–	–	–	–	n.a.	n.a.
Total Forest	6 264	2 994	48	14 142	44	21	5.9[1]	3.5
Total Côte d'Ivoire	9 300	5 095	55	32 237	29	16	4.6[1]	2.6

1. The population growth rates in Bouaké and Abidjan towns are not given by the source but are integrated in the totals, which are thus relatively high.
Source: DSREA, *Statistiques agricoles* 1983.
Estimates based on the 1975 population census and the 1974 agricultural census and extrapolations based on sample sureys.

Table V.2. **Trends in selected producer prices during the adjustment: 1980-89**

	Coffee[1]		Cocoa		Paddy rice		Cotton[2]	
	Nominal	Real[3]	Nominal	Real[3]	Nominal	Real[3]	Nominal	Real[3]
1980	300.0	300.0	300.0	300.0	65.0	65.0	80.0	80.0
1981	300.0	273.5	300.0	273.5	50.0	45.6	80.0	72.9
1982	300.0	237.5	300.0	237.5	60.0	47.5	80.0	63.3
1983	350.0	253.1	350.0	253.1	60.0	43.4	100.0	72.3
1984	380.0	265.4	375.0	261.9	80.0	55.9	115.0	80.3
1985	346.0	235.5	375.0	255.3	80.0	54.5	115.0	78.3
1986	369.6	245.3	400.0	265.4	80.0	53.1	115.0	76.3
1987	363.6	–	450.0	–	80.0	–	115.0	–
1988	363.6	–	400.0	–	60.0	–	115.0	–
1989	363.6	–	250.0[4]	–	60.0	–	115.0	–

1. Green coffee bean purchase equivalent (conversion factor 0.50).
2. Top quality cotton. Taking into account the cotton fertilizer price increase in 1985 (from 47 to 128 FCFA/kg), the effective price of cotton for the average producer amounted to 100 FCFA in that year.
3. Deflated by the manufactured goods price index.
4. The price was reduced twice in 1989. The latest price announced for 1989/90 is 200 FCFA.
Source: Based on MINAGREF, ministère du Plan.

Table V.3. **Minimum wage and price indices during the adjustment: 1980-88**

	SMAG 1				SMIG 5				Price Indices			
	Nominal		Real		Nominal		Real		Consumer	Food	Manuf.	Imports
		2	3	4		2	3	4	6	6	7	
1980	46.0	46.0	46.0	46.0	174.0	174.0	174.0	174.0	100.0	100.0	100.0	100.0
1981	46.0	42.3	43.6	41.2	174.0	159.9	165.1	158.7	108.8	105.4	109.7	115.4
1982	51.0	43.7	46.5	40.4	192.0	164.4	174.9	152.0	116.8	109.8	126.3	127.9
1983	51.0	41.2	44.5	36.9	192.0	155.2	167.5	138.8	123.7	114.6	138.3	135.1
1984	51.0	39.5	42.4	35.6	192.0	148.8	159.5	134.1	129.0	120.4	143.2	144.6
1985	51.0	38.8	41.7	34.7	192.0	146.1	157.0	130.7	131.4	122.3	146.9	146.7
1986	51.0	36.4	38.1	33.8	192.0	137.0	143.3	127.4	140.1	134.0	150.7	144.3
1987	51.0	34.6	–	–	192.0	130.1	–	–	147.6	–	–	142.5
1988	51.0	–	–	–	192.0	–	–	–	–	–	–	–

1. Minimum agricultural wage; there are four levels of SMAG depending on the sub-sector, fixed for an 8-hour working day. We have calculated an average hourly rate for reasons of comparability with the SMIG. The lowest rate applies to coffee, cocoa, cotton and rice farms (275 in 1980) and the highest to forestry work (480 in 1985).
2. Deflated by the consumer price index.
3. Deflated by the food price index.
4. Deflated by the manufactured goods price index.
5. Hourly rate, or 33 274 FCFA/month as from 1982.
6. Price index for African households in Abidjan.
7. This index has been constructed on the basis of group indices excluding food and housing, contained in ministère du Plan, *Memento chiffré de la Côte d'Ivoire 1985-86,* December 1987.
Source: ministère du Plan.

Table V-4. Lines of relative poverty by region

(adjusted per capita expenditure in FCFA 1985)

	The poorest 10%	30%
Côte d'Ivoire	95 681	170 766
Abidjan	213 482	349 859
Other towns	157 393	239 741
Western Forest	120 674	198 168
Eastern Forest	86 946	139 312
Savanna	59 509	95 681

Source: Glewwe 1987.

Table V-5. Regional price indices in Côte d'Ivoire (1985)

	Food prices	Non-food prices	General indices
Côte d'Ivoire	100.0	100.0	100.0
Abidjan	127.5	97.7	112.8
Other towns	98.1	97.7	97.8
Western Forest	84.3	100.8	92.3
Eastern Forest	90.9	98.5	94.7
Savanna	83.3	108.9	96.0

Source: Glewwe 1987.

Table V-6. Definition of household groups according to non-food monetary expenditures (*)
(FCFA 1985 per equivalent member)

	Poor	Middle	Rich
Abidjan	0-90 000	90 001-200 000	200 000
Other towns	0-50 000	50 001-120 000	120 000
Western Forest	0-35 000	35 001- 80 000	80 000
Eastern Forest	0-35 000	35 001- 80 000	80 000
Savanna	0-25 000	25 001- 50 000	50 000

* These expenditures include the following items listed in the survey: clothing, transport, health, school, equipment for the home, and transfers (gifts, donations, support for the family). The expenditures for the household as given in the survey have been recalculated for the equivalent member by counting as members of the household only those between 4 and 75 years old present in the household for more than nine months of the past year.

Table V.7. Restructured survey sample (1985)

Number of households

Expenditure category	Abidjan	%	Other towns	%	Eastern forest	%	Western forest	%	Savanna	%	Total	%
Poor	113	(33.8)	166	(48.5)	121	(58.7)	106	(36.9)	139	(62.3)	645	(46.3)
Middle	87	(26.0)	81	(23.7)	53	(25.7)	98	(34.1)	50	(22.4)	369	(26.5)
Rich	134	(40.1)	95	(27.8)	32	(15.5)	83	(28.9)	34	(15.2)	378	(27.2)
Total	334	(100)	342	(100)	206	(100)	287	(100)	223	(100)	1 392	(100)

Table V.8. Size of farms by region

Cultivated area	Number (%)		Total area (%)	
	Forest	Savanna	Forest	Savanna
> 5 ha	60.0	80.2	28.0	53.6
5-10 ha	27.1	15.7	34.8	30.8
< 10 ha	12.9	4.1	37.2	15.6
Total (number)	440 000	104 000		

Source: National agricultural census 1975.

Table V.9. Value of a day's labour for major crops in the forest zone (1985)

Crop	Cultivation method	Standard		Gross yield/ha	Charges/ha	Net income/ha	No. of days worked	Value of a day's labour (rounded)
		Tonnes/ha	FCFA/kg					
Cocoa	Extensive	0.3	400	120 000	25 000	95 000	37	2 600
	Semi-intensive	0.8	400	320 000	100 000	220 000	80	2 750
Coffee	Extensive	0.3	380	114 000	14 000	100 000	75	1 350
	Semi-intensive	0.8	380	304 000	28 000	276 000	150	1 840
Oil palm	(bunches)	8.0	15	120 000	30 000	90 000	50	1 800
Coconut	(coprah)	2.9	80	232 000	68 000	164 000	79	2 100
Rubber		1.75	150	262 500	80 700	181 800	69	2 630
Rice	Rain fed	1.2	80	96 000	25 000	71 000	120	590
	Irrigated	2.5	80	200 000	25 000	175 000	210	830
Maize		0.85	40	34 000	2 000	32 000	80	400
Ground nut		0.9	80	72 000	25 000	47 000	100	470

Source: M. Pescay, "Contraintes et potentialités des systèmes de production agricole en Côte d'Ivoire" in: ministère de la Coopération, 1986.

Table V.10. **Agricultural areas and their use**

	Average area in production (ha)	Fallow land available (ha)	Major cash crops (cocoa, coffee, cotton) %	Other cash crops (tobacco, rubber) %	Food crops total %	*of which:* rice %
Eastern forest:						
Large	20	7	72	2	26	2
Middle	11	5	64	3	33	4
Small	6	3	50	5	45	6
Western forest:						
Large	12	17	58	1	41	11
Middle	7	5	56	1	43	12
Small	6	5	46	2	52	17
Savanna:						
Large	9	1	23	0	67	9
Middle	5	1	19	0	81	11
Small	4	1	23	0	67	9

Source: 1985 Survey.

Table V.11. **Non-family labour by region and crop**

Per cent

	Type of employment				Employment by type of crop			
	Households with no non-family labour	Wage labour only	Share croppers only	Both	Export crops	Export crops + rice	Food crops	Everywhere
Eastern forest:								
Large	0	0	17	83	50	0	50	0
Middle	4	11	14	71	49	10	34	7
Small	18	11	44	27	17	6	45	32
Western forest:								
Large	0	0	10	90	64	14	0	22
Middle	0	4	26	70	28	28	18	26
Small	0	4	36	60	19	38	24	19
Savanna:								
Large	12	25	13	50	0	0	100	0
Middle	0	0	21	79	4	42	54	0
Small	19	8	41	32	2	59	39	0

Source: 1985 Survey.

Table V.12. **Monetary consumption expenditures in 1985**

Per equivalent member

Eastern forest

Socio-economic category: Sex of head of household: Number of observations:	Large m 32		Middle m 53		Small m 121		Chef f² 7	
	FCFA	%	FCFA	%	FCFA	%	FCFA	%
– food[1]	52 500	32	36 500	41	18 900	41	36 200	61
of which: rice		(5)		(5)		(5)		
bread		(3)		(3)		(3)		
– clothing	24 000	14	14 250	16	6 400	14	9 200	16
– maintenance	9 100	6	4 600	5	1 400	3	1 300	2
– transport	12 050	7	6 700	8	2 000	4	2 050	3
– school	13 000	8	6 300	7	4 900	11	5 200	9
– health	5 800	3	3 300	4	1 600	3	1 300	2
– funerals	9 300	6	5 500	6	1 700	4	1 100	2
– weddings	16 300	10	5 300	6	6 400	14	0	0
– gifts	6 300	4	1 250	1	1 000	2	0	0
– interest	1 600	1	500	1	250	1	200	1
– transfers	8 700	5	2 000	2	1 100	2	900	1
– other	7 200	4	2 800	3	700	1	1 550	3
Total	165 850	100	89 000	100	46 350	100	59 000	100

Western forest

Socio-economic category: Sex of head of household: Number of observations:	Large m 83		Middle m 98		Small m 106		Chef f² 6	
	FCFA	%	FCFA	%	FCFA	%	FCFA	%
– food[1]	68 300	42	45 200	49	29 150	57	15 900	58
of which: rice		(11)		(11)				
bread		(3)		(5)				
– clothing	17 500	11	11 000	12	4 900	10	2 400	9
– maintenance	9 000	6	3 100	3	1 350	3	1 850	6
– transport	14 100	9	5 400	6	2 200	4	1 000	4
– school	9 250	6	5 300	6	3 800	7	2 150	8
– health	5 600	3	2 700	3	1 500	3	700	3
– funerals	8 900	5	3 500	4	2 150	4	1 700	6
– weddings	11 500	7	6 000	7	2 700	5	0	
– gifts	3 100	2	2 000	2	900	2	10	
– interest	5 300	3	2 000	2	600	1	110	
– transfers	6 200	4	2 900	3	1 600	3	300	1
– other	3 400	2	2 850	3	700	1	1 400	5
Total	162 150	100	91 950	100	51 550	100	27 250	100

Table V.12.   (cont.)

Socio-economic category: Sex of head of household: Number of observations:	Large m 34		Middle m 50		Savanna Small m 139		Chef f² 6	
	FCFA	%	FCFA	%	FCFA	%	FCFA	%
– food¹	45 000	43	26 600	44	21 300	54	27 250	87
of which: rice	(15)	(5)	(18)	(16)				
bread				(5)		(3)		
– clothing	10 700	10	7 900	13	4 300	11	500	2
– maintenance	4 800	5	1 100	2	750	2	50	2
– transport	7 400	7	5 100	8	2 500	6	750	2
– school	5 900	6	4 300	7	2 000	5	1 500	5
– health	3 400	3	1 800	3	900	2	250	1
– funerals	6 200	6	3 900	7	1 500	4	530	2
– weddings	8 000	8	4 600	8	3 900	10	0	0
– gifts	2 500	2	500	1	750	2	50	
– interest	2 200	2	750	1	400	1	160	1
– transfers	6 300	6	2 400	4	750	2	200	
– other	1 900	2	950	2	700	1	0	0
Total	104 300	100	59 900	100	39 750	100	31 240	100

1. Excluding food grown by the family.
2. All socio-economic categories.
Source: 1985 Survey.

151

Table V.13. Trends in major non-food consumption expenditures: 1979-85

1985 FCFA/equivalent member

	Forest		Savanna	
	EBC 1979[1]	1985 Survey	EBC 1979[1]	1985 Survey
Clothing	8 437	10 846	5 162	6 083
Transport	1 066	5 913	2 061	3 830
Housing	11 727	3 850	5 974	1 445
Education	357	6 151	202	3 110
Health	851	2 926	474	1 482
Other	2 437	2 230	1 408	939
Total	24 875	31 916	15 281	16 889
Variation[2]		+ 28 %		+ 11 %

1. Values expressed in 1985 currency per equivalent member. A rate of 51 per cent has been applied for the price increase between 1979 and 1985. The 1979 per capita data are brought to equivalent member by dividing by a coefficient of 0.8.
2. Increase in volume, excluding food products. If food products are included the increases are 54 per cent for the forest and 36 per cent for the savanna. This expenditure has been excluded for reasons of comparability (see text).

Table V.14. Urban households by income level and occupation of head of household

Income level and sector	Abidjan		Other towns	
	N	%	N	%
Poor				
Civil servants and equivalent[1]	2	1.8	14	8.4
Private formal sector	24	21.2	19	11.5
Informal sector	85	75.2	132	79.5
Other[2]	2	1.8	1	0.6
Total	113	100	166	100
Middle				
Civil servants and equivalent[1]	17	19.5	14	17.3
Private formal sector	32	36.8	15	18.5
Informal sector	38	43.7	52	64.2
Total	87	100	81	100
Rich				
Civil servants and equivalent[1]	18	13.4	29	30.6
Private formal sector	72	53.7	33	34.7
Informal sector	44	32.9	33	34.7
Total	134	100	95	100
Overall breakdown				
Civil servants and equivalent[1]	37	11.1	57	16.7
Private formal sector	128	38.6	67	19.6
Informal sector	167	50.3	217	63.6
Grand total	332	100	341	100

1. Includes the military and employees of state enterprises.
2. Includes households subsequently excluded from the analysis because their members were absent for more than three months of the year.

Table V.15. **Expenditures on selected items affected by the adjustment measures**

Per equivalent member as a percentage of total monetary expenditure

	Poor	Middle	Rich
Abidjan			
Bread	2.6	2.8	4.2
	(4.7)*	(5.2)*	(7.8)*
Rice	7.1	5.3	3.4
	(12.8)*	(10.7)*	(6.8)*
School	9.0	6.7	11.4
Electricity	15.1	8.8	11.0
Water	6.6	5.4	3.3
Cigarettes	1	1	.1
Gasoline	.1	.1	.1
Other towns			
Bread	2.1	2.6	2.4
	(3.6)*	(5.2)*	(6.0)*
Rice	14.1	9.6	7.4
	(24.4)*	(18.7)*	(16.8)*
School	6.2	5.7	6.9
Electricity	9.9	7.5	5.8
Water	8.0	5.7	2.7
Cigarettes	1	1	1
Gasoline	.1	.1	.1

1. Figures of less than 0.05 %.
* The figures in brackets indicate the percentage of monetary expenditure on food.

Table V-16. **Annual monetary transfers between households**

(Average per capita in FCFA)

	Amount given	Amount received
Abidjan	34 362	56 613
Other towns	32 989	16 043
Western forest	7 372	3 537
Eastern forest	7 052	5 484
Savanna	10 844	8 920

Table V-17. **Proportion of men and women in the informal sector according to income level**

(per cent)

	Abidjan		Other towns	
	Men	Women	Men	Women
Poor	56	90	36*	56
Medium	42	72	38*	47
Rich	25	29	32	54

*   Excluding farmers who account for 43 and 28 per cent of the "poor" and "medium" respectively.

Table V.18. **Trends in enrolments in primary and secondary education: 1975-87**

Primary education

	1975	1976	1977	1978	1979	1980	1981	1982	1983	1984	1985	1986
Total enrolments	672 707	735 511	810 244	888 728	954 190	1 024 585	1 085 124	1 134 9_5	1 159 824	1 179 456	1 214 511	1 251 531
Annual increase (%)	9.3	10.2	9.7	7.4	7.4	5.9	4.5	2.2	1.7	3.0	3.0	n.a.
Of which: girls	253 582	277 846	310 617	344 407	375 233	409 859	438 367	461 9_5	476 170	485 875	502 672	n.a.
Girls (%)	37.7	37.7	38.3	38.7	39.3	40.0	40.4	40.7	41.1	41.2	41.4	n.a.
Private enrolments	125 177	125 324	133 959	137 569	141 839	143 049	143 616	139 6_1	133 268	130 196	n.a.	n.a.
Private (%)	18.0	17.0	16.5	15.5	14.8	13.9	13.2	12.3	11.5	11.0	–	–
Number of teachers	15 358	17 044	18 704	21 640	24 441	26 460	29 330	31 2_7	32 414	28 561	33 500	n.a.
Pupil/teacher ratio	43.8	43.2	43.3	41.1	39.0	38.7	36.9	36.5	35.8	41.3	36.2	n.a.

Primary education

	1977	1978	1979	1980	1981	1982	1983	1984	1985	1986	1987
Total enrolments	125 749	144 605	172 280	198 190	213 849	217 824	229 872	245 0_3	260 330	257 839	272 911
Annual increase (%)	15.8	19.1	15.0	7.9	1.9	5.5	6.6	6.2	–	1.0	5.9
Of which: girls	32 836	38 282	48 022	55 826	61 573	61 342	65 507	71 1_7	76 304	77 447	83 177
Girls (%)	26.1	26.5	27.9	28.1	28.8	28.2	28.5	29.0	29.3	30.0	30.5
Private enrolments	36 825	43 559	52 757	57 057	64 793	30 594	34 090	n.a.	n.a.	n.a.	n.a.
Private (%)	29.3	30.1	30.6	28.8	30.3	14.4	14.8	n.a.	n.a.	n.a.	n.a.

N.B.: No series available on the number of teachers in secondary education.
Source: UNESCO: Division of Educational Statistics and International Institute of Education Planning; ministère de l'Enseignement primaire: *Annuaire Statistique 1988*; ministère de l'Education nationale et de la Recherche scientifique. *Enseignement et formation en Côte d'Ivoire 1981/1982*; *La Côte d'Ivoire en chiffres*, édition 1986-1987.

155

Table V.19. **Trends in enrolments in higher education: 1975-87**

	1975	1976	1977	1978	1979	1980	1981	1982	1983	1984	1985	1986	1987
Total enrolments	7 174	8 701	10 201	12 470	14 418	19 633	18 732	18 800	18 872	19 660	20 480	21 330	22 200
Annual increase (%)	21.3	17.4	22.2	15.6	36.2	−4.6	0.4	0.4	4.2	4.2	4.2	4.1	
Of which: girls	1 218	1 543	1 800	2 180	2 543	3 450	3 290	3 300	3 300	4 000	4 165	4 340	4 500
Girls (%)	16.9	17.7	17.6	17.5	17.6	17.6	17.5	17.5	17.5	20.3	20.3	20.3	20.3

Source: UNESCO, Division of Educational Statistics, Paris, 1990.

Table V.20. **Educational level* of heads of household and their wives by age group and region**

Per cent

	Age						
		Male heads of household					
	Age	20-24	25-29	30-34	35-39	40 and over	No.
Abidjan		80.0	81.0	73.0	66.0	36.0	(294)
Other towns		80.0	72.0	79.0	55.0	77.0	(308)
Eastern forest		20.0	42.0	12.0	0.0	1.0	(199)
		Female heads of household					
	Age			20-29	30-39	40 and over	No.
Abidjan				44.0	64.0	30.0	(43)
Other towns				85.7	30.0	10.5	(36)
		Wives of heads of household					
	Age	15-24	25-29	30-34	35-39	40 and over	No.
Abidjan		20.7	40.0	37.0	26.0	12.0	(301)
Other towns		22.5	23.0	11.0	4.0	4.0	(373)

* At least CEPE (Certificat d'Etudes Primaires Elémentaires).
N.B.: Because of the very low response rate in rural areas, the Table is limited almost exclusively to urban areas. The age groups for the different categories are not always identical: this is to avoid very small groups and to make use of the data actually available.

Table V.21. **Proportion of boys and girls at school by income level and region**

Category of household	Percentage of school-age children attending school[1]		Number of school-age children	
	Boys	Girls	Boys	Girls
Poor				
Abidjan	68.0*	59.0*	146	137
Other towns	72.0*	58.0*	246	208
Eastern forest	51.0*	42.0	188	141
Western forest	62.0	60.0	130	131
Savanna	28.0*	18.0*	158	99
Middle				
Abidjan	86.0*	80.0*	97	105
Other towns	71.0	76.0*	113	113
Eastern forest	51.0	55.0	80	62
Western forest	48.0	40.0	126	114
Savanna	43.0	33.0	44	24
Rich				
Abidjan	92.0*	92.0*	103	110
Other towns	88.0*	92.0*	86	59
Eastern forest	76.0*	59.0	42	54
Western forest	59.0*	46.0	107	69
Savanna	50.0*	38.0*	20	24
Total				
Abidjan	80.0*	75.6*	346	352
Other towns	75.0*	68.4*	445	380
Eastern forest	54.0	48.6	310	257
Western forest	56.0	50.0	363	314
Savanna	33.0*	23.8*	222	147

* Statistically significant.
1. Between 6 and 21: this broad range takes account of the fact that schooling is often late in Côte d'Ivoire.
Note: The differences in the percentages may appear very large, but they are not always statistically significant. This is due to the small numbers involved. In particular, the differences between boys and girls are often not significant.

Table V.22. **Traditional distribution of major crops by ethnic group**

Growers/beneficiaries by sex

	Bete	Baule	Gouro	Senufo*
Food Crops				
Rice	M+F/M	F/F	M+F/M	F/[F]M
Maize	M+F/M	F/F	F/F	M+F/M[3]
Main vegetables and tubers	F/F	F/F[1]	F/F[2]	F/F[4]
Cash crops				
Coffee	M+F/M	M+F/M	M+F/M	p.a.
Cocoa	M+F/M	M+F/M	p.a.	p.a.
Cotton	p.a.	M+F/M[5]	p.a.	M/M[5]
Ground nuts	p.a.	p.a.	p.a.	M+F/M
Rice	M+F/M	p.a.	p.a.	p.a.

1. Except for yams, an identity lineage crop whose beneficiary is the male.
2. Except for yams where the beneficiaries are the elders.
3. for sorghum, but millet is a lineage crop with M/M distribution.
4. Except for yams, where the beneficiary is the male.
5. May also be a food crop with distribution F/F.
* Particularity: among the Senufo, tomatoes are a cash crop with M/M distribution.

Table VI-1. The macroeconomic closures

Market	Adjustment with flexible prices	Adjustment with price constraints
Labour	Agricultural labour Informal labour	Modern sector labour[1]
Goods	Traditional sectors[2] Informal sector[4]	Modern formal sector[3]
Money	Free interest rate	
Foreign trade	(Floating exchange rate in the SF simulation)	Fixed exchange rate

1. The modern wage is nominally unable to move down. The public sector wage is exogenous.
2. Primary exports and food crops.
3. Modern sector firms fix mark-up prices in order to maintain profits constant from one year to the next.
4. Informal sector workers receive the per capita value of their output.

Billions of CFA Francs

	Activities							
	Primary	Agriculture	Light Ind.	Heavy Ind.	Services	Informal	Gov't	Total
Activities								
Primary exports								
Agriculture								
Light Industry								
Heavy Industry								
Services								
Informal								
Imp (nc)								
Total								
Expenditures								
Primary exports	2.56	0.00	7.11	10.14	0.79	0.00		20.60
Agriculture	0.00	4.11	6.20	0.08	0.11	1.03		11.53
Light Industry	2.35	0.27	12.96	1.52	14.19	5.45		36.74
Heavy Industry	3.05	0.65	4.78	7.47	12.48	0.32		28.75
Services	14.43	3.60	15.66	9.03	30.11	6.25		79.08
Informal	2.80	0.65	5.07	1.75	8.60	1.71		20.58
Imp (nc)	0.00	0.00	3.21	2.82	7.59	2.06		15.68
Total	25.19	9.28	54.99	32.81	73.87	16.82	0.00	212.96
Factors								
Exports specific	14.04							14.04
Land		14.73						14.73
Capital			3.77	2.17	15.98			21.92
Labour *of which:*	17.13	18.04	7.23	2.01	41.77	13.54		99.72
Rural labour								
Modern labour								
Informal labour								
Total	31.17	32.77	11.00	4.18	57.75	13.54	0.00	150.41
Households								
Capitalists								
Big farmers								
Small farmers								
Modern workers								
Agric.workers								
Informal workers								
Total								
Government								
prod. tax	5.0	0.00	7.20	5.50	14.50	0.00		32.20
export tax	6.43							6.43
tariff								
income tax								
Total	11.43	0.00	7.20	5.50	14.50	0.00	0.00	38.63
Value added	36.17	32.77	18.20	9.68	72.25	13.54	0.00	182.61
Capital account								
Rest of the world								
Total	61.36	42.05	73.19	42.49	146.12	30.36	395.57	
Employment								
Rural	100.75	138.75						239.50
Modern			4.25	1.18	24.57		9.20	39.20
Informal						61.55	61.55	
Unemployed								11.10
Total								351.35

159

VI-2(b). Social Accounting Matrix (1980)
Billions of CFA Francs

				Commodities				
	Primary	Agriculture	Light Ind.	Heavy Ind.	Services	Informal	Imp (nc)	Total
Activities								
Primary exports	61.36	0.00						61.36
Agriculture		42.05						42.05
Light Industry			73.19	0.00				73.19
Heavy Industry				42.49				42.49
Services					146.12			146.12
Informal						30.36	30.36	
Imp (nc)							0.00	
Total	61.36	42.05	73.19	42.49	146.12	30.36	0.00	395.57
Expenditures								
Primary exports								
Agriculture								
Light Industry								
Heavy Industry								
Services								
Informal								
Imp (nc)								
Total								
Factors								
Exports specific								
Land								
Capital								
Labour *of which:*								
Rural labour								
Modern labour								
Informal labour								
Total								
Households								
Capitalists								
Big farmers								
Small farmers								
Modern workers								
Agric.workers								
Informal workers								
Total								
Government								
prod.tax								
export tax								
tariff	0.10	0.01	6.04	1.73	0.00	0.00	7.89	15.76
income tax	0.00	0.00	1.66	0.35	5.35			7.36
Total	0.10	0.01	7.70	2.08	5.35	0.00	7.89	23.12
Value added								
Capital account								
Rest of the world	3.29	1.85	17.74	13.54	6.08	0.00	44.50	87.00
Total	64.75	43.91	98.63	58.11	157.55	30.36	52.39	505.69
Employment								
Rural								
Modern								
Informal								
Unemployed								
Total								

VI-2*(c)*. Social Accounting Matrix (1980)

	Factors				
	Exp. specific	Land	Capital	Labour	TOTAL
Activities					
Primary exports					
Agriculture					
Light Industry					
Heavy Industry					
Services					
Informal					
Imp(nc)					
Total					
Expenditures					
Primary exports					
Agriculture					
Light Industry					
Heavy Industry					
Services					
Informal					
Imp(nc)					
Total					
Factors					
Exports specific					
Land					
Capital					
Labour *of which:*					
Rural labour					
Modern labour					
Informal labour					
Total					
Households					
Capitalists	4.41	0.32	16.44	2.84	24.01
Big farmers	3.79	7.54		8.31	19.64
Small farmers	3.51	6.86		21.70	32.07
Modern workers			2.19	68.78	70.97
Agric. workers				5.16	5.16
Informal workers				13.54	13.54
Total	11.71	14.72	18.63	120.33	165.39
Government					
Prod. tax					
Export tax					
Tariff					
Income tax					
Total					
Value added					
Capital account	0.13	0.01	0.22		0.36
Rest of the world	2.20		3.07	0.00	5.27
TOTAL	14.04	14.73	21.92	120.33	171.02
Employment					
Rural					
Modern					
Informal					
Unemployed					
TOTAL					

VI-2(d). Social Accounting Matrix (1980)
Billions of CFA Francs

				Households			
	Capit.	Big farm	Small f.	modern W	Agric. W	Inform. W	Total
Activities							
Primary exports							
Agriculture							
Light Industry							
Heavy Industry							
Services							
Informal							
Imp (nc)							
Total							
Expenditures							
Primary exports	0.22	0.34	0.0	0.61	0.0	0.0	1.17
Agriculture	0.94	4.41	8.90	11.95	1.70	5.15	33.04
Light Industry	2.53	3.20	5.82	17.66	1.40	3.93	34.53
Heavy Industry	2.05	2.56	2.15	8.93	0.18	0.04	15.90
Services	1.61	2.07	4.40	9.21	0.53	1.10	18.92
Informal	0.71	1.00	2.30	3.10	0.28	0.53	7.92
Imp (nc)	1.51	2.21	3.30	9.24	0.63	1.67	18.56
Total	9.56	15.78	26.87	60.70	4.71	12.41	130.03
Factors							
Exports specific							
Land							
Capital							
Labour *of which:*							
Rural labour							
Modern labour							
Informal labour							
Total							
Households							
Capitalists							
Big farmers							
Small farmers							
Modern workers							
Agric. workers							
Informal workers							
Total							
Government							
prod. tax							
export. tax							
tariff							
income tax							
Total							
Value added							
Capital account	14.45	3.86	5.20	10.27	0.45	1.13	35.36
Rest of the world							
Total	24.01	19.64	32.07	70.97	5.16	13.54	165.39
Employment							
Rural		56.57		148.06	34.87		239.50
Modern	2.0			48.30			50.30
Informal						61.55	61.55
Unemployed							351.35
Total							

Social Accounting Matrix (1980)

Billions of CFA Francs

	Govn't	Investmt	R of W	TOTAL
Activities				0.00
Primary exports				61.36
Agriculture				42.05
Light Industry				73.19
Heavy Industry				42.49
Services				146.12
Informal				30.36
Imp (nc)				0.00
TOTAL				395.57
Expenditures				
Primary exports	0.00	0.00	43.00	64.77
Agriculture	0.00	0.00	0.09	44.66
Light Industry	3.21	5.78	17.80	98.06
Heavy Industry	2.82	3.42	7.22	58.11
Services	7.58	41.52	10.46	157.56
Informal	2.06	0.00	0.00	30.56
Imp (nc)	2.12	16.0		52.36
TOTAL	17.79	66.72	78.57	506.07
Factors				0.00
Exports specific				14.04
Land				14.73
Capital				21.92
Labour *of which:*	20.61			120.33
Rural labour				0.00
Modern labour	20.61			0.00
Informal labour				0.00
TOTAL				171.02
Households				
Capitalists				24.01
Big farmers				19.64
Small farmers				32.07
Modern workers				70.97
Agric.workers				5.16
Informal workers				13.54
TOTAL				165.39
Government				0.00
Prod. tax				32.20
Export tax				6.43
Tariff				15.76
Income tax				7.36
TOTAL				61.75
Value added				
Capital account	23.35			
Rest of the world				87.00
TOTAL	61.75	66.72	78.57	1 394.03
Employment				
Rural				
Modern				
Informal				
Unemployed				
TOTAL				

Table VI-3 **Main parameters**

Households

    Consumption
        0.36 < elasticity of expenditure < 1.34[1]
        0.25 < Frisch[2] parameter < 2

effect of capital gains on consumption[3]	10%

    Portfolio
    Demand for money

Semi-elasticity with respect to interest rate	0.05
Income elasticity	1

    Arbitrage between physical and financial savings

Elasticity of physical/financial savings[4]	1
Average share of physical savings[4]	0.93

    Arbitrage between domestic and foreign assets

Elasticity of domestic/foreign bonds[4]	20

        40 < domestic share of total financial
        wealth < 100

Enterprises

    Technology

Elasticity of substitution in the production function (Cobb-Douglas)	1
Technical progress	1%
Depreciation	4%

    Portfolio

Elasticity of working capital with respect to sales	1
Elasticity of domestic/foreign loans[5]	20

    Foreign trade (price elasticity)
        1 < elasticity of export demand < 10
        0.6 < elasticity of import demand < 1.5

1.   The elasticities of expenditure of the different classes of household are within these two limit values.
2.   LES parameter, equal to the ratio of total income to income above the minimum consumption level.
3.   Proportion of the change in wealth that is consumed.
4.   This elasticity corresponds to ε in the expression

$$\frac{g}{1-g} = \psi \left(\frac{i^1}{i^2} \right) \varepsilon$$

where:
    g is the share of physical savings;
    i^1 is the yield on physical savings;
    i^2 is the yield on financial savings.

5.   This comes from the same expression as in Note 4, where:
    g is the share of domestic savings;
    i^1 is the yield on domestic assets;
    i^2 is the yield on foreign assets.

Table VI-4. **Summary of the scenarios**

BR: Reference simulation

Budgetary measures:

SI: Government investment fixed at FCFA 50 billion in 1981 and maintained at this level in subsequent years.

SW: Reduction in the nominal wage of public servants.

SG: Reduction in operating expenditures and public sector employment in the same proportions.

ST: Increases in taxes on production in all sectors except food crops.

SE: Increase in taxes on primary exports.

Devaluations:

SD: Devaluation of 20 per cent nominal with respect to the reference.

SF: Introduction of a floating exchange rate system and elimination of debt rescheduling.

Table VI-5. Simulations: main results

	BR	Budget policies					Devaluation	
		SI	SW	SG	ST	SE	SD	SF
GDP[1]	-0.45	-0.7	-0.5	-0.8	-0.6	-0.4	-0.4	-0.5
Budget deficit[2]	-6.7	-4.6	-4.8	-4.6	-4.7	-5.1	-3.3	-5.5
Current account[3]	-14.1	-12.0	-12.3	-12.6	-12.5	-14.3	-9.8	-11.2
Balance of trade[2]	-1.9	+5.4	+4.8	+5.0	+4.9	+2.7	-5.5	3.7
Public external debt[3]	47.4	39.2	40.3	40.4	40.5	46.6	32.5	37.1
Private external debt[3]	63.0	61.9	64.1	64.0	62.4	68.6	65.5	54.4
Interest rate[2]	10.0	9.9	9.8	9.9	9.7	9.8	13.6	12.2
Real devaluation	1.3	1.3	1.6	1.3	1.3	2.3	1.8	0.4
Inflation (CPI)[1]	7.3	7.2	7.2	7.2	7.0	6.3	9.8	4.1
(GDP)[1]	7.1	7.0	6.7	7.0	7.0	6.0	9.4	4.5
Private consumption[2]	57.9	57.8	56.4	57.5	56.7	56.7	55.8	56.8
Exports[2]	45.7	43.8	43.6	43.8	43.0	42.3	45.2	44.2
Imports[2]	37.0	36.6	36.9	37.0	36.6	36.6	35.9	36.5
Investment[2]	19.8	17.7	19.9	20.1	19.6	20.3	18.5	18.8
Capacity utilisation rate[2]	50.9	51.4	50.6	50.6	49.9	51.1	49.3	54.3
Unemployment rate[2]	5.4	5.7	5.6	5.8	5.7	5.5	4.6	5.0

1. Annual average rate of increase.
2. Average 1980-86.
3. 1986 level.

166

Table VI-6. Budgetary policy simulations: summary of results

	BR 80-83	BR 83-86	SI 80-83	SI 83-86	SW 80-83	SW 83-86	SG 80-83	SG 83-86	ST 80-83	ST 83-86	SE 80-83	SE 83-86
GDP[5]	-2.3	1.5	-3.0	1.5	-2.4	1.4	-2.8	1.3	-2.9	1.7	-2.3	1.6
Budget deficit[5]	-10.2	-4.0	-8.2	-1.6	-8.2	-1.6	-8.2	-1.6	-8.2	-1.6	-9.1	-2.6
Current account[2]	-22.6	-3.6	-19.4	-1.0	-20.8	-1.7	-20.8	-1.3	-20.1	-1.2	-22.8	-3.7
Public external debt[2]	76.1	47.4	72.9	39.2	74.5	40.3	73.4	40.4	76.1	40.5	79.0	46.6
Private external debt[2]	63.2	63.0	62.2	61.9	63.6	64.1	63.3	64.0	61.0	62.4	65.4	68.6
Interest rate[3]	7.0	14.2	7.0	14.2	7.0	14.1	7.0	14.2	7.0	14.2	7.0	19.2
Real devaluation[4]	12.9	-9.1	13.1	-9.3	13.7	-9.1	13.1	-9.3	12.8	-9.1	14.6	-8.6
Inflation[4]	0.2	14.4	-0.1	14.8	-0.7	14.6	0.0	14.6	0.0	14.4	-1.3	13.8
Household consumption[1]	-5.8	4.7	-6.6	5.2	-6.8	4.9	-6.6	4.7	-7.2	5.2	-6.5	4.6
Exports[1]	0.0	4.0	1.1	3.5	0.9	3.8	0.8	3.9	0.3	3.9	0.0	4.4
Imports[1]	-8.6	4.3	-9.7	4.6	-9.0	4.3	-9.1	4.2	-9.7	4.7	-9.0	4.2
Investment[1]	-6.5	-7.4	-10.7	-8.6	-6.5	-7.3	-6.6	-7.4	-7.8	-6.6	-5.5	-7.1
Unemployment rate[3]	5.6	7.2	15.3	7.5	5.9	7.3	6.0	7.6	6.1	7.5	5.7	7.6
Capacity utilisation rate	41.0	30.0	42.0	32.0	40.0	30.0	40.0	30.0	39.0	30.0	41.0	30.0

1. Annual average rate of increase.
2. As a percentage of GDP. End of period level.
3. End of period level.
4. Annual average.
5. As a percentage of GDP.

Table VI-7. Devaluation simulations: summary of results

	BR		SD		SF	
	80-84	84-86	80-84	84-86	80-84	84-86
GDP[1]	-1.6	1.9	-1.4	1.7	-1.4	1.4
Budget deficit[2]	-3.3	-2.3	0.9	3.0	-0.9	-5.0
Current account[2]	-8.5	-3.6	-16.7	0.7	-6.4	-7.5
Public external debt[2]	75.5	47.4	62.5	32.5	50.0	37.1
Private external debt[2]	61.4	63.0	68.2	65.5	64.6	54.4
Interest rate[3]	9.5	14.2	13.5	18.3	10.0	8.7
Real devaluation[4]	6.8	-8.8	8.8	-2.5	7.0	-11.6
Inflation[4] (GDP)	4.8	11.8	7.7	12.7	5.0	7.2
Household consumption[1]	-4.5	15.3	-5.2	7.2	-4.2	9.3
Exports[1]	2.5	1.0	4.4	-0.6	3.0	-4.6
Imports[1]	-6.7	6.9	-7.2	6.6	-6.5	8.8
Investment[1]	-10.7	2.2	-12.4	5.1	-11.0	15.6
Unemployment rate[3]	6.5	7.2	5.6	5.6	5.7	6.8
Capacity utilisation rate[3]	34.0	30.0	32.0	22.0	38.0	32.0

1. Annual average rate of increase.
2. As a percentage of GDP. End of period level.
3. End of period level.
4. Annual average.

MAIN SALES OUTLETS OF OECD PUBLICATIONS – PRINCIPAUX POINTS DE VENTE DES PUBLICATIONS DE L'OCDE

Argentina – Argentine
Carlos Hirsch S.R.L.
Galería Güemes, Florida 165, 4° Piso
1333 Buenos Aires   Tel. (1) 331.1787 y 331.2391
           Telefax: (1) 331.1787

Australia – Australie
D.A. Book (Aust.) Pty. Ltd.
648 Whitehorse Road, P.O.B 163
Mitcham, Victoria 3132   Tel. (03) 873.4411
           Telefax: (03) 873.5679

Austria – Autriche
OECD Publications and Information Centre
Schedestrasse 7
D-W 5300 Bonn 1 (Germany)   Tel. (49.228) 21.60.45
           Telefax: (49.228) 26.11.04
Gerold & Co.
Graben 31
Wien I   Tel. (0222) 533.50.14

Belgium – Belgique
Jean De Lannoy
Avenue du Roi 202
B-1060 Bruxelles   Tel. (02) 538.51.69/538.08.41
           Telefax: (02) 538.08.41

Canada
Renouf Publishing Company Ltd.
1294 Algoma Road
Ottawa, ON K1B 3W8   Tel. (613) 741.4333
           Telefax: (613) 741.5439
Stores:
61 Sparks Street
Ottawa, ON K1P 5R1   Tel. (613) 238.8985
211 Yonge Street
Toronto, ON M5B 1M4   Tel. (416) 363.3171
Federal Publications
165 University Avenue
Toronto, ON M5H 3B8   Tel. (416) 581.1552
           Telefax: (416)581.1743
Les Éditions La Liberté Inc.
3020 Chemin Sainte-Foy
Sainte-Foy, PQ G1X 3V6   Tel. (418) 658.3763
           Telefax: (418) 658.3763

China – Chine
China National Publications Import
Export Corporation (CNPIEC)
P.O. Box 88
Beijing   Tel. 44.0731
           Telefax: 401.5661

Denmark – Danemark
Munksgaard Export and Subscription Service
35, Nørre Søgade, P.O. Box 2148
DK-1016 København K   Tel. (33) 12.85.70
           Telefax: (33) 12.93.87

Finland – Finlande
Akateeminen Kirjakauppa
Keskuskatu 1, P.O. Box 128
00100 Helsinki   Tel. (358 0) 12141
           Telefax: (358 0) 121.4441

France
OECD/OCDE
Mail Orders/Commandes par correspondance:
2, rue André-Pascal
75775 Paris Cédex 16   Tel. (33-1) 45.24.82.00
           Telefax: (33-1) 45.24.85.00
           or (33-1) 45.24.81.76
           Telex: 620 160 OCDE
Bookshop/Librairie:
33, rue Octave-Feuillet
75016 Paris   Tel. (33-1) 45.24.81.67
           (33-1) 45.24.81.81
Librairie de l'Université
12a, rue Nazareth
13100 Aix-en-Provence   Tel. 42.26.18.08
           Telefax: 42.26.63.26

Germany – Allemagne
OECD Publications and Information Centre
Schedestrasse 7
D-W 5300 Bonn 1   Tel. (0228) 21.60.45
           Telefax: (0228) 26.11.04

Greece – Grèce
Librairie Kauffmann
Mavrokordatou 9
106 78 Athens   Tel. 322.21.60
           Telefax: 363.39.67

Hong Kong
Swindon Book Co. Ltd.
13 - 15 Lock Road
Kowloon, Hong Kong   Tel. 366.80.31
           Telefax: 739.49.75

Iceland – Islande
Mál Mog Menning
Laugavegi 18, Pósthólf 392
121 Reykjavik   Tel. 162.35.23

India – Inde
Oxford Book and Stationery Co.
Scindia House
New Delhi 110001   Tel.(11) 331.5896/5308
           Telefax: (11) 332.5993
17 Park Street
Calcutta 700016   Tel. 240832

Indonesia – Indonésie
Pdii-Lipi
P.O. Box 269/JKSMG/88
Jakarta 12790   Tel. 583467
           Telex: 62 875

Ireland – Irlande
TDC Publishers – Library Suppliers
12 North Frederick Street
Dublin 1   Tel. 74.48.35/74.96.77
           Telefax: 74.84.16

Israel
Electronic Publications only
Publications électroniques seulement
Sophist Systems Ltd.
71 Allenby Street
Tel-Aviv 65134   Tel. 3-29.00.21
           Telefax: 3-29.92.39

Italy – Italie
Libreria Commissionaria Sansoni
Via Duca di Calabria 1/1
50125 Firenze   Tel. (055) 64.54.15
           Telefax: (055) 64.12.57
Via Bartolini 29
20155 Milano   Tel. (02) 36.50.83
Editrice e Libreria Herder
Piazza Montecitorio 120
00186 Roma   Tel. 679.46.28
           Telex: NATEL I 621427
Libreria Hoepli
Via Hoepli 5
20121 Milano   Tel. (02) 86.54.46
           Telefax: (02) 805.28.86
Libreria Scientifica
Dott. Lucio de Biasio 'Aeiou'
Via Meravigli 16
20123 Milano   Tel. (02) 805.68.98
           Telefax: (02) 80.01.75

Japan – Japon
OECD Publications and Information Centre
Landic Akasaka Building
2-3-4 Akasaka, Minato-ku
Tokyo 107   Tel. (81.3) 3586.2016
           Telefax: (81.3) 3584.7929

Korea – Corée
Kyobo Book Centre Co. Ltd.
P.O. Box 1658, Kwang Hwa Moon
Seoul   Tel. 730.78.91
           Telefax: 735.00.30

Malaysia – Malaisie
Co-operative Bookshop Ltd.
University of Malaya
P.O. Box 1127, Jalan Pantai Baru
59700 Kuala Lumpur
Malaysia   Tel. 756.5000/756.5425
           Telefax: 757.3661

Netherlands – Pays-Bas
SDU Uitgeverij
Christoffel Plantijnstraat 2
Postbus 20014
2500 EA's-Gravenhage   Tel. (070 3) 78.99.11
Voor bestellingen: Tel. (070 3) 78.98.80
           Telefax: (070 3) 47.63.51

New Zealand – Nouvelle-Zélande
GP Publications Ltd.
Customer Services
33 The Esplanade - P.O. Box 38-900
Petone, Wellington   Tel. (04) 5685.555
           Telefax: (04) 5685.333

Norway – Norvège
Narvesen Info Center - NIC
Bertrand Narvesens vei 2
P.O. Box 6125 Etterstad
0602 Oslo 6   Tel. (02) 57.33.00
           Telefax: (02) 68.19.01

Pakistan
Mirza Book Agency
65 Shahrah Quaid-E-Azam
Lahore 3   Tel. 66.839
           Telex: 44886 UBL PK. Attn: MIRZA BK

Portugal
Livraria Portugal
Rua do Carmo 70-74
Apart. 2681
1117 Lisboa Codex   Tel.: (01) 347.49.82/3/4/5
           Telefax: (01) 347.02.64

Singapore – Singapour
Information Publications Pte. Ltd.
Pei-Fu Industrial Building
24 New Industrial Road No. 02-06
Singapore 1953   Tel. 283.1786/283.1798
           Telefax: 284.8875

Spain – Espagne
Mundi-Prensa Libros S.A.
Castelló 37, Apartado 1223
Madrid 28001   Tel. (91) 431.33.99
           Telefax: (91) 575.39.98
Libreria Internacional AEDOS
Consejo de Ciento 391
08009 - Barcelona   Tel. (93) 488.34.92
           Telefax: (93) 487.76.59
Llibreria de la Generalitat
Palau Moja
Rambla dels Estudis, 118
08002 - Barcelona   Tel. (93) 318.80.12 (Subscripcions)
           (93) 302.67.23 (Publicacions)
           Telefax: (93) 412.18.54

Sri Lanka
Centre for Policy Research
c/o Colombo Agencies Ltd.
No. 300-304, Galle Road
Colombo 3   Tel. (1) 574240, 573551-2
           Telefax: (1) 575394, 510711

Sweden – Suède
Fritzes Fackboksföretaget
Box 16356
Regeringsgatan 12
103 27 Stockholm   Tel. (08) 23.89.00
           Telefax: (08) 20.50.21
Subscription Agency/Abonnements:
Wennergren-Williams AB
Nordenflychtsvägen 74
Box 30004
104 25 Stockholm   Tel. (08) 13.67.00
           Telefax: (08) 618.62.32

Switzerland – Suisse
OECD Publications and Information Centre
Schedestrasse 7
D-W 5300 Bonn 1 (Germany)   Tel. (49.228) 21.60.45
           Telefax: (49.228) 26.11.04
Suisse romande
Maditec S.A.
Chemin des Palettes 4
1020 Renens/Lausanne   Tel. (021) 635.08.65
           Telefax: (021) 635.07.80
Librairie Payot
6 rue Grenus
1211 Genève 11   Tel. (022) 731.89.50
           Telex: 28356
Subscription Agency – Service des Abonnements
Naville S.A.
7, rue Lévrier
1201 Genève   Tél.: (022) 732.24.00
           Telefax: (022) 738.87.13

Taiwan – Formose
Good Faith Worldwide Int'l. Co. Ltd.
9th Floor, No. 118, Sec. 2
Chung Hsiao E. Road
Taipei   Tel. (02) 391.7396/391.7397
           Telefax: (02) 394.9176

Thailand – Thaïlande
Suksit Siam Co. Ltd.
113, 115 Fuang Nakhon Rd.
Opp. Wat Rajbopith
Bangkok 10200   Tel. (662) 251.1630
           Telefax: (662) 236.7783

Turkey – Turquie
Kültur Yayinlari Is-Türk Ltd. Sti.
Atatürk Bulvari No. 191/Kat. 21
Kavaklidere/Ankara   Tel. 25.07.60
Dolmabahce Cad. No. 29
Besiktas/Istanbul   Tel. 160.71.88
           Telex: 43482B

United Kingdom – Royaume-Uni
HMSO
Gen. enquiries   Tel. (071) 873 0011
Postal orders only:
P.O. Box 276, London SW8 5DT
Personal Callers HMSO Bookshop
49 High Holborn, London WC1V 6HB
           Telefax: 071 873 2000
Branches at: Belfast, Birmingham, Bristol, Edinburgh,
           Manchester

United States – États-Unis
OECD Publications and Information Centre
2001 L Street N.W., Suite 700
Washington, D.C. 20036-4910   Tel. (202) 785.6323
           Telefax: (202) 785.0350

Venezuela
Libreria del Este
Avda F. Miranda 52, Aptdo. 60337
Edificio Galipán
Caracas 106   Tel. 951.1705/951.2307/951.1297
           Telegram: Libreste Caracas

Yugoslavia – Yougoslavie
Jugoslovenska Knjiga
Knez Mihajlova 2, P.O. Box 36
Beograd   Tel. (011) 621.992
           Telefax: (011) 625.970

Orders and inquiries from countries where Distributors have not yet been appointed should be sent to: OECD Publications Service, 2 rue André-Pascal, 75775 Paris Cédex 16, France.

Les commandes provenant de pays où l'OCDE n'a pas encore désigné de distributeur devraient être adressées à : OCDE, Service des Publications, 2, rue André-Pascal, 75775 Paris Cédex 16, France.

OECD PUBLICATIONS, 2 rue André-Pascal, 75775 PARIS CEDEX 16
PRINTED IN FRANCE
(41 91 17 1) ISBN 92-64-13654-1 - No. 45935 1992